COMPUTERS FOR LIBRARIANS

An introduction to the electronic library

Third edition

Stuart Ferguson

with Rodney Hebels

Topics in Australasian Library and Information Studies, Number 22

Centre for Information Studies
Charles Sturt University
Wagga Wagga New South Wales

ISBN 1 876938 60 9
ISSN: 1030-5009

National Library of Australia cataloguing-in-publication data

Ferguson, Stuart, 1953- .
    Computers for librarians : an introduction to the electronic library.

    3rd ed.
    Includes index.
    ISBN 1 876938 60 9.

    1. Libraries - Automation.   2. Information storage and retrieval systems.   I.
    Hebels, Rodney, 1969- .   II. Charles Sturt University--Riverina. Centre for
    Information Studies. III. Title. IV. Title : Computers for Australian librarians.
    (Series : Topics in Australasian library and information studies ; no. 22).

025.04

This edition published in 2003
First published in 1993 as 'Computers for Australian librarians'

Editorial direction: G. Eyre
Copy editor: J. Harris
Text processor: L. Campbell
Cover design: K. Reid
Printer: Active print, Wagga Wagga.

Centre for Information Studies
Locked Bag 660
Wagga Wagga NSW 2678
Fax: +612 6933 2733
Email: cis@csu.edu.au
http://www.csu.edu.au/cis

Contents

collections - Records management systems - Management information systems (MIS) - Collection evaluation - Other management information - Decision support systems (DSS) - Executive information systems - Library management systems and the electronic library - References - Review questions - Further resources

Figures

Preface

Anyone who reads about information provision in the information technology literature is bound to come across predictions about a state of information abundance, in which the end-user is offered direct and 'seamless' access to a huge body of publications, electronically stored and transmitted on request. Sometimes this electronic library of the future is graced with mythological significance, with names like the Electronic Alexandria (a reference to the famous record repository of classical Alexandria). In the literature of library and information management, the corresponding vision is the so-called library without walls or virtual library, where the user can access this world of information from his or her desktop computer.

This paradigm owes much to the ideas of Vannevar Bush, senior Science Advisor to US President Roosevelt. In 1945, in what is regarded as a seminal work, 'As we may think', Bush propounded the idea of a scholarly workstation or *memex*, that would store an extensive library of scientific publications on microfilm and permit the scholar to index publications, record annotations and create associative links between documents. Many see Bush's *memex* as a visionary idea which was merely waiting for computer technology. With the development of computer systems and technology, computer networks and user-friendly retrieval tools, such as the World Wide Web, it could be argued that Bush's idea of a memex has been realised. When the first edition of this book was published in 1993, such a statement might have seemed hyperbolic, but ten years later it seems an unremarkable claim.

Where do libraries fit into this apparent world of information abundance? The first few chapters of this edition present an overview of how computers and computer networks are used in the library environment and how developments in information and communications technologies (ICTs) provide opportunities for improving library service. Areas covered include:

- provision of access to web-based resources, commercially available databases and the growing number of electronic journals and electronic books being published
- the use of computer systems and networks to support much of the collection management transacted by libraries
- the development of digital library collections.

The focus, in other words, is computer applications in libraries.

Chapter 1 is devoted to the Internet and examines the range of information resources available on the Internet, use of the Internet for communications, and information retrieval on the Internet, with particular reference to the World Wide Web. (It perhaps gives some idea of the rate of change to note that in 1993, when this book was first published, the Web was newly established!) Basics of the Internet and the Web are covered, including the principal search tools available and their main features. The chapter closes with some observations on attempts by librarians to improve access to Internet resources, and some of the main issues to consider in the development of a library website.

In Chapter 2, the focus shifts from the Internet to library and information services, which utilise a range of information resources – those accessed electronically, increasingly via the Internet, and those (electronic, print and audiovisual) that are purchased by libraries in line with their collection development policies. Resources discussed include online information databases, 'portable' databases such as CD-ROM information sources and inhouse resources. The main services covered are the virtual reference library – which aims to provide an information service twenty-four hours a day, seven days a week – and document delivery, which involves obtaining resources for users that are neither available locally nor accessible electronically. The other main topics covered are the digitisation of existing collections (in other words, copying them into a format that can be stored and transmitted electronically) and the impact of electronic publishing.

Chapter 3 discusses the impact of ICTs on the provision of access to information resources. Much of the focus is on catalogues and shared cataloguing. As long as libraries have collections, catalogues will remain one of the principal information retrieval tools used in libraries. Cataloguing was one of the earliest library operations to be computerised, and this chapter looks at the various forms of library catalogue in use and at attempts by librarians to pool their cataloguing effort through the formation of bibliographic networks. It also explains the use of MARC formats (MAchine-Readable Cataloguing, or Code) in the exchange of bibliographic data. Finally, newer alternatives to information access are explored, such as the 'metadata' standard known as Dublin Core – means of improving resource discovery on the Internet and sharing information about information.

Chapter 4 introduces the idea of an information system, which is a system that represents objects in a physical system, for example, information resources in a library collection (a catalogue). The focus here is library management systems, which are used to manage library collections: their acquisition, their cataloguing (identification, description and location) and their circulation (recording and controlling the movement of individual items in the collection). The remainder of the chapter discusses two main topics, the management of special materials, such as serials and short-loan collections, and the generation of management information; information that can assist library directors in performance evaluation. Finally, it discusses the place of library management systems in the wider library and information environment, and the need for library systems to adhere to some of the standards discussed in earlier chapters.

In Chapter 5, the focus shifts from library specific software, such as library management systems, to generic software that is used in the wider community for data management but which can be adapted to library use. The two main types of software discussed are text retrieval systems and database management systems. These offer quite different approaches to data management and are discussed and compared in some detail. The remainder of the chapter outlines four other types of software that have particular relevance in the library environment: hypertext, expert (or knowledge-based) systems, personal bibliographic software and spreadsheet packages.

Up to this point, the discussion is largely (though not entirely) taken up with computer applications in libraries and has avoided talking about computers in much detail. This has been deliberate, because the plan is to provide a gentle introduction to computers in libraries by outlining how they are used in libraries before considering how they actually perform these functions. Some do argue that computer systems have become so easy to use, compared to earlier systems, that librarians do not need to know how computers work, any more than someone driving a car needs to know anything about its mechanics. The approach taken here is that knowing something about how computers work helps librarians make more effective use of their computerised systems, helps them keep abreast of computer and communications developments (
on which the library literature has much to say) and helps them communicate intelligently with the computer systems people, many of whom see no need to familiarise themselves with library operations.

Chapter 6 therefore is a brief introduction to computer systems and technology, which assumes no previous knowledge of computing. A computer system is taken to comprise three main components:

- data, which are the raw facts that are stored and processed in a computer system, e.g., data about books, library users, loans transactions or library suppliers
- computer hardware, which is the equipment used to enter data into the system, store or process data, and display data to users
- computer software, which consists of sets of instructions (programs) that cause the hardware to perform actions, such as data processing, as required by the human operator.

Each of these components is discussed in turn, starting with the different categories of hardware. In order to understand computer processing, it is necessary to know something about the way in which data are represented in a computer, and Chapter 6 introduces this crucial topic. It also covers computer software, both applications software, such as the library management software described in Chapter 4, and the operating systems that control the hardware on which the applications run. Finally, it discusses different types of computer system and the different types of user interface – the combination of hardware and software that allows the user to maintain a dialogue with a computer system.

Chapter 7 examines data communications and networking, a field in which some of the most exciting developments in library services are taking place. Topics covered include network models, the media used in the transmission of data and data transmission methods. It also discusses protocols – sets of conventions or rules used in data transmission – and provides an overview of many of the standards that are most important to libraries. It concludes with a brief explanation of some of the hardware required for data communication.

The final chapter examines the development of computerised library systems. It builds on the previous chapters, which dealt first with computer applications in libraries and then with the supporting technology and standards. It outlines the main options for systems development facing library managers and introduces the traditional systems analysis and design approach, before focusing on the way in which most libraries go about acquiring new systems, which is to purchase prewritten software packages. Specific aspects of systems development are examined, including project management, development of specifications, system selection, implementation of systems and the final systems evaluation.

This edition of *Computers for librarians* differs from previous editions in including case studies, with a view to providing concrete examples of system development and thereby putting the theory and principles discussed in the preceding chapters into some form of context. These include systems development in a polytechnic library over a twenty-year period; the processes of upgrading a library management system in a public library; catalogue enhancement using information from online bookstores; Kinetica; the development of online multimedia library collections and services in a university library; reconstruction of a university library (Universidade Nasional Timor Lorosae); and the development of a digital library for a general community.

Like previous editions, the approach taken is a top-down one, in which applications are discussed first, before the more technological topics. This is not the approach taken by standard texts on computers in libraries. These invariably start with computing concepts, such as bits and bytes (or even semiconductor technology!), and work their way up through software and data management concepts to applications. The reason for taking a top-down approach is that, for those readers who have a poor understanding of computer technology, it makes more sense to start with what computers do and to build an understanding of how systems operate within the context of the applications. This approach has been used to great effect in a number of courses, including library and information management programs.

The book is aimed primarily at students of library and information management and at those library and information service professionals who feel the need for a text which will give them a broad overview of computer applications and systems in their field. It provides self-learning aids, such as learning objectives, keywords and review exercises for the benefit of students, but it is not only a textbook – it is intended as an exploration of where we have reached in the development of the electronic library. No attempt has been made to compile lengthy bibliographies, since resources in this area date so quickly, but at the end of each chapter there are a few suggestions for further reference, which include books, conferences and websites that the authors think particularly worth exploring.

Finally, this is not a substitute for reading some good computer and communications texts, but it is intended as a gentle introduction to systems, technologies and networks for those who find such texts intimidating. It is not intended as a handbook, with practical advice and checklists. There are plenty of such handbooks, aimed at specific markets, such as microcomputer buyers or school librarians (a couple of which are included in the 'further resources' lists). What the book does provide is a survey of where we are with the electronic library and, it is hoped, some idea of where we are going.

Acknowledgements

No book is written in a vacuum, and the authors acknowledge their debt to those who have previously written texts on computers for librarians, such as Jennifer Rowley, Lucy Tedd and William Saffady, and to David William Walker, whose *Computer based information systems* (1989) took the top-down approach to computing adopted in this book. They must also thank a large number of colleagues who made helpful comments during the writing of this and earlier editions, most notably Geoff Fellows, Edward Stow, Ken Dillon, John Mills, Ashley Freeman, Ken Eustace, Ross Harvey and Joseph Meloche, all of Charles Sturt University, School of Information Studies, at the time. They also acknowledge the information retrieval skills of Alice Ferguson and David Pietsch of Charles Sturt University, Division of Library Services, who provided invaluable support during the writing of the second edition. Alice is also an excellent source of information and impassioned opinion on topics such as the virtual reference library and the special challenges of providing library services to remote users.

Special thanks also go to Philip Hider, now at CSU, who generously provided a detailed review of the second edition – *most* of his comments have been addressed in this one – and to Karin Smith of CSU, Division of Library Services, who read the third edition and added further suggestions. Jill Harris's copy editing was excellent and timely, and both she and Lynne Campbell made a significant contribution to the final version of the book. The authors are also grateful to those who generously took time off from their busy schedules to contribute case studies – Fang Sin Guek, Kelly Brennan, Tommy Yeung, Owen Tam, Roxanne Missingham, Karen Myers and Alan Dawson – in the process enriching what otherwise threatened to be a rather dry, theoretical work.

It goes without saying – but writers prefer to point it out anyway – that any shortcomings in the book are the responsibility of the authors and no-one else.

Writing, even collaborative writing, is an essentially anti-social activity. Stuart wishes to thank Alice for her optimism and Seon and Ross for letting him on the Internet once a week (and for even allowing him to use their wonderful XP-based system). Rodney would like to thank his wife Jillian for her patience and support while he spent numerous nights conversing with a computer screen and keyboard instead of her.

Stuart Ferguson
School of Information Studies
Charles Sturt University

Rodney Hebels
Information Technology Division
TAFE New South Wales – Riverina Institute

CHAPTER 1
The Internet and the Web

It may seem strange to start a book about computers for librarians by focusing on neither. The Internet, however, has had an enormous impact on libraries over the past few decades and promises to continue revolutionising library and information services. Much of what is discussed in later chapters about library applications and about computer systems, technology and networking, is affected by Internet developments, and it would help put the use of computers in libraries into some sort of context by outlining first the main features of the Internet. It is also a topic that continues to absorb librarians, which in itself is a good reason for starting with it.

Learning objectives

At the end of this chapter, you will be able to:

- outline the types of information resource available on the Internet
- discuss different means of communicating across the Internet
- explain some basic networking principles and standards
- discuss different ways of searching the Internet, including the World Wide Web, and
- discuss specific features of the World Wide Web, such as hypertext and HTML.

Keywords

Internet
Network
Electronic publishing
E-book
Electronic mail
Discussion list
Newsgroup
Internet chat

Protocol
Client/server model
World Wide Web
Web server
Hypertext
Hypertext Markup Language
Hypertext Transfer Protocol
Uniform Resource Locator

Web browser
Search engine
Boolean searching
Subject directory
Portal
Intranet
File Transfer Protocol
Invisible Web

What is the Internet?

The Internet is a worldwide network of interconnected computers which enables computer users to communicate with each other and to share resources and services. To be more literal, it is a network of computer networks: the word is a combination of 'inter' (between or among) and 'network'. This begs the question, of course:

What is a network?

A network is an arrangement of computers, computer peripherals (for example, printers) and communication media, designed to share data, information or components of a computer system (such as a printer). It also includes a control mechanism, to ensure that the parts of the network can actually communicate (see Chapter 7). One of the devices used to transmit data between other devices, such as computers, or between networks is a device called a router, hence Harry Bruce's interesting notion that 'the Internet is really a collection of routers that talk the same language and pass data back and forth' (2002, p. 9).

Networks can be any size, from a *local area network* (LAN) that encompasses computer parts and cabling within a single building (for example, the public library) to a *wide area network* (WAN) that encompasses separate computer systems in different organisations in different parts of the country. The following are the main types of wide area network:

- cooperative networks, such as the bibliographic networks, formed by libraries to allow the exchange and sharing of bibliographic data or, in other words, data describing their information resources (see Chapters 2 and 3)

- corporate networks, shared by the parts of a corporate body such as a company that has branch offices in different parts of a country (corporate libraries are likely to be part of such a network)

- academic and research networks, such as the many national networks linking academic and research institutions (which may be used by academic libraries), and

- commercial networks, which provide network services to personal and corporate subscribers, for example, CompuServe in the USA.

The Internet falls into none of these categories. It can be thought of as the backbone of countless networks throughout the world; that which links these other kinds of network together. It may help to put the Internet in context by considering briefly its genesis. It was started in 1969 by the US military with the aim of decentralising its computing infrastructure. It realised that its current structure was vulnerable in wartime because of its centralisation. Later, the network (ARPANET) was joined by scientific and academic institutions in the US and by networks from other countries (hence the term 'internetworking') and it grew from there. Because of this, there is no governing body of the Internet. As you will read elsewhere, 'Anarchy is at its heart'.

Individual users can:

- connect their computers directly to the Internet and form part of the network
- use their computers to connect to a host computer that itself is directly connected to the Internet
- connect to the Internet via a constituent network of the Internet, for example, one of the academic and research networks, or
- subscribe to an Internet Service Provider (ISP), sometimes also referred to as an Internet Access Provider, which is a company that will provide connections and the necessary software to connect to the Internet.

The Internet can also be thought of as more than simply the *means* by which networks are linked world-wide: it also includes the beginnings of a vast electronic library or archive. (Sometimes the means are collectively referred to as the Net, while the resources that it links are referred to collectively as the Web, a term that is discussed later in this chapter.) The interconnection provided by the Internet encourages many organisations and individuals, talented or otherwise, to self-publish. Here, the term 'publish', is used in the basic sense of 'making public'. The Internet has considerably facilitated the process of self-publication, making it easy for authors to reach end-users directly, without intermediaries such as traditional publishers and booksellers. This is not to say that traditional publishers and distributors play no part on the Internet. The publisher of this book, for example, uses the Internet to promote its products and services. Recent years have also seen the emergence of new electronic publishers that publish on behalf of authors, like any print-based publisher, while print-based publishers increasingly turn to electronic publishing.

What information resources are available on the Internet?

Before exploring some of the technical aspects of the Internet, it would be worth considering some of the information resources – the actual content – available via this network of networks (or collection of routers).

Commercial information resources

These are commercially produced and distributed information resources which often, but not necessarily, duplicate the kind of information purchased by librarians in print format, for example, periodical indexing and abstracting sources, directories and, to an increasing extent, full-text information resources (see Chapter 2). They are made available on remote 'host' computers, can be accessed and used, by subscription, and are usually password protected. Such resources predate the Internet (many of the well-established information sources and services, for instance, Dialog, have been around since the 1970s) – before the Internet they were accessed via the telephone systems using what was called 'dial-up' access. These are dealt with in more detail in the next chapter.

Electronic journals and newsletters

These cover a range of publications, some available without fee but others costing as much as the print equivalents. They include scholarly electronic journals, many of them prestigious, refereed publications, like their print equivalents; electronic versions of existing print publications; and the archived back-issues of discussion lists, messages that have been sent by one member of a discussion list to other members on the list. (Discussion lists are dealt with later in this chapter.) Many print publishers also provide selected articles free of charge, as part of a promotions strategy, along with contents pages. There are useful directories of electronic journals available on the Internet, for example, the American Association of Research Libraries' *Directory of Electronic Journals, Newsletters and Academic Discussion Lists* or the more specialised *Library-Oriented Lists and Electronic Serials*. Another useful source is *Current Cites*, which has a team of librarians and other library staff monitoring the information technology literature and distributing electronically citations and short annotations for those items regarded as 'best' (about ten to fifteen in each monthly 'issue').

Electronic reference works

These are the electronic equivalents of the reference resources used by libraries, such as directories, dictionaries and encyclopedias, for example, *Britannica Online*, and are usually available for a fee. There are many directories on the Internet that help users to locate useful resources, for example, the two mentioned above. Directories suffer from a problem common to many Internet resources, namely that it is not always obvious how up to date, comprehensive or authoritative they are. As for print publications, the producer of an electronic publication is one indicator of the quality of a publication, but it is not as easy to identify producers as it is in a clearly delineated commercial print market. There are sites on the Internet that provide a selection of reference resources. Libraries are an obvious example because their main business is to provide their communities of users (geographical, academic or corporate communities) with access to useful resources.

Electronic books

The best-known attempt to develop a collection of electronic books is *Project Gutenberg*, which provides more than 3,000 works that are in the public domain, free of charge. (Such names, of course, contain the inflated, but common, notion that the Internet will have as important an impact on human consciousness as the invention of printing. The 'Gutenberg' in this case refers to Johann Gutenberg, who established his commercial printing business in Mainz in 1445. Other projects include:

- *Questia*: (www.questia.com/), which offers over 400,000 books, journals and articles, including scholarly material from over 235 acclaimed publishers in the humanities and social sciences, and, to 'complement the library', a range of search, note-taking, and writing tools designed for students

- *ebrary*: (www.ebrary.com/) – offers products and online services to libraries and publishers, including database collections with more than 20,000 books and other authoritative documents from over 150 academic, trade and professional publishers
- *netLibrary*: (www.netlibrary.com/).

NetLibrary is probably the most interesting from a library perspective. Now under OCLC, it specifically targets libraries. It was one of the so-called dot-com companies that looked as if it had collapsed in 2002. There was speculation at the time that libraries would be left without access to the collection, but OCLC made a successful bid for the company and guaranteed continued access. OCLC also provides MARC records for the netLibrary e-books.

It is worth noting that commercially produced (and priced) electronic books or e-books are available, such as RCS's Gemstar, but these are designed for use with dedicated machines, for example, Gemstone readers (formerly Rocket eBook Reader) and the Everybook Reader, which offer extra facilities: adding annotations, bookmarking and providing access to reference tools. E-books are being produced that closely resemble 'regular books', and there are currently reports of experiments with electronic ink (Deegan & Tanner 2002, p. 77). There are many bibliophiles who remain convinced that these will not replace 'regular' books (not surprisingly they seem reluctant to 'curl up' with an electronic book), but it is worth noting that Monroe County Library System in New York experimented with e-book readers in five of its libraries, and reported that some 35% of people surveyed stated that they would prefer to use e-books to the print ones (Deegan & Tanner 2002, p. 78).

It is especially worth noting the role of leading libraries, such as the Library of Congress in the USA, the British Library and the Bibliothèque Nationale in France in converting large parts of their print collections into electronic format. The Library of Congress National Digital Library Project, for example, is intended to create a 'virtual library' of images of books, drawings, manuscripts and photographs that can be transmitted across computer networks (discussed towards the end of this chapter). It is perhaps also worth mentioning the current attempt by Australian university libraries to make higher degree theses available online.

News reports

Many people use the Internet to obtain up-to-date news reports. Some of the broadcast media, for example, provide news summaries, for instance, the British Broadcasting Corporation, and there are many newspapers that can be accessed, in full or in part, on the Internet, for instance, the *Sydney Morning Herald*, which offers recent issues on the Internet and provides an archives search service for a fee. Commercial organisations such as Reuters also provide newswire services, geared primarily for the news media, including television, radio and newspapers.

Government publications

Many governments and government agencies use the Internet to disseminate government, political and legal information. In the UK, for example, the *CCTA Government Information Service*, provided by the Central Computer and Telecommunications Authority, stores information for a number of British government departments and agencies and provides links to those which have their own sites. In Australia, users can access primary legal material in electronic format courtesy of the Australian Legal Information Institute.

Commercial information

Many commercial organisations also use the Internet to disseminate information about themselves, their products and services. An example, already mentioned above, is print publishers, who provide catalogues of their publications, contents pages and sample publications. Another example, familiar to librarians, is booksellers and subscription agents, who use the Internet to advertise and enable customers to order material electronically (see Chapter 4).

Library catalogues

Library catalogues are not regarded as information resources, in the sense that they do not give the end-user the answer required (unless the user simply wants to know, for example, who published a particular title), but they are useful information retrieval tools. Many library catalogues are in electronic format and can be made available on the Internet. One problem facing users is that there are many commercial suppliers of electronic catalogues, and some catalogues were even developed 'inhouse', with the result that there is no uniform set of procedures for interrogating a catalogue. It is not easy, therefore, for users to move from one catalogue to another. One solution is to develop computer software (sets of instructions that tell a computer what to do – discussed in a later chapter) which, regardless of catalogue, provides users with a uniform set of search facilities – see Chapter 7, on the so-called Z39.50 standard.

People

Librarians are generally accustomed to the idea that, although their main information sources are published resources, they can also make use of people whose personal knowledge may never have been published as an information product or resource. The so-called 'invisible college' has grown in terms of size, significance and geographical distribution with the development of a range of electronic mail facilities (see below). Librarians, like any other group with Internet access, can benefit from getting together electronically with colleagues who have similar professional interests and problems – particularly (but by no means exclusively) those working in small, one-professional libraries. See the discussion below about electronic means of communication.

Software

Finally, the focus above has been on information resources or, in the case of library catalogues, information retrieval tools, but there are other resources available on the Internet. It is worth particular mention that the Internet is also used by many, particularly those interested in information systems and technology, to search for computer software, especially freeware and shareware. Freeware is computer software that is quite often written by an enthusiastic individual and is offered to others for no charge. Shareware is similar, except that it is typically accompanied by a request for payment in return for which the purchaser often receives extra functionality or documentation.

Why are librarians so excited about the Internet?

Librarians can make use of the Internet in the following ways:

- electronic mail for communication, for example, for inter-library loans
- exchanging information and ideas with colleagues, for example, through newsgroups and discussion lists
- retrieving electronic publications, such as journals or legal publications
- subscribing to electronic information retrieval tools, such as indexing services
- accessing library catalogues
- searching the catalogues of suppliers and subscription agents and ordering titles
- subscribing to electronic journals, conferences and newsletters
- extending library services, for example, making library or commercial databases available to distance learning students
- publishing documents relating to the library, for example, library guides.

Most of the remainder of this chapter discusses the following Internet facilities:

- communicating over the Internet, including electronic mail
- finding Internet resources, including connecting to remote sites
- the World Wide Web (WWW)
- search engines and subject directories: key retrieval tools
- fetching stuff over the Internet (file transfer protocol)
- describing Internet resources
- providing 'one-shop stops' on the Internet: portals.

Communicating over the Internet

Earlier it was suggested that people are an important information resource. The main kinds of interpersonal communication on the Internet are:

- electronic mail
- discussion lists
- newsgroups or forums
- interactive ('live') forms of conferencing
- webcasting.

Electronic mail

The term electronic mail (email) refers to a variety of means of electronic messaging, for example, via a direct computer to computer link, via a local area network (LAN), via wide area networks like those mentioned earlier, or across separate networks. It is generally used to describe messaging between specific electronic mailboxes, but on some networks there is a facility to send messages between a computer and a facsimile or fax machine (for example, to send an inter-library loan request to a library that has no email address).

An email 'posting' will contain an Internet address (discussed below), the text of a message, plus information such as a subject header (provided by the sender), the sender's name and/or email address, and the time and date the message was sent. When the receiver opens his or her mailbox, some of this information is displayed, making it possible to delete unwanted mail without opening it – often a good move with mail that does not have an obvious and known source, because of the dangers of computer 'viruses'.

The software package used to handle electronic mail is sometimes referred to as a mailer. Examples include *Pegasus*, *Pine*, *Eudora* and Microsoft *Outlook*. Generally, a mailer enables users to

- read mail
- print mail
- save or delete mail (including block deletion, which means selecting postings from a list and deleting the whole selection)
- create electronic 'folders' in which to save mail (and in which to find it again!)
- forward and redirect mail
- reply to mail
- send new mail
- send mail with electronic documents and other information 'objects' attached (for instance, images)
- create distribution lists, in order to send postings to more than one mailbox simultaneously (for example, a city librarian may want to contact all branch libraries)

- save copies of outgoing mail
- store and retrieve mail addresses from a special address file
- archive mail.

Mailers generally only handle text, but there is a standard, MIME (Multipurpose Internet Mail Extension), which enables people to send non-textual documents. This requires that both the sending mailer and the receiving one support the MIME standard.

One of the main benefits of email is its speed. In libraries the main application is the sending and receiving of requests, for example, reference enquiries, inter-library loan requests and, in the case of some academic libraries, requests from distance learning students. There are also benefits in librarians being able to communicate quickly with colleagues, for example, through discussion lists (below) or with outside agencies such as booksellers and subscription agents.

Addressing email messages

If mailboxes on the Internet are to receive email, they must have unique addresses and there are Internet conventions for ensuring this. These conventions specify that each site on the Internet is identified by a unique number (just as people have a telephone with a unique number), called an IP or Internet Protocol number. These are discussed in Chapter 7. Here it is simply noted that most email addresses are alphabetical or alphanumerical (a mixture of alphabetical text and numbers), but that when people use an alphabetical or alphanumerical address to send an email, their mailers automatically translate that address into an IP number. This is a simply matter of convenience, because alphabetical (and alphanumerical) addresses are easier to remember than IP numbers.

Take an example: the email address for the Australian publisher of this book, the Centre for Information Studies, has an email address that looks like this:

cis@csu.edu.au

This is made up of

- a user identifier, in this case 'cis' stands for the publisher's name
- the 'at' symbol, @, linking the other two main elements in the address, and
- the site address, which in this case is made up of three domains (each helping to identify where the host computer that stores the email 'account' is to be found):

  - 'csu', which indicates the institution in which the server is found (in this case, Charles Sturt University)

  - 'edu', which indicates the type of institution, in this case, an educational organisation (some countries, such as the UK and New Zealand, use 'ac' to denote educational institution), and

  - 'au', which indicates the country in which the institution is located, in this case Australia (absence of a country domain indicates a US address).

In this instance, the name of the 'host' computer does not actually appear in the email address. This is mainly for convenience. Once a message reaches the institution's mailer, it will be directed to a particular computer using an internal address that includes the name of the host computer on which the mailbox is stored. (Bear in mind that an institution may have more than one computer dedicated to electronic communication.) Internet addresses are discussed again later in the chapter, when you read about the World Wide Web, and Chapter 7 attempts to explain some of the main communication 'protocols' involved, such as the IP one just mentioned.

Discussion lists

A *discussion list*, or *mailing list*, is a form of electronic mail in which messages from one member of a group are sent to all members of the group. It is like the distribution list mentioned above in that it is a one-to-many form of communication, but, whereas any individual can set up a distribution list on his or her own computer, a discussion list is a cooperative venture, generally set up by a group of people who wish to exchange views and information on a particular topic, such as music librarianship or library automation. Each member of the list can send messages to the other members and receive all their postings. Discussion lists can be a useful way in which to keep up to date with one's profession and even to receive help. OZTL_NET, for example, is a discussion list in Australia with more than 2,000 members, consisting of teacher librarians, school library consultants, teacher librarianship educators and other professionals with an interest in teacher librarianship and school library issues.

Normally, the discussion list will be mounted on a server (host computer), which will employ special software to distribute incoming postings to current members of the list and to handle additions to, and deletions from, the list. Members of the list will receive copies of all postings successfully submitted, including (in some cases) messages from non-members, and are able to post their own contributions.

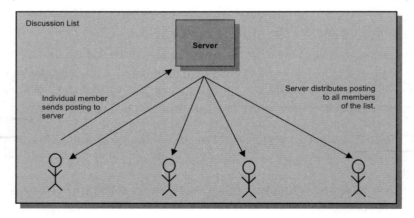

Figure 1.1: Discussion lists

In some cases, not all messages are distributed to members because there are *moderated* lists in which editors check incoming postings and block those considered inappropriate. The majority of discussion lists, however, are unmoderated, primarily because editing lists is so time-consuming. There is also a perception that moderation is a form of censorship. Some lists accept contributions from non-members, but others are closed to outsiders.

LISTSERV is a common piece of mail server software and sometimes the term is used in speech as another synonym for discussion list or mailing list. The International Federation of Library Associations (IFLA), for example, uses the LISTSERV software and provides general information on LISTSERVs and on IFLA discussion lists, as well as references to LISTSERV guides and resources, including where to find lists of discussion lists. One example of a list of discussion lists, available on the Internet, is *PAML - Publicly Accessible Mailing Lists*.

Because of the impersonality of email, for example, the lack of non-verbal signals, it is easy for misunderstanding to occur. There are even suggestions in the computing literature that email can become quite abusive (abusive messages are sometimes referred to as 'flames' in the growing Internet jargon). There are informal rules of etiquette ('netiquette'; another piece of jargon) which new members of discussion lists are advised to observe. Much of it is commonsense, for example, the need to avoid troubling professional colleagues with trivia or promotional material.

Clearly, there can be benefits in belonging to a discussion list but there are also drawbacks for busy professionals. One of the common complaints from members of discussion lists is that they increase the volume of email messages dramatically and, since most lists are unmoderated, a large proportion of messages are likely to be of little or no interest. People who come back to work from leave are likely to find too many messages to handle and are often forced to block delete messages (in other words, select a group of messages and delete them all). It is generally advisable to unsubscribe from discussion lists before going on leave. One option to keep down the volume of postings is the digest facility provided by most discussion list software, which batches and sends postings that arrive over a specific time period (for example, a day) as a single posting.

Newsgroups

Newsgroups, sometimes called forums, are similar to discussion lists in that groups of people use email to communicate on topics of interest. The main difference is that, whereas messages sent to discussion list servers are redistributed to members of the list, messages sent to newsgroup servers are stored on the servers or host computers for people to access at their convenience.

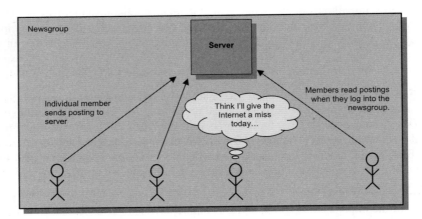

Figure 1.2: Newsgroups

For some, this can be a disadvantage, because it means that they have to make a point of checking the server, whereas discussion list postings are waiting in their email for them. Busy professionals, however, may decide that accessing newsgroups is preferable to having an overload of email, much of it of little interest, but of course, if they fail to access their newsgroups regularly, they may miss postings and lose some of the current awareness benefits associated with both discussion lists and newsgroups.

Newsgroups require special software, called newsreaders, which allow users to display the names of newsgroups and to move between them. Newsgroup postings resemble other email postings, such as those distributed by discussion lists, except that, where people respond to particular postings, their postings are displayed under the original one, with a common subject header. The original posting and responses to it (and any responses to these responses, and so on) are known collectively as a *thread*. Threading can be a useful means by which subscribers of a newsgroup can identify and follow particular debates among their colleagues and, of course, post their own contributions. Newsreaders normally allow users to mark postings as 'read', which means that the next time they access that particular group they see only those messages posted since the ones that have been read.

The largest grouping of public newsgroups on the Internet is a US one called USENET, with the result that one will sometimes see newsgroups referred to as USENET groups. These are organised into main categories, such as 'comp' for computers, which are then subdivided hierarchically into topics, for example, 'comp.internet' (if one is interested in that sort of thing). As well as groups which are of professional interest, there are groups which may provide personal help, such as coping with menopause or helping to give up smoking.

Newsgroups have a somewhat mixed reputation, not least because of the publicity given to the 'alt.sex' categories of newsgroup, but there are some useful groups in the library and information science area. Like discussion lists, newsgroups can be moderated, but in general they are not. Some newsgroups post a FAQ (Frequently-Asked Questions) document, which answers the more straightforward questions likely to be asked, and new users are well advised to check this before posting a question.

As suggested earlier, the archives of discussion lists and newsgroups can constitute a useful information resource.

Interactive conferences

The types of interpersonal communication discussed so far, person-to-person messaging, discussion lists and newsgroups, are not, generally, 'live' forms of communication, such as speaking to someone on the telephone. There are, however, forms of interactive communication on the Internet, notably:

- videoconferencing, which is possible via the Internet using MBONE, or IP Multicast Backbone (IP or Internet Protocol is discussed in Chapter 7)
- chat, which is a form of conferencing in which participants communicate using a keyboard instead of speech, and
- MOOs (MUD Object-Oriented), which have role-playing elements (see below).

'Chat' is currently the most popular form of synchronous communication on the Internet. In this context, the word synchronous denotes the fact that the people communicating with each other are doing so simultaneously. This contrasts with asynchronous forms of communication such as email, which involves leaving a message for someone. The 'chatroom' is a piece of imagery commonly associated with online chat, giving the idea that people come together via the Internet to have a 'live' conference. Once people join a chat group they can select a topic or 'channel' and communicate with others in the group by entering words into their computers by use of the computer keyboard. Internet Relay Chat (IRC) is a common piece of computer chat software, available on the Internet free of charge. Chat has widespread application, both as a recreational service and as an educational one. It also has some application in the library and information environment, because the 'live' aspect allows for immediate feedback, unlike email in its various forms.

MOOs resemble Chat on a superficial level. They are so called because they are based on MUDs (Multi-User Dungeon): a form of multi-user 'virtual environment' game in which participants play out roles such as elves, wizards and other strange characters. MOO stands for MUD Object-Oriented environment and is a form of Internet conferencing based loosely on the role-playing model provided by MUDs. Clearly MUDs do not offer the kind of role-playing activities which would engage serious-minded librarians, but MOOs offer more than internet chat in that they allow users to create virtual objects as they interact within the MOO environment. They have a couple of applications that are of interest to librarians: first, their use for online tutorials aimed at remote users (for example, in distance learning to explore information retrieval tools such as online databases) and, second, their use in interactive online reference services.

Probably the best-known MOO in the library environment is the Internet Public Library MOO. The Internet Public Library is an attempt to bring to the Internet long-standing librarianship skills such as finding good information resources, organising them and making it easier for users to find them.

Webcasting

Webcasting, as the name suggests, is a one to many form of communication (like broadcasting), which allows users to 'publish' multimedia presentations (including video, audio and powerpoint) via the Internet. It is therefore an especially powerful communication tool in the corporate sector. It is treated separately from the preceding forms of communication because it can be both viewed live, with interaction between webcaster and viewer (for instance, via a chatroom), or it can enable webcasts to be archived and presented to users on demand. As the distinction between publisher and library (traditionally a purchaser and repository of publications) becomes blurred – a notion that will be revisited later – and libraries use the Internet to publish their own material, webcasting offers attractive features, not least in the area of user education or what is increasingly termed information literacy (a broader concept).

Finding Internet resources

So far, the discussion has focused on communication. In the earlier section on information resources, however, it was suggested that there are a great many information resources, information retrieval tools and computer software packages that can be accessed on the Internet. This section discusses various means of retrieving Internet resources, including the World Wide Web, which for some people has become (mistakenly) synonymous with the Internet.

Before discussing the retrieval of Internet resources, it would be worth considering the client/server model, which underlies many Internet facilities. Only network *concepts* are considered here, however: the basic technological infrastructure is not discussed until Chapter 7.

Client/server model

The term client/server model may sound a bit daunting for those unfamiliar with computer concepts, but the concept itself is straightforward. For a user to access the Internet resources outlined earlier, there generally needs to be cooperation between two computer systems: the client and the server. The client is the user's local system, which will typically comprise a personal computer, computer peripherals (for example, a computer screen on which to display the data exchanged) and software. These components allow the user to communicate with the client and the client to communicate with the server. Note that if this book mentions 'clients' it is referring to such systems, and not to users (for which 'clients' is sometimes synonymous in librarianship literature). The server, which is a 'remote' system (it may be on another continent or in the next building), stores the data that the user wishes to access, retrieves data requested by the user and transmits them to the client. (The server is sometimes referred to as a host, especially in the case of the commercial servers discussed in the next chapter.)

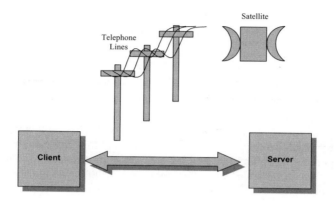

Figure 1.3: The client/server model

The operation of the client/server model, therefore, involves the use of two sets of computer software: client software, such as the software that helps the user communicate with the computer system (see, for instance, the web browser discussed later in this chapter), and server software, such as the retrieval software (consider, for example, search engines, also discussed later). The server is generally a more powerful computer system than the client and would be expected to deal with more than one client simultaneously. One of the main advantages of the client/server model is the fact that, provided the clients and servers can understand the data passing between them, it doesn't matter what kind of computer system is used for the client. An IBM-compatible server (a computer designed according to the same standards as those of the IBM company) may be accessed, for example, by clients that are not IBM-compatible, such as Apple Macintosh computers. This depends on networking standards, one of the main topics of Chapter 7.

Telnet

If users are to access files or applications on a remote server, there needs to be a convention by which users can log in to the server. *Telnet* is widely used on the Internet for remote login. It opens a link between the telnet client and the server, enabling the user to access the server as if he or she were actually at the remote site and to log in to a file or application (assuming login is permitted). The way of doing this is for the user to enter the 'telnet' command followed by a site address.

Once the Telnet connection is opened, the user then has to *log in* by identifying the file or application required and entering a 'login', usually an identifier (a username) and a password. Opening a connection using the Telnet protocol does not necessarily gain the user access to files and applications on a remote server, since these may not be for public access. Nonetheless, many are available for access, particularly electronic library catalogues and at some of these sites, a login will be displayed to users.

Once the user has logged in, the client behaves as if it were a *terminal* of the remote system. A terminal is an input/output device that allows a user to communicate with a computer system. Typically, this consists of a keyboard, which allows the user to input data (such as a catalogue search), and a computer screen, to display both the data input and the response of the system (for example, search results). A simple terminal, usually called a dumb terminal, merely acts as an input/output device and relies on the computer to which it is connected for storage and processing of data. In telnetting, however, a client computer is acting like, or emulating, a terminal and it is necessary for the server to know which particular type of *terminal emulation* (for example, VT100) is being used for the two to communicate meaningfully. For this reason, once a user has telnetted to a server, he or she will be asked about the client's terminal emulation. Some communication may be possible if the client and server are using different emulations, but if there are problems, it is generally best for the user to quit the application, telnet again and try a different emulation.

Many Internet users will be unaware of telnet if they use the World Wide Web (discussed below) for finding remote servers.

World Wide Web (WWW)

The Web (sometimes also shortened to WWW or W3) has become synonymous, for many people, with the Internet but, whereas the term Internet tends to refer to the actual network of networks, Web is generally used to refer to the actual resources that can be accessed via the Internet. A working definition of the Web might be that it comprises the large number of Internet servers that use *hypertext* to store and link files.

Hypertext, HTTP and HTML

Since hypertext is an important component in the Web, it is worth pausing to consider the difference between an information resource that uses hypertext in its publication and one that is published in the 'traditional' way. The use of the word 'pausing' betrays the fact that the authors are steeped in traditional forms of writing, because they are saying, 'right, before we discuss the Web, we're going to have to digress and discuss hypertext.' Hypertext writers, on the other hand, would present a section or chunk of information (called a node) about the Web and a separate node on hypertext. Since the publication is intended to be a learning resource, they would create a link between the two nodes, so that readers who are unfamiliar with the concept of hypertext could follow a link from the node on the Web to the one on hypertext, and read up about it. The link between the nodes would be made apparent to the reader by highlighting the term 'hypertext' in the node about the Web and could be selected by the reader by pointing to the term and indicating the selection to the computer system. The node on hypertext would, in turn, have links, for example, one back to the node on the Web and another to a third node that discusses the computer pointing device used to select links (typically a mouse; not discussed until Chapter 6 of this book).

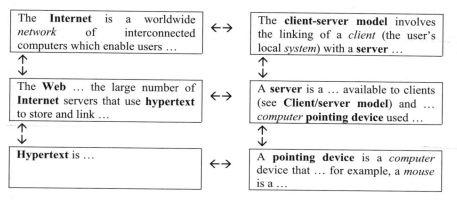

Figure 1.4: The web-like nature of hypertext

One way of distinguishing between traditional printed text and hypertext is to think of text that is presented in linear and non-linear sequences. Traditional text is written in a linear sequence and the reader is more or less confined to following that sequence. A book such as this one, for example, is generally read in a linear sequence, starting at the Preface and finishing with the final chapter, or perhaps appendices (or index in the case of conscientious reviewers). The reader *may* be directed to other sections of text (for example, the reference to another chapter at the end of the last paragraph) or even to another text altogether (for example, the earlier reference, 'Bruce 2002, p. 9'), but these references tend to be of an incidental nature. Hypertext, on the other hand, encourages the reader to follow links to other nodes. Typically these nodes express a single idea or concept, for example, an entry in an encyclopedia would constitute a node and might present a variety of links for the reader to follow.

Hypertext has been combined with multimedia (itself a combination of traditionally separate media, such as graphics, sound and video) to create *hypermedia*, which allows users to follow associative links, not just to other nodes of text, but also to other media presentations, such as sound and video, for example, an encyclopedia entry on kookaburras could provide a link to a node storing an image illustrating the bird and another to a sound recording of the its distinct laughing call.

The Web has its origins in a hypertext publishing project at CERN (the European Particle Physics Laboratory) in Switzerland. In Web publishing, the nodes or chunks of text, referred to earlier, are called pages or web pages. Each page contains links to other pages within the publication, similar conceptually to the reference earlier to Chapter 6. Each page may also contain links to publications elsewhere on the Web, similar to the Bruce reference earlier, which referred the reader to a book by another author. In practice, of course, the reader of a print-based resource may have difficulty retrieving the actual resource to which reference was made, whereas a reader who is presented with a hypertext link, or hyperlink, on a web page can actually follow the link and access the second publication electronically (all being well). Readers of a Web version of this chapter, for example, could follow links to those Web-based resources referred to in the course of the chapter, even though they are stored at completely different websites in a variety of countries.

For documents to be mounted on the Web, there needs to be a standard for their publication. One standard, central to the Web, is *HTTP* (HyperText Transfer Protocol), which, as the name suggests, is the protocol (the set of rules or conventions) used to move copies of hypertext files between Web servers and Web clients. It is a communications protocol, like Telnet (discussed earlier), and will be discussed in Chapter 7.

The other principal standard associated with Web publication is *HTML* (HyperText Markup Language), which is a code that is used to determine the format of Web pages and to embed links to other pages/publications in specified text. The use of the HTML standard means that when someone uses an HTTP client to download a publication from an HTTP server, the client is able to identify the various parts of the document and present them to the user correctly. Each element in a page (such as title, heading, paragraph, picture or textual link) is marked with an HTML *tag*, which carries instructions about what is to be done with the tagged element, for example, highlighting of text with embedded links. Each element will be flanked on either side by an HTML tag so, to take an example, the title of this work as it appears on the publisher's website will be preceded by certain HTML tags indicating how it is to be presented (for instance, font style) and followed by another tag indicating that the previous instruction has ceased to apply. To take the example of font colour, the tags and element might look like this:

<font color="#FF9933">Computers for librarians </font>

Each tag is enclosed in the '<>' symbols. The diagonal slash in the second of the two tags indicates that this particular instruction ends here, and is a common piece of HTML practice. Note, too, that this instruction relates solely to font colour, and there will be other pairs of tags dealing with other aspects of the presentation of this particular element, title, such as the actual font style.

The original HTML format and tags were created by Tim Berners-Lee when he developed the HTTP protocol. They were an application of an earlier, and much more complex, markup language called SGML or Standard Generalized Markup Language. As the simple example above demonstrates, a markup language specifies characteristics of electronic text such as the font style and layout of a data element. Prior to the use of generalised tags, specific electronic documents would have been marked up by publishers for output in the required formats and styles. Interest in generalised languages began in the late 1960s and resulted first in GML (Generalized Markup Language) and then SGML, first published as a working draft in 1980 and by 1986 an international standard: ISO 8879:1986 (SGML

Users' Group 1990). Because it is independent of specific computer systems and non-proprietary – and because it is extremely comprehensive language – SGML has become a very widely adopted standard. (The ISO is the International Standards Organisation, which is a major source of many of the protocols used by the library and information sector.)

The downside of SGML's comprehensiveness is that it is extremely complex. It uses a range of what are called Document Type Definitions (DTDs) to define the tags and syntax used for individual formats, such as journal articles, architectural drawings or novels. DTDs are sets of rules that define the elements that make up a document and encode them in such a way that text within the document can be retrieved, displayed and exchanged across different platforms (in other words, irrespective of the user's computer hardware/system software). Encoded Archival Description Document Type Definition (or EAD DTD), for instance, was developed specifically to designate the intellectual and physical elements of archival finding aids.

HTML is essentially an application – in other words, a DTD – of SGML. One of its strengths is its simplicity compared to a language like SGML (a benefit that library web developers can appreciate). That simplicity can also be a disadvantage, and it can be used for purposes for which it was not designed. As new features are added by web designers it becomes less of a standard, and some users' web browsers (see below) may be unable to cope with the developments. Different varieties of HTML have begun to emerge, which poses the danger that it could become 'a series of proprietary formats' (Deegan & Tanner, 2002, p. 125), and thus cease to be a standard.

XML (Extensible Markup Language) is another important standard, a subset of SGML specifically developed for use with the Web. It was developed under the auspices of the World Wide Web Consortium (or W3C): a grouping of vendor-neutral organisations which recommends to members the standards and protocols that underlie the Web. It has been designed as the universal format for the exchange of structured documents and data on the Web. The intention was that XML would enable SGML to 'be served, received, and processed on the Web in the way that is now possible with HTML' and that HTML itself would become an XML application, as distinct from an SGML one. Its primary purpose is 'as an electronic publishing and data interchange format':

> XML is primarily intended to meet the requirements of large-scale Web content providers for industry-specific markup, vendor-neutral data exchange, media-independent publishing, one-on-one marketing, workflow management in collaborative authoring environments, and the processing of Web documents by intelligent clients. It is also expected to find use in certain metadata applications (Cover Pages 2003).

Because of the insistence on using the Unicode character set (see Chapter 6), XML can be used for the publishing of Asian and European languages, so it is very much an international standard.

It is sometimes suggested that XML might replace HTML, for instance, in the area of professional web development (see, for example, Kochtanek & Matthews 2002, p. 105), but it is worth being aware of the development of XHTML, a version of HTML that is based on XML and not SGML, and which is intended to provide some of the advantages of both markup languages.

Web servers

A web server is the computer device and the software required to run it which together store website files and respond to messages that have been submitted using HTTP (or an associated protocol). Often only one server is used, but for very busy sites it is quite normal to use more than one server, in order to spread out the load. A 'daemon' is a specific kind of computer software that processes enquiries as they come in. Web servers typically need to be powerful computers in processing terms and in terms of memory. Text files are relatively compact, but image files are more 'data intensive' (see the account of data representation in Chapter 6) and other formats, such as video, can require even more computer memory.

URLs (Uniform Resource Locators)

Just as email accounts are given unique addresses through the use of IP numbers (described earlier), Internet resources are given using a unique address, known as a Uniform Resource Locator or URL: for example, the Australian publisher of this book has a site on the Internet with the following URL:

> http://www.csu.edu.au/faculty/sciagr/sis/CIS/cis.html

The URL is made up of three main elements:

- the retrieval method, in this case 'http' or HyperText Transfer Protocol, which is used for accessing Web resources (mentioned above)
- the host and domain name, here 'www.csu.edu.au', and
- the so-called pathway, in this case 'faculty/sciagr/sis/CIS/cis.html', a hierarchical directory type of address on the host computer or server itself.

Note the two elements between the retrieval method and the 'pathway' on the host computer: the host name and the domains. The host name identifies the actual server, while the domains indicate where the server is to be found. The host name in this case is 'www', which is a common (but not universal) name to find in URLs. The name 'www' indicates that the server is a Web server, but in this case no host name is found necessary. The domains in this example are the same ones found in the earlier email example:

- 'csu', which indicates the institution in which the server is found (in this case, Charles Sturt University)
- 'edu', which indicates the type of institution, in this case, an educational organisation, and
- 'au', which indicates the country in which the institution, and therefore the server, is located, in this case Australia.

The third element in the address, the pathway, locates on the server the actual webpage, or set of webpages, identified by the address, in this case a university publisher's website. The directory-type pathway, 'faculty/sciagr/sis/CIS/cis.html', for example, places the Centre's webpages within those of a specific university faculty (Science and Agriculture). Clearly this can lead to long and complicated web addresses, but some organisations will provide an 'alias' that points to the full, hierarchical address – in this case, 'www.csu.edu.au/cis/' is used as an alias for the full web address given above. (A similar practice can be observed with email addresses.) Finally, in the case of Web resources the 'pathway' usually generally ends in 'html' (unless the file naming convention of the computer is to use three letters, in which case 'htm' would be used).

It is worth noting, too, the URN or Uniform Resource Name. One of the main problems with URLs is that they do change, and if someone searches an out-of-date link (such as many of the links contained in the second edition of this book!) they reach only a broken or 'dead' link or, in other words, a screen advising them that the link cannot be found. The idea of a URN is that it will provide a more permanent form of identification than the URL and so solve the problem of broken links. Clearly, URNs will be much more difficult to implement than URLs, because of the need to provide unique and agreed names, but they are of great interest, not least in libraries which would like to improve access to Internet resources for their users (see below). International Standard Bibliographic Numbers (ISBNs) and International Standard Serial Numbers (ISSNs) are examples of library-related identifiers that have been registered as URNs. Finally URIs (Uniform Resource Identifiers) represent an attempt to establish a uniform public naming system (see Chapter 3).

Web browsers

In order to look at Web resources, users need a piece of client software called a browser (not to be confused with a web server). When a user selects a particular browser (typically by selecting an icon on the computer screen), he or she is presented with a 'home page', which provides links to other web pages for users to follow, as well as the opportunity to enter directly the URLs of other Web sites. The home page could be any HTML page, but typically would be provided by the user's Internet Service Provider (ISP), or by the producer of the browser or by the user's organisation: for instance, a librarian might have for her or his home page the Library home page, with hypertext links to other library webpages, webpages of the parent institution and to selected pages outside the parent body; a university student might be provided by the university with a personal home page, with links to useful sites such as the university library or student services and with the option of adding customised links.

Following hyperlinks from one resource to another is what is popularly referred to as 'surfing' the Internet. Users are able to move backwards and forwards between pages and to move directly back to the home page (a useful facility if they get lost on the Web; something that is easy to do in the hypertext environment). Web browsers provide the opportunity to *bookmark* (record) those sites to which the user would like to return, so that she or he can access the site directly, by activating the bookmark. Bookmarking provides libraries with the opportunity to record links to resources that particularly match their users' information needs, for example, law librarians might bookmark relevant full-text electronic legal resources available on the Web. (On Microsoft's Internet Explorer, the term 'favorites' is used.)

The first Web browser was *Mosaic* (developed at University of Illinois at Urbana-Champaign), which attracted considerable attention because it could run on a 'graphical user interface' or GUI, which allows users to select actions, commands or options that are displayed on the computer screen as graphical representations or 'icons'. This is a form of interface (discussed in Chapter 6) that is particularly appropriate for the navigation of hypertext. Hypertext links on the Web can be textual (as in the case of highlighted text and lists of options) or graphical (for example, images and 'buttons', such as a 'go back' button). Since *Mosaic* was made available in 1993, other browsers have been developed, such as Netscape's *Navigator* and *Communicator* (based on the Mosaic model) and Microsoft's *Internet Explorer*. Some of the commercial networks, such as CompuServe also provide browsers for their users.

Most web browsers have a feature called cache memory. This is discussed in Chapter 6 (which outlines different types of computer memory), but here it is worth knowing about its specific application in web searching. It can take time to download webpages from websites (in other word, copy them from the server to the client), but where cache memory is used the browser will check to see if a webpage has previously been downloaded. If it has then the browser can read the page from the client's cache memory, saving the time that would be spent retrieving the page from the Web.

Intranets

Intranets are essentially internal networks that employ Web standards and technologies, such as HTML, HTTP and the use of a web browser client. They are generally available only to employees and to those outsiders who are granted special login or access privileges, and are typically protected from outside 'invasion' by firewalls and the use of 'proxy' servers (explained in Chapter 7). Intranets are an important tool in the so-called knowledge management environment, allowing enhanced communication within an organisation; the sharing of data, information and expertise; collaboration with partners and suppliers; and the sharing of electronic resources and services such as multimedia products and videoconferencing. Many librarians have been keen to use organisational intranets to disseminate its resources and services – typically to users' desktops (their computers) – and on some occasions have even been active in the development of their organisations' intranets. One of the benefits of using web-based technologies is the fact that users can access resources on the intranet via browsers such as Netscape Navigator or Internet Explorer, regardless of the user's computer system.

It was suggested that intranets might on occasion be opened to select outsiders. An extension of this, in which two or more organisations share space on a common server, is called an extranet. At the time of writing, these appear to have little application in the library environment, because of issues such as security and intellectual property, but it is as well to be aware of their existence and development.

Search engines

There is now an extremely large number of HTML servers on the Internet and there can be great problems finding appropriate information resources on the Web. There are so many Web-based resources, ranging from those of governments and large corporations to personal home pages, that 'surfing the Net' by following hyperlinks can be incredibly time-consuming. The Web, however, has search tools that index the contents of the Web. These are search engines, which automatically search out websites, index words it finds there and then follow the hyperlinks embedded in that site to other sites on the Web, adding to the index and following still further links, until it compiles a large computer file of keywords and links. Well-known examples of search engines include Lycos, WebCrawler, Alta Vista, Infoseek, Excite, Open Text, Google and Hotbot. The index is made available to users for searching, using special retrieval software provided by the producers of the search engine. Essentially, there are three main components in a search engine:

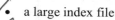

- the program that searches the Web periodically to collect and update links –referred to as a robot (sometimes shortened to 'bot') or spider
- a large index file
- retrieval software.

There is considerable variety amongst search engines: some will index only certain elements in a web page, such as title, URL and the first paragraph, but some, such as WebCrawler and Lycos, will index the full contents of websites (a process that is sometimes described as 'harvesting', after a particular piece of software). Search engines also differ in the search facilities that they offer users (discussed below). The ones mentioned above vary significantly in the facilities offered. There are also search tools such as Yahoo that are not developed automatically like these search engines. (These are also discussed below.) It is important to realise that no one search engine indexes the whole of the Web – even the largest of them indexes a surprisingly small proportion of what is available. Further, while size of index may seem like a very important criterion in selecting a search engine, it is not the only one: for example, a small index may be more useful for one's needs because the method it uses to rank search results on the user's screen (the computer algorithm) may be better than that of a search engine with a larger index, with the result that the user finds relevant search results more quickly. Time, in the work environment, is money. There are some useful websites at which search engines are evaluated and compared, but here is a summary of the main criteria used:

- size of index
- subject coverage: whether the search engine is subject-specific or covers a broad range of resources
- level of indexing: whether the full contents are indexed or not
- currency: how often the index is updated, because, despite the robotic nature of search engines, they may not update as quickly or as regularly as users expect
- geographical area covered and, linked to that, language
- search facilities (discussed below) and whether they cater for different levels of user expertise (for example, a choice of basic and advanced searching)
- ranking of search results and, linked to that, whether websites that include several 'hits' (in other words, a search term occurs several times at that site) results in separate listings among the search results
- ease of use, which includes factors such as intuitive instructions, 'help' information and screen design (some are cluttered with advertisements)
- speed, not usually a factor with the leading engines, but one should be aware of speed as a possible criterion for evaluating search engines
- scope: whether only websites are covered (some search engines will include other resources, such as newsgroups or discussion lists (or ftp sites, which are discussed below)

At present, there are considerable differences between search engines and users need to be able to compare and evaluate them. There is little point in doing this here in any great detail because this is an area in which change does occur especially rapidly, but after some of the basics of searching are discussed (below), there is a brief and indicative comparison of selected search tools.

The invisible Web

It is worth bearing in mind that no one search engine indexes the whole of the Web. Indeed, there are areas of the Web that are not indexed by any search engines: the so-called Invisible Web. This includes webpages that are 'created on the fly by querying a database of information (for example, a product catalogue on a commercial site); sites and pages that are constantly being updated (for example, news of current events); sites that use 'frames';[1] sites that use languages which require non-Latin character sets; web pages that are restricted to certain users; web sites which, or part of which, have been 'blocked' by their

---

[1] Frames were developed by Netscape and allow website developers to design a fixed screen layout in which certain frames appear in all webpages. There are disadvantages to use of frames but one of the advantages is that the user sees the same layout, with only content selections changing.

Web masters, with the result that search engine robots cannot index what has been blocked; sites that are simply not detected by search engine robots (for example, if there are no links to it from other sites); and 'yet to be indexed' sites in the search engine's weeks-long backlog (Sauers 2001, pp.43-51).

It is worth emphasising the importance of these areas of the web to librarians, who may need to find specific information and to understand where to find it in the invisible Web

Meta search engines

Meta search engines are popular with some users. These are search engines that will send users' search terms to a group of different search engines (such as the ones mentioned above) and then display the search results from each. Examples include Dogpile, MetaCrawler, SUSI, Ixquick and Inference Find. Since search engines differ in what they search, the level at which they search and their search facilities, there is an obvious benefit for users in that meta search engines should provide a wider range of search results than a single search engine. Moreover, they are useful in the sense that novice users are presented with a single search interface (that with which the user is presented and interacts on the computer screen: a specific screen design, textual information and instructions, graphical representations, choices and so on – see Chapter 6) instead of having to cope with a different interface for each search engine. Meta search engines may save time and duplication if users do wish to use different search engines, but many users are satisfied with the results from a single search engine, and meta search engines do take longer to search than a single search engine and use up much more in terms of local Internet communication. They are also of less interest to the experienced searcher who can customise complex search strategies using the advanced search options of a single search engine.

Subject directories

Subject directories are often treated as if they are much the same as search engines. Technically they are quite different, because subject directories consist of hierarchically-organised lists of websites that have been compiled by human developers and not by robots or 'spiders'. What the user is presented with, therefore, is not a choice of search strategies but a list of subject topics from which to select. Once a selection is made there is generally a list of sub-topics from which to make a further choice, and so on until the user reaches the subject descriptor in which she or he is interested, and checks the hyperlinks listed under the descriptor. These hierarchical arrangements are sometimes referred to as subject trees.

These are often better search tools for users who have a fairly well-defined topic on which they want information. It is also fair to say that because subject directories are compiled by humans there is a good chance an element of evaluation has gone into the selection, whereas search engines display search results based simply on a computation of some kind (for example, frequency with which search terms occur in a document) and will even put to the top of the search results sites that pay for the privilege of being listed first. A website will generally also appear only once in a subject directory, whereas a search engine may list the same website many times, if the search term used appears frequently on the website, making it more difficult for the user to sort through results. There are, however, disadvantages to using subject directories. Because they are compiled by humans, they are much smaller than search engine indexes (although, on the other hand, the human indexers will sometimes find sites on the 'invisible Web' that robots cannot find). They are typically less up to date than search engines, which regardless of their backlogs can index much more quickly than a human. There are also the problems that are encountered with any hierarchical arrangement, namely that specific topics may appear quite logically in more than one place in the hierarchy and, through human oversight, contain different sets of sub-topics or hyperlinks. Consider the following example.

Subject 'scatter'

Take, for instance, a search for educational publishers. (In this case the Google directory has been used, but similar subject 'scatter' can be found on any number of directories.) The 'Business' link at the top level lists 'Publishing and printing'. Selecting that link leads to a set of publishing and printing links plus a set of Publishing and printing sub-topics. The latter includes 'Publishers' which, if selected, shows a set of links to publishers and a further set of sub-topics, including 'Nonfiction', which in turn has links to nonfiction publishers and set of further sub-topics – including Education. Here is the pathway through the directory to educational publishers:

> Business > Publishers > Nonfiction > Education

The point is that before one reaches the level of Education in the directory, one finds relevant publishers – such as Longman Educational Language Teaching (under 'Publishers') and Patricks Press (under 'Nonfiction') – that are not listed under 'Education'. As with any other directory, therefore, one cannot be sure that the Education page lists all the publishers in which one might be interested (although one may well have a much more relevant and comprehensive listing than one would using a search engine and the boolean search techniques discussed below).

As the above Google example demonstrates, although search engines and subject directories are quite distinct in terms of functionality (what they do) there is not always a clear separation when these tools are used. Some search engines will offer a limited hierarchy of subjects or even a proper directory for their users and of course subject directories such as *Yahoo* will offer users the option of conducting a search using a search engine.

Basic search features

Reference has been made to the variety of search features that search engines offer, so it is worth considering the basic features here in order to understand the retrieval power of search engines and the main problems associated with them. One also needs a sound understanding of search features if one is to make any judgement on the value or otherwise of a specific search engine.

One of the points highlighted in the preceding discussion is that when search engines 'crawl' the Web compiling their indexes they list occurrences of specific keywords. How a computer-based index of this kind actually works is discussed in Chapter 5. Here, it is simply worth noting that when a user conducts a search using a search engine, the software is required to retrieve webpages in which specific keywords or combinations of words occur. This is an invaluable facility in the case of rarely used words, but searches on frequently used terms such as 'computing' or 'management' can generate huge lists of search results. What is generally required, therefore, is some means of narrowing a search, in order that a smaller and (one hopes) more relevant set of search results is retrieved.

To take an example: although some search engines allow users to search indexes of the complete contents of webpages, it may be advisable for users to specify that they want to search specific information-rich elements in a page, such as URL or title, in order to narrow retrieval and cut down on the sheer amount of websites retrieved. Here, the experience of librarians searching full-text databases (of the kind discussed in the next chapter) comes in useful, because in searching the full text of documents there are frequently occasions on which it is necessary to refine and narrow down searches. There are other ways in which to limit a search (other than specifying the element in which to search), including specifying date ranges, such as the previous two years, or particular formats (for example, image files only) or particular languages. One of the most common devices for refining searches, however, is the search operator.

Boolean searching

Search operators are devices that are used to combine individual search terms, which has the effect of either narrowing or broadening a search. The most common search operators are the boolean operators 'and', 'or' and 'not' (so called after the mathematician and logician, George Boole). The sets of results retrieved using these operators are commonly demonstrated using Venn diagrams:

AND

The use of the operator AND to link two search terms will produce a set of documents which contains *both* terms entered. In the diagram below, the rectangle represents the complete database, one circle represents a set of documents containing the search term 'computers' and the other circle represents a set of documents which contain a different search term, 'libraries'. The intersection of the two sets (the shaded area) represents those documents that contain *both* search terms. In other words, the boolean search 'computers AND libraries' will retrieve only those documents that contain both terms (and exclude those which contain neither term or only one of them). The AND operator, therefore, *narrows* a search.

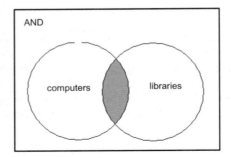

Figure 1.5: The AND operator

The notion that the AND operator *narrows* a search seems to defy everyday logic, because the word 'and' sounds inclusive, as if it would widen one's options. In fact, if one uses the AND operator (given as + in some search engines) one is effectively instructing the search engine that one wants to retrieve webpages in which ALL the following terms appear, and that is precisely what some search engines offer: instead of requiring their users to use the AND operator, they offer the chance to 'search for sites that contain all the following terms'.

OR

By using the operator OR to combine search terms, the searcher can *widen* a search. In plain English (offered by some search engines) this translates as 'Search for sites that contain ANY of the following terms' (in other words, 'it doesn't matter which of the following terms you find, bring up links to the website'). The set of documents offered to the searcher will contain *one* or *both* of the specified terms. This may be desirable in the case of synonymous terms, for example, 'elderly OR aged', or antonyms (opposites) like 'unemployment OR employment'. In the diagram below, documents from both sets (represented by the shaded area) are retrieved. The OR operator widens a search, which may not always be desirable in the Web context.

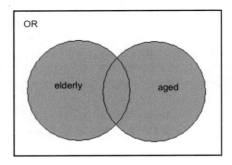

Figure 1.6: The OR operator

NOT

The operator NOT narrows a search by *excluding* documents that contain a specified term, for example, 'automation NOT office' will find documents that contain the term 'automation', search this set of documents for the second term, 'office', exclude from the first set those documents that also appear in the second set, and in this way retrieve only those records that do *not* contain 'office'. As before, the shaded area in the diagram below represents the documents retrieved, while the unshaded intersection represents those documents containing the term 'automation' which were excluded because they also contained the term 'of

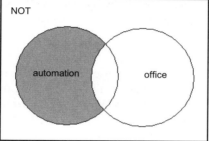

Figure 1.7: The NOT operator

Sometimes systems that provide boolean searching are referred to as *post-coordinate* systems, which signifies that terms are brought together (in other words, coordinated) at the search stage, as distinct from some indexing languages, in which terms are coordinated at the indexing stage.

For those who have some elementary mathematics and understand a bit of set theory, it is possible to combine different boolean operators using *nesting*, a term that in general terms refers to the embedding of a smaller element in a larger one. An example should make that a bit clearer:

health AND (elderly OR old OR aged)

If one were interested in finding documents on the health of elderly people, one might conduct a keyword search like this, in which one is specifying that one wants documents that contain the keyword 'health' *as well as* any of the following (nested) keywords. Of course, one could construct a still more complex search: for example, include 'illness', the antonym of 'health':

(health OR illness) AND (elderly OR old OR aged)

In these examples, one is both widening a search, by use of the OR operator, and narrowing the search, by use of AND.

Proximity operators

Many information retrieval systems also provide *proximity operators*, which allow the searcher to specify how closely terms appear in a record, for example:

- within a specified number of words from each other;
- together, in the same element, for example, in the title
- adjacent (that is, next to each other).

Like the boolean operator AND, these proximity operators will have the effect of narrowing a search, thus reducing the set of records retrieved.

Ranking of search results

Earlier it was suggested that one of the criteria used to evaluate search engines is the way in which they rank search results. This is an especially critical criterion when huge sets of results are retrieved – research shows that very few people are willing to search through page after page of search results.

With one notable exception – where producers of search engines are actually paid by other organisations to present their websites at the top of the results lists – search engines make some attempt to rank results by relevance. In the world of information retrieval, however, relevance is a difficult quality to define with any confidence. Relevance is in the mind of the searcher (in other words, it is a subjective factor), and search engines need to employ an objective measure. The criteria that search software use to rank documents vary: for instance, the frequency with which search terms appear in a document, their position in the document (appearing early in the document may be considered significant) or their occurrence in important, content-rich elements, for example, title. At the time of writing – a dangerous way to begin a sentence in a fast-changing field like this – Google has for some years been the favourite search engine for librarians, because the algorithm (set of rules) used to calculate relevance by Google is generally seen to have been much more effective in terms of relevance ranking than those employed by other search engines.

A further relevance facility is based on feedback from the user, who can specify which documents in a set of search results are particularly relevant and ask to see similar documents.

Search engine functionalities: a 'snapshot'

Search engine functionalities change relatively quickly, so there is little point in trying to itemise them here. It may, however, be helpful to outline the basic features that can currently be expected. Reference will be made to three search engines: Google (for the reasons mentioned above), AltaVista (a well-established search engine for many years) and Alltheweb. There is no attempt to evaluate the three search engines to which reference is made, nor is there any claim to present an exhaustive listing of their features. They are included purely as indicative examples. If that sounds like a disclaimer, so be it. Features include:

Choice of basic and advanced search

This provides novice users with the option of conducting a relatively straightforward, basic search, while offering experienced users the chance to construct complex search strategies, using boolean and proximity searching. This choice is available to Google and Alltheweb users.

Boolean search

Google provides boolean searching, including '+' in place of AND and '-' for NOT. In advanced search, the user is also presented with AND, exact phrase, OR and NOT, plus searches that are expressed in English and not in terms of near-mathematical operators: for instance, "Find results related to **all** of the words …" has the same effect as 'AND' or '+'. Alltheweb includes the extra boolean query 'rank', which indicates that the term before 'rank' is the important one that must appear, and it provides intuitional word filters, such as 'Must include' and 'Must not include'. AltaVista, too, offers, English-type searches such as 'all of these words' and 'any of these words'.

Proximity search

AltaVista allows users to search for websites in which the specified search terms are NEAR each other.

Phrase searching

Google allows phrase searching through the enclosure of phrases within inverted commas, as does Alltheweb. In advanced search, AltaVista offers the option of retrieving results 'with the **exact phrase**'.

Search of specific elements

AltaVista, Alltheweb and Google all allow users to search for words and phrases within specific elements, such as the text of a webpage, the page's title or its URL. AltaVista and Alltheweb searches can also include such technical elements as specified Java applets (special small programs, written in Java, that produce special features such as animation – see Chapter 6 for computer languages).

Search for specific types of object

Google will search for images and newsgroups (Usenet discussion archive), as well as websites; AltaVista also searches for images, audio, video and news; and Alltheweb searches for news, images, video, audio and FTP files (see below for an explanation of FTP files).

Search limitation

Google allows users to specify that they want results from specific domains: for instance, specifying that the URL must contain 'edu'. It also permits the restriction of search results to specific time periods (for instance, last six months). Alltheweb has domain filters that allow the user to include *or exclude* results from specified domains, include only results from specific IP addresses or IP ranges, or restrict results to those from specified regions or from specified date ranges. AltaVista allows the user to restrict searches to specified file types, languages, date ranges and locations (including domains).

Presentation of results

Google is especially noted for its ranking of search results, using criteria such as number of times a site is visited. It also provides statistics on the number of results found and the amount of time taken to conduct the search. Alltheweb and AltaVista display the number of search results but not the time taken. Alltheweb lists only one page per website, with the option of seeing other pages from the website – this does cut down on the clutter that can face a user when many of the results listed come from the same website. Google and Alltheweb include the option of customising one's search results: for instance, setting the number of search results for display per page (more results per page sounds good, but longer pages take longer to load) or setting language preferences.

Translation

Currently Google offers translation for pages published in Italian, French, Spanish, German and Portuguese. AltaVista provides translation to and from several languages ('Babel Fish Translation'), a feature that one can add to one's own website.

Other features

Other features noted include:

- Google provides a directory
- AltaVista uses 'stemming' but Google makes a point of not doing so. (Stemming is discussed in the following chapter – it involves entering only part of a word in order to widen one's search: for instance, in some information retrieval tools, 'comput' will find 'computers' and 'computing'.)
- Google will give the user a 'search similar pages' option – AltaVista offers 'related pages'
- Google will prompt the user with alternative spellings: for instance, a search on 'technlogy' will prompt the reply, 'Did you mean: technology'. Alta Vista will 'correct' the spelling without actually informing the user that there may have been a problem. In the case of the example above, Alltheweb automatically searched for the correct spelling but also presented a website high in its listing that had misspelt the word 'technology'.
- Alltheweb has sets of fairly detailed FAQs (Frequently Asked Questions) that searchers would find useful: for instance, 'Why am I having trouble downloading songs?'
- Alltheweb will allow the user to narrow a search using the set of search results already retrieved, as will Google.

This is a 'snapshot' of search engine features, provided as indicative examples only – for evaluations of search engines, there is no shortage of material on the Web (see 'Further resources' at the end of this chapter).

File transfer protocol (FTP)

So far, the emphasis has been on tools that allow users to search the Internet. Before leaving this general discussion of the Internet, however, it would be worth mentioning File Transfer Protocol or FTP, which is an important tool for copying resources found on the Internet.

The term protocol refers to a set of rules or conventions that governs the use of communication channels. Telnet is an example of a communication protocol that has already been mentioned. Protocols are examined in more detail in Chapter 7, but it is worth noting here that if a variety of computer systems and networks is to communicate over the Internet, there need to be conventions. Many of the Internet facilities described in this chapter require internationally accepted protocols.

Whereas Telnet allows users to connect to remote sites, FTP goes further, enabling users to copy or *download* files, such as electronic documents or computer software, to the client (provided, of course, that the owner of the server permits files to be copied). It was mentioned earlier, for example, that there is shareware on the Internet that is publicly available. FTP is a set of conventions that allows users to transfer electronic files between computers that are not necessarily compatible. Where the owner of a server does permit downloading of files (that is, transferring copies to clients), users are generally able to use the login 'anonymous'. For this reason, such sites are often referred to as *anonymous FTP* sites.

It may take considerable time to download a file, because of its size (or, some might say, because of the limited capacity of the communication channel or 'bandwidth'). At some sites, however, some files are compressed, particularly non-text files, such as computer software programs. When a file has been compressed, repeating elements in the file are removed and need to be recovered, once the file has been copied to the client, using special software. Compressed files are easily identified by the 'extension' that appears, in the case of IBM-compatible computers, after the filename (separated from it by a period), for example, 'wc4demo.zip'. There is a variety of compression software packages to use, which may create problems for the user once files are downloaded, for example, a file with the extension 'zip' will need special 'unzip' software in order to open it.

In this context, FTP is primarily a tool for users to copy files from remote servers to their own 'client' systems or, in other words, *download* files. It is worth noting, however, that it is also the protocol that is used to *upload* files from a local system to a server: for example, someone developing a website is likely to transfer a copy of the files that are to be worked on from the server to a local system (perhaps two copies, storing one as a backup, in case of problems), make the required changes and upload the amended files to the server.

Libraries and the Internet

Since the second edition of this book was published five years ago, the Internet and the use of the Internet have changed dramatically. Very few people would like to predict what changes will take place in the next five years. The Web may look quite different and the means of actually finding Web resources will undoubtedly have developed considerably. One aspect that librarians will continue to watch eagerly is the growth of electronic publishing, since the main business of libraries remains what it has been since the development of the printing press: namely, providing their users with access to published information resources. There is a misconception that the Internet will make librarians redundant, since users will be able to search for their own resources and will not need to rely on libraries. It is a misconception (or at least it appears a misconception in the early years of the twenty-first century) because there are simply so many resources on the Internet, and they are of such variable quality, that there is still a place for information intermediaries, like librarians, to help users find relevant resources and to help evaluate them. There is also a continuing need for the 'value-added' activities provided by librarians, who can apply their information knowledge and skills to do more than the average Internet user.

One of the growth areas in the library and information management sector has been the emergence of, and growing interest in, web-based libraries of various kinds. Different terms are used to describe these developments: principally electronic library, virtual library and digital library. There is very little difference between any two of these terms. The term *digital library* tends to be associated with the idea of digital collections, which often involves the process of digitising print-based resources (turning them into computer-readable format). The term *virtual library* appears to be more popular in the literature of library and information management (at present!) than the competing terms 'electronic library' and 'digital library', and is generally taken to cover more than digital collections and to include a variety of Web-based *services*: for example, the reference services discussed in Chapter 2 are taken to include 'virtual reference services' (the terms 'digital reference' and 'electronic reference' do not appear to have any currency). The English language is not always precise, of course, and with new terms like these lexicographers arrive at definitions on the basis of use. Picking an imprecise path through the semantics, it is assumed in this book that *electronic library* is a term with a slightly broader meaning than the other two, since it might be taken to include the automated systems discussed in Chapter 4, and it is suggested that, as regards developing a Web-presence, libraries have witnessed or participated in two main kinds of development: digital libraries and virtual library services.

Many leading libraries, such as national libraries, state or provincial libraries and large university libraries have initiated digitisation programs that aim not just at providing access to new electronic publications but also at converting existing print-based resources into digital form. One of the best-known attempts to develop a digital collection is Michael Hart's *Project Gutenburg* (1971), mentioned earlier as a source of electronic books. The aim of this project was to convert classic texts to electronic format, where permitted by copyright laws to do so. In the United States, the Library of Congress's digitisation program predated the Internet, when in 1982 the Library began making some print and pictorial material available on videodisk. (Optical disk technology is discussed in Chapter 6.) The benefits of this program were two-fold: greater accessibility to pictorial material and greater opportunities for preservation (Kochtanek & Matthews 2002, p. 242). Since 1994 Library of Congress has led a digital library initiative, currently called the National Digital Information Infrastructure and Preservation Program (NDIIPP) – a collaborative program that involves other organisations from the library, university, archival and private sectors and other federal agencies in the 'preservation of America's digital heritage'. Through its own National Digital Library (NDL) Program, it is claimed, the Library of Congress 'is also one of the leading providers of noncommercial intellectual content on the Internet' (Library of Congress 2003).

In Australia, the National Library of Australia's Preserving Access to Digital Information (PADI) initiative is also supported by a number of agencies and organisation, such as the National Archives of Australia, the Australian Department of Communication, Information Technology and the Arts, ScreenSound Australia, the Commonwealth Scientific and Industrial Research Organisation (CSIRO) and the National Museum of Australia. The PADI website is described as a subject gateway to digital preservation resources, with an associated discussion list on digital preservation issues and a set of criteria for the selection of resources for PADI (National Library of Australia 2003).

Leading libraries such as the National Library of Australia have also established *portals* for the communities that they serve. The word portal may conjure up the picture of a science fiction story in which the heroes disappear into a portal or gateway of some kind and re-emerge in another planet or a parallel dimension. A portal on the Internet may not be quite so dramatic, but the name suggests that the portal is a gateway of some kind on to an information environment. In general terms it can be regarded as a website that offers its users a range of resources and services. Many of the search engines and subject directories discussed earlier have established themselves as portals, offering more than just the search facilities that characterise them: for example, free email and information services such as news and stock market reports. In other words, they are not unlike 'virtual libraries'. Typically, these information services are funded by advertising revenue, and invite customers to use their websites as their homepages, in other words, the site to which the user's web browser links when it is first activated.

Many libraries have been involved in the development of portals: a form of 'one-stop shop' for their user communities, giving them a good resource from which to start exploring the Internet. Indeed, if libraries are doing a good job of developing portals their users are likely to bookmark them – if not as points from which to start their Internet searches (perhaps a bit ambitious), then certainly one of a set of useful gateways on to the Internet. These virtual libraries share with the subject directories discussed earlier the fact that the organisation of web links has a human, and not a robotic, origin. The need for both subject directories and virtual libraries stems from the anarchical nature of the Internet and the fact that it is so difficult to find 'good' resources – or, to say the least, it is so easy to find a lot of 'poor' resources. Web sites developed by librarians, and other human agents, not only provide an organised set of links but carry the expectation on the part of their communities of users that the links will lead to resources to which their human creators consider it worthwhile to provide access. In other words, the resources found via these portals have been through some kind of evaluation process.

Libraries and access to the Internet

More specific issues relating to libraries and the Internet will be taken up in later chapters: for example, the impact of the Internet on library acquisitions; but it would be appropriate to discuss in general terms the response on the part of the library and information management sector to the opportunities offered by the Internet. Near the beginning of this chapter there was a reference to the anarchical nature of the Internet. Librarians have information organisation and information retrieval skills that could be brought to bear. There is dissatisfaction with search engines and their effectiveness in searching a large and chaotic electronic resource like the Web, and there is considerable enthusiasm among librarians for the development of standards for describing resources on the Internet, similar to those developed by cataloguers for bibliographic description. In other words, Internet resources should be 'indexed' in much the same way in which the resources of libraries have been catalogued in the past.

Attempts by librarians to 'organise' the Internet fall into two categories. The minimalist approach is for libraries, like many other institutions, to act as gateways to the Internet for their users and to extend their value-added cataloguing effort to include Internet resources, thus helping their users locate a selection of Internet resources previously identified, described and, presumably, considered potentially useful to the user community: for example, law librarians identifying full-text legal resources on the Internet. One of the problems with such attempts is that the Internet changes so quickly – for example, changing URLs or websites disappearing altogether, although this is not entirely new to cataloguers, who already have to describe a range of on-going publications, such as serials that change name. The OCLC Cooperative Online Resource Catalog (CORC) is an example of an attempt by libraries to describe Internet resources (see Chapter 3).

A more ambitious approach is to develop *metadata* sets that could be embedded in the web resources themselves. The term metadata is often used to refer to structured data about data, required to describe Internet resources and represent their content. It was first used in computing to refer to datasets, but some librarians have been quick to claim that bibliographic data, such as the data contained in library catalogues, represent a form of metadata. Clearly, it is an approach that contrasts with the anarchical nature of Internet development already alluded to and is much less likely to be adopted than Internet cataloguing projects, because it would require cooperation from millions of web publishers, many of them enthusiastic individuals. One of the best-known attempts to develop a metadata set, particularly in the library community, is the so-called Dublin Core Metadata Element Set. Use of metadata standards is discussed in some detail in Chapter 3, which focuses on the provision of access to information resources.

Libraries and education

The educational role that librarians have played in the past, particularly, but not exclusively, in school and other academic libraries, is of growing importance, as many users need guidance to information resources and to the *means* of accessing those resources. There is no evidence (so far!) to indicate that school students starting university or college courses have the requisite level of information literacy and, until there is, school, college and university librarians have an important educational role to share. Education no longer needs to take place in the library, of course, since librarians can go to the users, for example, to academic and research staff or distance learning students, in order to show them electronic facilities that their libraries offer via the libraries' webpages (themselves a form of publication). Indeed, much as one might regret the lack of human contact, much effort in recent years has gone into the development of computer-based user education and instruction packages that users can access and try at their own pace, without ever setting foot in a library (see Chapter 2). This educational role is not confined to academic librarians, of course. Special librarians, for example, can enhance their contribution to organisational goals by helping to educate users and by providing a value-added service by guiding overworked executives to particularly useful resources. Last, but not least, public libraries currently have a role to play in providing access to information resources to the 'information poor' in the community and clearly access to the Internet and instruction in its use fall within that function.

Librarians may have a growing role as educators, but for their own part they also face a increasing need for continuing professional development. Since the Internet is a growing part of the business of librarians, it goes without saying that the knowledge and skills base associated with librarianship has widened correspondingly. Librarians need to be familiar with the technologies, software and networking tools required, for example, to find Web-based resources, transfer files, describe electronic resources, instruct users in Internet use and create Web pages. The implications have not been lost on educators, trainers and those with an interest in continuing professional development. In Australia, for example, the professional association (ALIA) is currently reviewing educational needs and the means of meeting these needs, and it seems quite incontrovertible that there will be an increased emphasis on CPD.

The lessons of the dot-com bubble

What relevance could the dot-com bubble experience possibly have for librarians? Well, it could be summed up in the need to avoid the 'build it and they will come' approach that characterised much early website development. A presence on the Internet is not enough – one needs to establish and maintain an attractive website and to have a realistic business plan. The dot-com experience, according to some commentators, demonstrated the inability on the part of many of the new companies to identify their market, believing (mistakenly) that the technological breakthrough had created the conditions for completely new industries (*New economy or old economy* 2001). It has also been suggested that the dot.com experience 'underscored the importance of adding depth to applications rather than simply offering cliché-ridden value propositions' (Robinson 2002).

Going back to the comment that search engines and subject directories want customers to return to their portals and to make them their homepages, libraries too need to ensure that if they are going to go to the trouble and expense of developing their own websites – and arguably they should because the communities they serve have come to expect it – then they have to do more than simply present basic information, such as opening hours, and a catalogue. The following questions are well worth considering:

> Will the site provide more than simple information about the library and access to the library's Web OPAC? ... Can users ... customize the site? ... What will keep a user on your site? Does your site provide access to subject pathfinders with links to recommended Web sites? Can the library patron interact directly with a reference librarian using e-mail, instant messaging, or chat? Is the library adding content-rich information resources on an ongoing basis? (Kochtanek & Matthews 2002, p. 189)

Some specific aspects of virtual reference services are considered in the next chapter, some of the general points raised in the discussion by Kochtanek and Matthews are worth noting: the need, for example, for a website search engine; locally developed information; avoidance of 'dead links' (links to URLs that are no longer used, resulting in user frustration); good organisation of webpages; consistent use of navigational aids between pages; avoidance of large graphics that take web browsers too long to load; currency; and authority, as for the library's other resources (2002, pp.190-5).

Finally the need for marketing and engaging the community served by the library should be emphasised. As David Lankes notes in his introduction to *Implementing Digital Reference Services*, the success stories, such as Cleveland Public Library's 24/7 service, the Internet Public Library and AskERIC, owe much to good marketing – 'These services are out there to be seen, targeted to their user base and not hidden twelve layers down on a Web site' (2003, p. 3).

Having established a few basic facts and principles about the Internet and the positioning of libraries in this virtual environment, it is worth turning to libraries themselves, beginning with a survey of the information resources and services provided by libraries, how information and communication technologies have affected these services and how libraries have responded, and are responding, to the new opportunities offered by these ICTs.

References

Bruce, H 2002, *The user's view of the Internet*. Scarecrow Press, Lanham, MD.

Cover Pages 2003, *XML: Overview*, viewed 5 April 2003,
    <http://xml.coverpages.org/xml.html#overview>.

Deegan, M & Tanner, S 2002, *Digital futures: Strategies for the information age*. Library Association Publishing, London.

Kochtanek, TR & Matthews, JR 2002, *Library information systems: From library automation to distributed information access solutions*. Libraries Unlimited, Westport, CT.

Lankes, R D, McClure, C R, Gross, M & Pomerantz, J 2003, *Implementing digital library services: Setting standards and making it real*. Facet Publishing, London.

Library of Congress 2003, *News from the Library of Congress*, viewed 12 April 2003, <httpp://www.loc.gov/today/pr/2003/03-022.html>.

National Library of Australia 2003, *About PADI*, viewed 12 April 2003, <http://www.nla.gov.au/padi/about.html>.

New economy or old economy, a shakeout is a shakeout 2001. *ebizChronicle.com*, 8 March 2001, viewed 6 Jan. 2003, <http://www.ebizchronicle.com/wharton01/29_shakeout.htm>.

Robinson, T 2002, Lasting benefits of the dot-com bubble. *E-Commerce Times*, 15 July 2002, viewed 6 January 2003, <http://www.ecommercetimes.com/perl/story/18570.html>.

Sauers, MP 2001, *Using the Internet as a reference tool: A how-to-do-it manual for librarians*. Neal-Schuman, New York.

Review questions

1. What is a listserv?
2. How is it possible to follow discussions that have taken place in a newsgroup?
3. Explain the client/server model.
4. What does it mean if you telnet?
5. Explain what a protocol is and give four examples from this chapter.
6. Which search operators discussed in this chapter have the effect of narrowing a search?
7. What does HTML do?
8. Explain what a URL is.
9. What is a web browser?
10. Which parts of a web page are indexed by the common search engines?

Further resources

Bradley, P 2002, *Getting and staying noticed on the web: Your web promotion questions answered*. Facet Publishing, London.
A step-by-step guide to creating a professional webite and attracting visitors to that site, once established. Aimed at the beginner, it includes examples of websites to underline points.

Henninger, M 2003, *Hidden Web: Quality information on the Web*. University of New South Wales Press, Sydney.
Maureen Henninger, author of *Don't just surf: Effective research strategies for the Net*, aims to provide strategies for uncovering valuable information from the vast number and variety of websites confronting users.

Internet library for librarians (http://www.itcompany.com/inforetriever/)
A Web site which aims to provide a portal for librarians who wish to locate Internet resources related to their profession, such as ready reference tools and resources covering the major fields of library and information management (including the Internet, library automation systems and library software).

Poulter, A, Hiom, D & Tseng, G 2000, *The library and information professional's guide to the Internet*. 3rd ed. Library Association, London
One of several excellent guides to the Internet aimed specifically at librarians. It contains a mixture of background information, explanation, helpful hints and details of Internet resources.

Search engine watch (http://www.searchenginewatch.com/)
This site is aimed at both specialist groups, such as webmasters, and at generalists, such as librarians and researchers. It provides a range of information, for example, how search engines find and rank pages, how to make effective use of search engines and how search engines are performing in particular areas.

Usability First (http://www.usabilityfirst.com/)
One of a number of websites that provides useful information and resources for key issues related to usability in website and software design. Its resources include courses, books, links, applications, groupware and a glossary.

World Wide Web Consortium (http://www.w3.org/)
W3C is a key organisation in the development of interoperable technologies for the Web (specifications, guidelines, software and tools). Its website has a wealth of information and links to W3C technologies. See especially the Web Accessibility Initiative (WAI), which includes technology, guidelines, tools, education and outreach, and research and development.

CHAPTER 2
Information sources and services

In the last chapter, the focus was the Internet, with some reference to the uses to which libraries can put it. This chapter focuses on the ways in which systems, technology and networks support information provision in libraries. In other words, attention shifts from the so-called virtual library, in which the library resembles a subject directory or any other portal in acting as a switching centre that connects with primarily Web-based resources world-wide, to the 'hybrid' library, in which libraries provide users with access to a range of electronic, audiovisual and print information resources through the complementary strategies of *access* and *acquisitions*: that is, the provision of access to information resources via the Internet, in response to specific requests for information, and the development of 'collections' of resources (many of them still print-based), in anticipation of requests for information.

Learning objectives

At the end of this chapter, you will be able to:

- discuss the development of virtual reference services
- explain what an online database is
- outline the information services provided by online vendors
- discuss the strengths and limitations of online retrieval systems
- discuss the strengths and limitations of portable databases, such as CD-ROM databases
- outline the development of inhouse databases, and
- describe developments in the delivery of non-electronic information resources.

Keywords

Virtual reference services
Frequently asked questions (FAQs)
Database
File
Record
Field
Online vendor
Text retrieval software

SDI services
Front-end software
Gateway
CD-ROM
Reference advisory system
Computer assisted instruction
Conspectus
Document delivery services

The reality for most librarians is the development of a hybrid library that both provides access to and collects information resources in a multiplicity of formats. Collection development is taken to mean more than the purchase and organisation of a physical collection, and to include subscription to e-journals, purchase or subscription to other electronic resources and even the digitisation of existing materials (which often has implications for the dissemination of these resources). This chapter focuses on the resources and services used by reference or information librarians, as they have been affected by ICT developments. The term 'resources' refers to the wide range of information resources used in information work, such as dictionaries, encyclopedias, directories, indexes, catalogues, monographs, government publications, journals, newspapers and legislation. These may be electronic resources stored on remote servers, electronic resources stored on 'portable' media (such as CD-ROM), electronic resources developed by libraries themselves, or 'traditional' print-based and audiovisual resources such as books and microfilms. The term 'services' refers both to the services that libraries provide to their user communities, such as the virtual reference services mentioned at the end of the last chapter, and to the various activities that support the work of information librarians, such as the commercial provision of electronic information resources (including search facilities) and document delivery services.

The chapter begins where the last chapter ended and outlines developments in the so-called virtual library.

Virtual reference library services

Much of the activity associated with the development of virtual reference library services is concerned with providing library users either with the electronic means of finding the information or resource for which they are searching, or with improved means of communicating with information librarians. Typical developments include:

- direct access to the electronic resources which the library holds or to which it subscribes, such as databases (discussed below)
- search tools, such as search engines or search facilities developed inhouse, for example, subject guides or pathfinders
- guides to the search tools, including databases and catalogues
- 'Frequently Asked Questions' or FAQs
- access to information librarians via asynchronous modes of communication, such as email
- access to information librarians via synchronous modes of communication, for example, chat
- online request forms
- 'Ask-a-Librarian' services
- collaborative '24/7' reference services
- 'Virtual Reference Desk' services

These services resemble the commercial portals discussed in the last chapter in that they provide users both with links to useful resources, such as the library's 'collection' of databases and electronic journals, and with a range of value-added services, such as instructional media and access to (human) help. Many of the electronic resources are purchased or provided on subscription by commercial suppliers (see below), but librarians too are involved in the production of online resources, such as subject guides or pathways, not unlike the directories discussed in the last chapter, and instructional packages that help users become proficient in the use of library catalogues, online databases and search engines. (These packages are discussed later in this chapter.) The use of FAQs (Frequently Asked Questions) is common on the Internet, and reflects a fairly common strategy in reference librarianship of maintaining ready-reference files – the difference is that the frequently asked questions and their answers can be published on the library website for the website for the benefit of its users (and, it is always hoped, its overworked librarians).

Use of email to put 'remote' users in touch with information librarians goes back as far as the late 1980s, so in a sense there is nothing new about virtual reference services, other than the name. There are a couple of problems with use of email. The obvious one is the lack of synchronicity – the library user simply does not (generally) receive an immediate answer. Email is a like voicemail or answer-phone services in that the message is recorded and usually addressed by the recipient later. Following from that problem, if it is seen as a problem, is the lack of interaction or, in other words, the difficulty of conducting the traditional 'reference interview', in which the information librarian establishes the user's information needs and any other requirements. Many libraries, especially in the academic sector, have therefore developed online request forms which, if they are well designed, help to gather much of the information that would 'traditionally' have been established during the reference interview: for example, the date by which the information requested is required. In the 1990s some libraries developed Ask-a-Librarian services, similar to non-library 'Ask-a' services available on the Internet, such as AskERIC, which is well known in the academic sector. These services generally use both online forms and email.

The use of synchronised forms of communication such as Internet Chat, from the late 1990s overcame some of the problems associated with the asynchronous modes. It meant that information librarians could obtain immediate feedback from users and return to something like the reference interview (without the worry about body language which seems so important to some writers on library education) – something close, in fact, to the telephone interview. The use of synchronous modes does generally make communication more efficient, not least in those cases where the user does not need help with a particular request, but needs instruction on using library facilities, such as its databases. It stretches the ingenuity of academic librarians, for example, to use an asynchronous mode like email to impart this kind of knowledge (as distinct from information). Internet chat is therefore an increasingly popular option, especially in academic libraries. There are those who argue that MOOs (discussed in Chapter 1) are even more appropriate in an instructional setting, because of the ability to manipulate virtual objects. Some libraries have tried introducing video reference services, but of course these are more expensive and are not easy either for librarians or users, and so require training.

Where synchronous forms of communication come to be the norm or, in other words, users become used to the idea that they will have access to reference services twenty-fours a day, seven days a week, libraries face a logistical problem of how to staff such a service. One solution, typical of libraries over the years, has been to collaborate with other libraries. One of the best-known ventures of this kind is *QuestionPoint*, a joint project by Library of Congress and the Online Computer Library Center (OCLC), with input from members of the Global Reference Network (an international network of organisations committed to virtual reference services). *QuestionPoint* is designed to enable libraries to:

- respond to, track and manage reference questions from patrons via the Web
- refer unanswered questions to other libraries in the library's cooperative as needed based on availability and expertise
- refer still-unanswered questions to expert resources through a global web-based network in which an automated 'request manager' routes questions from one library to another, based on metadata about the question and predefined profiles of the collection, subject and staff strengths of members of the network, etc.
- provide libraries with tools to add simple links from any page in their library portal to support a locally branded and customizable question-asking service including: Web-based submission forms, email-based interaction and live chat for their patrons
- integrate QuestionPoint's global reference network with alternative service providers the library might be using to address their local needs
- search a global knowledge base of previously asked and answered reference questions (QuestionPoint 2003).

Another development worth noting here is the existence of software products such as Virtual Reference Software and 24/7, which have been adapted for use in libraries. Functionalities of these products include:

- an interface (the medium through which the user communicates with the computer) that is customisable
- text-based chat interfaces
- 'page pushing', which allows librarians and users to 'push' pages to each other (allowing, for example, a librarian to demonstrate a search strategy to a user)
- 'predefined or standardized responses'
- email, in case no librarian is available
- 'system stallers', which consist of text that is sent automatically to users when they have been waiting a for predefined period
- queue information
- the ability to 'route' questions
- user-specific information
- 'co-browsing' which allows user and librarian to see what the other is seeing

- user feedback
- statistics maintenance (Wells 2003, pp.100-2).

Finally, here, as in other points in this book, it is worth noting the importance of standards. Wells mentions, for example, QuIP or Question Interchange Profile, a proposed standard developed jointly by the ERIC Clearinghouse on Information & Technology and the National Library of Education, that is written in XML (Extensible Markup Language) and looks as if it is becoming a standard in library data sharing applications (2003, p. 106).

Online information services

One of the ways in which libraries provide their users with access to electronic information resources is through the purchase of, or subscription to, large datasets provided by external vendors, typically commercial companies. The vendor is not necessarily the same organisation that produces the electronic datasets, although some producers do offer direct access to their own data, for example, Lexis/Nexis. Most electronic datasets, however, are supplied by third-party vendors, who mount other organisations' datasets, and sometimes some of their own, on to their own servers and sell access to them. For this reason vendors are sometimes called online hosts and their servers are referred to as host computers. Indeed, the large vendors, such as Dialog, which supplies a wide range of databases, are sometimes referred to as supermarket hosts. Some of these vendors began operating in the early 1970s.

It is worth noting here the part played by many national libraries in the development of database access, particularly in the case of databases that are of national interest and not available through major US vendors such as Dialog. Ozline, for example, was established in 1987 by the National Library of Australia, and provided databases covering subjects as diverse as law, architecture, politics, economics, cultural and ethnic affairs, criminology, science, industrial relations, education, medicine, agriculture, natural resources, history, geography, language, engineering, sport, religion, literature and librarianship (see ALISA – Australian Library & Information Science Abstracts). Dissemination of these databases passed to RMIT, as one of its Informit online products, following the development of the National Library's Kinetica system (see Chapter 3). The National Library of New Zealand too developed an online information service, called Kiwinet, now available via Te Puna

Charging varies according to vendor and is subject to change, but may include connect time (length of time connected to the server) or charging according to the quantity of search results. More typically, however, many of the newer, specialised and Web-based information services (for example, those offering financial data for business) offer subscriptions. Those who subscribe to their services are given user names and passwords to access the desired files.

Selective dissemination of information (SDI)

Selective dissemination of information or SDI represents an important value-added service because it is the means by which librarians can keep users informed about the latest literature on topics of specified interest, thus helping them keep on top of the so-called information explosion – indeed, it is a service by which librarians themselves can keep up to date. An SDI service is greatly facilitated by computerisation. It is typically based on a set of user-profiles consisting of data such as topics of interest, associated keywords and some sample citations for literature considered by the user to be of primary interest. Typically, users' search strategies are saved for the purpose of receiving updates. SDI services are supplied by some database producers, as well as database vendors like Dialog, which generally encourage users to set up their own profiles. At regular intervals, search results are either delivered to on-site printers or mailed. The normal end-result is a regular list of citations, but some services offer copies of the source documents. Lexis/Nexis, for example, has an Electronic Clipping Service (ECLIPSE). Some SDI services are referred to as alert services.

Aggregator services

The term 'aggregator' refers to services that sell publications from a variety of publishers as a single package. Typically libraries will pay a licence to access the aggregator's database. Some developed out of early online information services such as Dialog and BRS. The larger ones are known to negotiate licenses with more than 5,000 publishers and offer these to customers as a package (Arms 2000, p. 93). Although there are clear advantages to libraries in having only one or more aggregator with which to deal, there are also disadvantages, such as the fact that the libraries' users may not need access to all of the thousands of journals included in the package. Further, there may be considerable overlap between the titles on different aggregators' databases, although it may be possible to determine the level of overlap by using JAKE or Jointly Administered Knowledge Environment (http://jake.med.yale.edu/) – 'a freeware metadata management system and online database used to find, link, and compare journal titles and union lists' (Pettijohn & Neville 2003, p. 25). Another problem commonly reported is the problem of accessing back-issues in the event of cancellation or in cases where a particular journal is sold to another publisher. In the case of cancellation, some aggregators do allow libraries access to back-issues for the years they 'purchased', but librarians need to check contracts if this is likely to be an issue. At the time of writing, some aggregators insist on including paper versions of journals, which can obviously be a drawback for libraries.

Some libraries save effort by forming consortia that share 'collections', which has the added benefit of giving them extra negotiating power. Arguably, such arrangements are not detrimental to the aggregators because they have less customers with which to deal and, in any case, they generally charge extra rates where their databases are networked, charging either by network size or by the number of simultaneous users permitted. A further advantage of consortia is the opportunity to share hardware (an issue discussed in later chapters).

Other issues to consider are copyright restrictions and authentication of users. Copyright requirements need to be checked to see if they are going to cause problems for the library, because they are likely to place restrictions on copying and lending of the journals under license. Academic libraries, for example, many of which have set up 'electronic reserve' collections consisting of material highly recommended to students by academic staff, may find copyright unduly restrictive. (Of course, as more material becomes available in full text, the need for 'e-reserve' collections diminishes.) Methods of authentication include 'automatic login using ID and password, automatic login using IP address, library authentication, and proxy server login' (Pettijohn & Neville 2003, p. 26). (IP numbers and proxy servers were discussed briefly in Chapter 1; see also Chapters 6 and 7.) The situation becomes complicated where databases are shared by a consortium, and even moreso in the case of academic libraries that have distance learning students to serve – in such a case, use of the library's range of IP addresses is not going to help a remote student.

Online retrieval systems

What are the main components of the online information services used by librarians? They are:

- the database or files, containing the data required by librarians and library users (see below)
- the search software, which enables the user to retrieve the information/data required (discussed in the section following databases)
- the computer terminal or microcomputer, with which the user (either the librarian or the library user) searches the database
- the communications link between the vendor's server and the user's terminal or microcomputer
- the communications software, which allows the user's terminal or microcomputer to connect with the host computer and communicate with it.

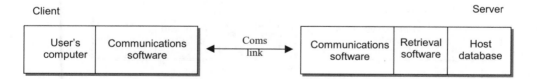

Figure 2.1: Online information services

Software is not discussed in detail in this chapter (it is discussed later in the book). At this point, it is enough to recall that software is the set of programmed instructions that directs the computer hardware to perform the tasks required by the user of the computer system.

Here, the focus is on text retrieval software, which is a form of software that enables the user to search the computer file or database for the occurrence in the database of specified text or character strings. Typically, a character string is merely a series of alphabetical characters, such as a keyword, but it can be a numerical sequence, such as a book's International Standard Book Number, or an alphanumeric sequence (a mixture of alphabetic and numeric characters). The search software discussed here is most accurately described as text retrieval software, although the term is not universally used in the library science literature.

Front-ends and gateways

Over the years there has been an increase in end-user searching, as distinct from use of a library-based intermediary, with the development of more user-friendly interfaces, a shift in pricing structures and a change in the way in which the databases are accessed. There has been an effort on the part of the online industry to cultivate the end-user, especially in view of the wide use made of numeric and directory databases by that end of the market and in view of the increasing use of the Internet by the corporate sector. Guidance for inexperienced users has improved over the years, with help facilities, for example, and online thesauri to help users use the best search terms (in other words, the ones preferred by databases' human indexers). 'Front-ends' and 'gateways' also make it easier for a user to search for and retrieve information from an online database.

A front-end is a type of computer software that acts as an intermediary between a user and a computer system, in this case, an online host computer using text retrieval software. The front-end provides a more user-friendly interface than that offered by a command driven system and translates the user's responses into the language of the specific text retrieval system. Front-end software is generally geared towards the inexperienced user, offering more in the way of menu-type prompts. (Human-computer interfaces are discussed at the end of Chapter 6.)

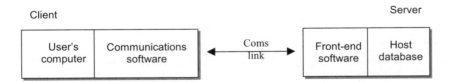

Figure 2.2: Server front-end software

Many front-ends are supplied by the commercial vendors themselves and are obviously geared towards use of those vendors' products. Much of the impetus for front-ends came from the growth in microcomputing in the 1980s, and there is a selection of front-end software for the microcomputer.

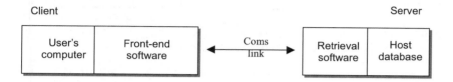

Figure 2.3: Client front-end software

The main facilities offered by front-end software are:

- logging users on to the required database (that is, going through the process of establishing a connection between the client and the host server and gaining access to the required file using commands and passwords) and logging out of the file at the end of a session

- helping the user to formulate a search strategy (which can be done offline, if a microcomputer-based product is used) and to upload the strategy to the online retrieval system

- providing a user-friendly interface between the user and the text retrieval system, for example, by use of a uniform set of menus and prompts

- helping users to download search results to the local system and to clean up the records, which typically involves using special bibliographic software to format citations, once they have been downloaded, and to produce bibliographies that conform to international bibliographic styles (see Chapter 5)

- helping users manipulate data retrieved from a numeric database, for example, business and financial data contained in downloaded records

- helping users select an appropriate database: thus emulating, to a limited degree, the role of an experienced searcher

- ranking of search results, for example, by allowing the user to assign weights to search terms and presenting search results in decreasing order of weight, and

- tutorial material, for example, microcomputer-based products, which can be run offline and then used to help users search in online mode (note, especially, the increasing availability of web-based tutorials that can be downloaded).

One of the criticisms leveled at some front-ends is that in catering for the inexperienced user and presenting a user-friendly, menu-driven interface, they lose some of the useful interactive qualities associated with the expert intermediary's use of a command-driven system. This interactive quality is maintained, and indeed emphasised in the *intelligent front-end*, which represents an attempt to incorporate into the front-end the knowledge and skills of a human intermediary. This is achieved through the use of expert system software (part of the area of computing known as artificial intelligence). Expert systems are an attempt to reproduce human expertise through development of a knowledge base (in this case, knowledge of the databases, their terminology, conceptual relationships among terms, indexing policies and search strategies) and a set of rules for using this knowledge (see Chapter 5 for a more detailed description of expert systems).

Whereas front-end is a generic term for search assistance software, a *gateway* is a facility that provides the searcher with access to more than one online service. In offering the user a choice of databases, the gateway service will typically offer many of the user-friendly features of front-end software (for example, use of common commands regardless of which text retrieval system is being accessed). A gateway is a third-party service that provides access to other agencies' databases.

Figure 2.4: Use of a gateway

Typically, the user of the gateway service will be able to search the other (host) database using the commands and prompts that are used to communicate with the gateway.

Databases

In the last chapter, resources found on the Internet were referred to rather indiscriminatingly as files, whether they were actual information resources, such as electronic documents, or software resources. Many of the information resources discussed in this chapter are described as databases. The term database refers to a collection of related computer files. *File* is taken here to refer to a set of records systematically organised and stored in electronic format. Perhaps the best way in which to explain how these terms relate to each other is to consider an example.

The computer-based library catalogue is a type of database, at the heart of which is a bibliographic file, in which each record represents a specific work, such as a book in the library collection. The bibliographic file may not be the only file in a library catalogue, for example, there may be a holdings or item file which gives users item-specific information, in other words, it will give details of individual copies of a work. It is not important to think about holdings files here. (They are more important in Chapter 4, as part of circulation systems.) The point to note is that, strictly speaking, the term database is more generic than the term file. In practice there is some confusion between the terms. Information librarians sometimes use the term database to refer to a single file, but a database might normally be expected to contain more than one file, for example, a legal database may store a set of discrete, full-text electronic documents, like those mentioned in the last chapter.

It was suggested above that a file is a set of records, for example, a set of bibliographic records, each representing a work in a library. Sometimes catalogue records are referred to as surrogates, indicating that they merely *represent* information resources and are not themselves information resources (in that they do not *generally* give users the answers that they are looking for). Each record, therefore, provides a description of a work, namely, descriptive elements that identify a work (its title, publication date etc.) and descriptive elements that help a user establish whether or not a work is likely to be useful (for example, subject descriptors or classification numbers). To use the work you are reading as an example, descriptive elements might include:

TI	Computers for librarians: an introduction to the electronic library
ED	3rd edition
AU	Ferguson, Stuart; Hebels, Rodney
PU	Wagga Wagga, NSW: Centre for Information Studies, 2003
SE	Topics in Australasian Library & Information Studies, no. 22
NU	1-876938-54-4
SU	Libraries - Automation; Information storage and retrieval systems

Figure 2.5: Sample bibliographic record

Each of these data elements (or attributes) is called a field. In this example, the fields are represented by keys: TI = title; ED = edition statement; AU = author; PU = publishing (imprint) details; SE = series statement; NU = standard identifying number; SU = subject descriptor.

Fields are sometimes referred to as the smallest data elements to make sense to a user, unless of course one counts subfields, such as publisher's name in the sample above. (In the next chapter, there are examples of bibliographic standards that would break the 'PU' field above into subfields.) All the records in a file would normally contain much the same fields. One would expect a library to use its bibliographic file to store representations of its information resources and not, in the case of a public library for instance, to store information on community organisations. This would be stored in a separate file.

A database is regarded here, therefore, as a collection of related computer files, each of which is a set of similar records containing similar fields or data elements. The relationship of these elements can be expressed hierarchically:

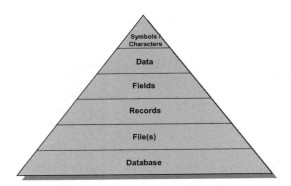

Figure 2.6: Organisation of a database 1

Another way of representing the relations among these elements would be to imagine a file as a matrix, in which each row represents a discrete record within the file, while each row represents a field or data element that is shared by most of the records in the file.

	Author Field	**Title Field**	**Publisher Field**	**Date Field**
Record 1	Frow, John	Marxism and literary history	Blackwell	1986
Record 2	Lukács, Georg	The historical novel	Merlin	1989
Record 3	Lukács, Georg	The theory of the novel	Merlin	1971
Record 4	Vazsonyi, Nicholas	Lukács reads Goethe	Camden House	1997

Figure 2.7: Organisation of a database 2

Each cell (the rectangular intersection of a row and a column) in this matrix contains a single datum (the singular of data, strictly speaking): for example, an author's name or a title.

Databases in which data are organised in this way are often referred to as *structured databases*. Most of the databases used by information librarians are of this kind. They generally fall into one of three categories:

- external or remote databases, which can be accessed online, typically over the Internet (the information stored on such a database often, but not necessarily, duplicates the kind of information previously purchased by librarians in print format)

- portable databases such as those held on optical disks, for example, on CD-ROMs (these typically, but not necessarily, duplicate external databases that were already available online), and
- locally stored or inhouse databases, generally accessed online (these are most often catalogues or indexes to local collections, but might also consist of community information systems).

Optical disk resources and inhouse databases are discussed later in the chapter.

Bibliographic databases

The first online databases to be developed were bibliographic databases, particularly indexing and abstracting services like *Index Medicus* and *Chemical Abstracts*. Like the simple bibliographic file above, these contained 'surrogates', representations of information resources, in this case (most often) periodical articles. Beginning in the 1960s, many publishers in this area turned to computer-based text-editing and phototypesetting techniques to help produce and publish their indexes. Since data were held in machine-readable form, the computer could be used to perform literature searches, and large commercial organisations were able to acquire data on magnetic tape and perform searches on their inhouse computer systems. With the development of online processing systems and retrieval software, for example, ORBIT (Online Retrieval of Bibliographic Information Time-Shared), it became possible to offer an online search service, a move facilitated by developments in telecommunications in the 1970s.

There are three main types of online bibliographic database:

- catalogues, both individual catalogues and union catalogues
- bibliographies, such as the New Zealand National Bibliography, and
- indexing and abstracting services, such as *Chemical Abstracts*.

Many bibliographic databases are indexing and abstracting services, with several hundred world-wide. Most of these cover scientific and technical literature. Medline, for example, was publicly available as early as 1971, and now contains more than twelve million references, dating back to 1966 and covering 4,600 biomedical, clinical science and (increasingly) life science journals in the US, currently in thirty languages (National Library of Medicine 2003). The fields that make up a bibliographic citation are similar to those in a catalogue, in that they consist of elements of bibliographic description and subject description, although of course the elements of bibliographic description vary slightly (for example, volume, number and pagination of journal articles). Many of these services include abstracts with the bibliographic citations, which, like subject descriptors, assist selection of resources, particularly where the resources cited are not available locally and need to be ordered from elsewhere. Where abstracts are provided, they are stored in a searchable field and offer users a subject-rich set of text for retrieval purposes.

Other types of online database

There are probably as many taxonomies of online database as there are directories of databases. Most directories, however, refer to four main types:

- the bibliographic databases described above
- full-text databases, which provide documents themselves in machine-readable format and not simply citations
- numeric databases, which contain numerical as distinct from textual data, and provide statistical and financial data for government and business: for example, *AUSSTATS* (provided by the Australian Bureau of Statistics)
- directory databases, which provide the user with information about individuals or organisations, for example, *Business Who's Who*.

Full-text, numeric and directory databases are sometimes referred to as source databases, because the user can obtain the required information online instead of being referred elsewhere. On a superficial level, directory databases are similar to bibliographic databases, in that each record in a bibliographic database represents an information resource, such as a journal article, while each record in a directory database represents an actual person or organisation. In a sense, each record in a directory database is therefore a surrogate. The fields in such a database refer to specific elements associated with the entities described, for example, (in the case of an organisation) corporate name, address, product listings and contact numbers. Nonetheless, a user does find substantive answers in a directory database and it could arguably be regarded as a form of full-text database.

Full-text databases are a more recent development than bibliographic databases, but have grown considerably in number over the past few years. They are an interesting development, not least because they represent an important step towards the digital library referred to in the last chapter. The main areas for full-text development have been:

- legal resources, for example, Lexis/Nexis databases
- business sources, for example, *Harvard Business Review/Online*
- scientific and technical journals, for example, *Chemical Journals Online*
- newspapers, for example, the *Sydney Morning Herald*
- news wires and summaries, for example, Reuters Financial Report
- reference works, for example, *Britannica Online*, which is available on the Internet.

These resources are commercially produced and are generally available for a price, but it is worth noting that there are many other types of electronic source, including the government publications, academic journals, news releases, research reports, newsletters and magazines mentioned in the last chapter. Another point worth noting is that the term full-text does not necessarily denote that the whole of an information resource is available in electronic form. A full-text journal, for example, may include only the longer articles that appear in the print equivalent.

Most of the full-text databases used by libraries are structured, in the sense that they have fields that correspond to those in a bibliographic database, with bibliographic and subject descriptions of the documents represented, but, unlike a bibliographic database, they also contain a field or fields in which the actual text of the document itself appears.

Text retrieval software

The text retrieval systems described here are used to search the online databases discussed so far and the 'portable' databases described later in this chapter. The categories of database outlined above (which apply also to portable databases) are examples of *structured* text retrieval systems. An example of unstructured text retrieval software would be retrieval software that is used to search word processed documents, for example, in correspondence files (see Chapter 5). Structured text retrieval systems allow users either to search for text under specified fields (for example, under title or subject descriptor) or to conduct free text searches across all or most of the fields in a file. Normally, the user will be able to search the file for specified keywords, but, in some cases, it may also be possible to search under a phrase, for example, title proper, a multi-term subject descriptor (for example, 'Information storage and retrieval systems') or an author's name.

The availability of keyword and phrase searching will depend on the parameters established by the designers of a particular system. (Parameters are sets of variable values that can be established by the system designers before data are entered on to the database, for example, searchable and non-searchable fields.) Most of the text retrieval systems with which librarians are familiar operate on the principle that every time a set of terms is added to a text file, terms required for retrieval purposes are added to a separate index file by the system, complete with details of their occurrences (see Chapter 5, where text retrieval systems are discussed in more detail). The system selects terms for indexing based on the parameters set by its human designers. The most common parameters are:

- not all words are indexed, for example, common words such as articles and prepositions are not indexed (these are known as stop words)
- certain fields may not be considered worth indexing (from an economical point of view), for example, publisher's name, in the case of a set of conference proceedings
- some fields, for example, title or subject heading fields, may be searched under keyword or phrase, in which case both will be indexed by the system.

It is worth recalling that the term held by the system in its index file is merely a character string, a chunk of text as it was entered on to the database – in other words, if it is misspelt by the person entering the text, it will not be retrieved, unless the searcher happens to make an identical spelling mistake. The system will not create a link between singular and plural versions, or indeed any other version, of a term. Similarly, the system itself exerts no vocabulary control, with the result, for example, that a free text search (searching for a keyword across fields) will fail to uncover synonymous terms, quasi-synonyms or indeed antonyms (for instance, documents containing the term 'employment' may be of interest to someone looking for material on unemployment). In such cases, the user may wish to widen the search beyond one search term and combine groups (or sets) of references. Similarly, there are cases where the user, conducting a free text search, retrieves too many references and wishes to narrow the search and reduce the set retrieved.

As mentioned in the last chapter, there are a number of techniques for either widening or narrowing a search. The main ones are:

- truncation, which allows the user to search for variations of a term, thus widening a search: for example, a search under 'comput*' (the symbol differs according to system) will find variations such as computer, computers and computing (truncation like this, at the end of a word, is sometimes referred to as *stemming*); similarly 'labo*r' should retrieve both American and non-American spellings

- field specification, that is, specifying that the term sought must occur in a specified field, is a means of narrowing a search

- field delimiters, which are devices that may be used to reduce the number of records in a set: common examples are an 'equals' symbol (for example, 'language = English') and a 'greater than' symbol (for example, 'date > 2000')

- search operators, which are devices used either to widen or to narrow a search by combining search terms: these are worth considering in more detail.

The so-called boolean features of some Web search engines, described in Chapter 1, derive from developments in text retrieval pioneered by the vendors of online information services. BRS Search is an example of a text retrieval system, originally developed to search the BRS database (later CDP), but sold subsequently as a text retrieval package that supports modules such as library management systems (see Chapter 4) and records management systems.

Because of the large amount of text which these text retrieval systems have to search, including (typically) an abstract field and (increasingly) full text, there is considerable need to narrow searches and reduce the number of search results, hence, for example, the use of proximity operators, which allow the user to specify how closely terms appear in a record, for example,

- within a specified number of words from each other
- in the same sentence
- in the same paragraph
- in the same field
- adjacent (that is, next to each other).

In the past, online searching of databases such as Dialog was almost exclusively the preserve of the reference librarian, or even special sections, particularly because of the costs associated with searching, for example, connect time charges and long-distance telephone charges, and the difficulties associated with online searching – the early systems were command-driven (see Chapter 6) and required users to be familiar with the commands, operators and even the field names used by particular systems.

The librarian became an intermediary between the user and the information stored on the database. For a number of years there has been a weakening of this role, with the development of more user-friendly menu-driven interfaces and subsequently the use of the graphical user interfaces (GUIs) associated with the Web, changes in pricing structures and a growth in access via the Internet – all resulting in an increase in end-user searching, as distinct from use of a library-based intermediary. Increased use of online databases by inexperienced or infrequent searchers makes it important that online help is available. Help facilities include:

- online help documentation (the searcher can request help information relating specifically to what he or she is trying to do at the time)

- access to the index file (the searcher may be able to browse through the index file and discover what terms appear in the main file and the frequency of their appearance)

- online thesauri (some systems will allow the searcher to explore the thesaurus of terms used to establish vocabulary control in the subject descriptor field).

Access to a thesaurus should not be confused with access to the database's index file. What appears in the index file is a mere list of terms (words and phrases) that are present in the main file. A thesaurus, however, is the means by which an indexer is provided with a *controlled* vocabulary with which to describe documents. In practical terms it comprises a list of terms (words and phrases) in which preferred terms are indicated, non-preferred terms are listed with references to the appropriate preferred terms (thus facilitating control of synonyms), and hierarchical relationships between terms are indicated (the reference structure generally including broader terms, narrower terms and related terms). Thesauri can be used by searchers to explore the controlled vocabulary used by the indexers. Unfortunately, some are available only in print form, but some vendors provide online access to thesauri.

Limitations of boolean searching

So far, the positive aspects of boolean searching have been stressed. For librarians and end-users who can remember searching manually through volume after volume of printed reference resources, boolean searching has provided obvious advantages, for example, the benefit of being able to search one file (as distinct from separate annual cumulations), fast search facilities and many more access points than printed resources. Nonetheless, it does have serious limitations. The main criticism concerns the all-or-nothing nature of boolean searching. As soon as the searcher retrieves a set of documents, the file is split into two sets, those considered relevant and those not considered relevant. The problem is that users do not have such a clear-cut sense of relevance. In the course of narrowing a search, users may push records that they might consider relevant into the irrelevant set. The set retrieved, on the other hand, will contain irrelevant records. Moreover, there is no way of ranking items in the retrieved set, which must be further refined or reviewed in full.

As suggested in Chapter 1, various solutions to the limitations of boolean searching have been developed. One approach, adopted by search engines, is for the system to rank the records retrieved, basing the ranking on the frequency with which search terms appear in the records. The searcher can start reviewing the top rankings and go as far down the list as required. Word frequency can also be used to indicate the degree to which documents are alike and to cluster records according to the degree of similarity. The searcher will then be offered the opportunity to review related clusters. Considerable effort has gone into researching such probabilistic approaches to information retrieval, and there are some applications (discussed later). Another variation is to permit the user to assign weights to search terms, so that the retrieved records can then be weighted by the system, which will offer only records with more than a specified 'weight'.

Post-retrieval features

Once a set of records has been retrieved, there is a range of further options:

- printing search results – either printing online or requesting printouts from the vendor
- downloading search results to the searcher's computer, assuming the vendor permits records to be downloaded – one advantage of downloading records is that the searcher does not have to wait for a printer to print the results of the search before quitting the commercial database
- saving search strategies, either to be used at a later date or in another file
- bibliography production – where search results are downloaded to the searcher's computer, the data often need to be tidied up and formatted before a polished bibliography can be produced
- manipulation of data from a numeric database (similar to the ability to tidy up data from a textual database)
- document delivery services – some vendors provide the documents to which bibliographic citations refer (see below)
- selective dissemination of information or SDI services (discussed above)
- offline services, for example, some database producers provide subsets of their online databases on diskette (floppy disk) for microcomputer use (see below).

Portable databases

So far, the discussion of information resources and services has focused on remote online resources. It was noted, however, that offline, 'portable' databases, such as CD-ROMs, are also available. A portable database is simply a database that has been transferred to an auxiliary storage medium in order that it can be acquired by libraries and other users. The media used to store such databases are either:

- magnetic media, such as magnetic tape and floppy disk (or diskette); or
- optical disks, such as CD-ROMs and videodisks.

Most of the attention here focuses on CD-ROM, since it is a medium that has found wide use in library and information services. Since the first CD-ROM products became available in 1985, the market has grown steadily. Although there are other offline computer-based information resources (for example, database subsets on magnetic diskettes), CD-ROM is the main electronic alternative to online information resources. It can also be a useful supplement to online services. Alternative portable resources are discussed later.

CD-ROM databases

First, what is CD-ROM? CD-ROM stands for Compact Disk Read-Only Memory. It is a type of optical disk technology, based on the compact disk technology used for sound recordings (CD-Audio). Indeed, the relatively favourable price structure for CD-ROM products reflects the commercial success of CD-Audio. The ROM part refers to the fact that once a CD-ROM has been produced it cannot be altered. In other words, it can be read but not written to. (Some other types of optical disk can be written to – see Chapter 6.)

The disk itself (12 cm. in diameter) is plastic, covered on one side with a thin layer of aluminium, on which data or information are encoded in a format that computers can manipulate. This chapter does not explain how the data are stored (see Chapter 6). For the purposes of this overview, it is enough to know that it is possible to store a considerable amount of data on a disk and that the data are read by a special device called a CD-ROM drive. The read head (the part of the CD-ROM drive that performs the reading function) is based on laser technology and does not have to come into contact with the disk, with the result that CD-ROMs are *relatively* robust. Unlike CD-Audio, however, a CD-ROM drive must be linked to a computer, so that users can retrieve, manipulate and analyse the data stored on disk.

As with online databases, there is a wide range of CD-ROM information resources, including: bibliographic databases (catalogues, bibliographies and indexes), directories (particularly in the business area), numeric databases and finally, full text databases, for which CD-ROM, with its large storage capacity, is well suited. There is occasionally a fifth category of database, which is neither numeric nor textual: cartographic databases (for instance, DeLorme's *Eartha Global Explorer*).

The basic *CD-ROM workstation*, that is, the configuration of computer equipment and software required to search a CD-ROM database, consists of:

- a CD-ROM drive, which reads the data on the disk itself and converts those data into a form that a computer can handle
- a microcomputer
- an interface between the two devices (see Chapter 6)

- text retrieval software, similar to the software used to search online databases, and
- a printer, in order to print out search results – the alternative to printing out results is to download them to a magnetic diskette in order that the user can take results away.

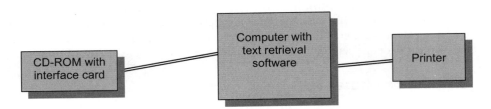

Figure 2.8: Basic CD-ROM workstation

In practice, most libraries go beyond that single workstation, partly because they may have a large number of CD-ROM databases which need to be exchanged in the CD-ROM drive and partly because such a configuration allows only one user per workstation. In this situation, libraries can use devices such as disk-changers, towers and jukeboxes to store their CD-ROM collections, which can then be accessed via one powerful microcomputer (the server) from a variety of microcomputers – provided of course that the library has a license from the CD-ROM producer to share it among different workstations. Indeed, users outside the library (for example, staff and students in an academic institution) can access library CD-ROM collections via computer networks.

Note, however, the technical support required to maintain such networks. Many libraries, as a result, have opted for Internet access to databases in preference to the networking of CD-ROM databases.

Other portable databases

CD-ROM is the principal offline computer-based alternative to online search services. It is worth remembering, however, that CD-ROM is not the only offline product available. Some online database producers, for example, have on occasion provided subsets of their databases on magnetic diskette for microcomputer use. It is feasible for customers of such a service to supply a profile of interests and, on the same principle as SDI, receive a custom-designed subset of the database for local use. One reason for the use of floppy disk for such services, and not CD-ROM, is that at present it is more appropriate for the delivery of information that requires frequent updating. All that is required is one person with a microcomputer and diskettes to create and update a database (and a postal service for delivery).

In the reference environment, CD-ROM is the main optical disk resource. The only other optical disk mentioned in surveys of optical disks in libraries – as far as information resources are concerned – is the videodisk, which is larger than a CD-ROM and enjoyed a small market niche as an interactive multimedia product, for example, in computer-assisted learning packages, as well as an entertainment market.

Hypertext search facilities

Typical CD-ROM search facilities are much the same as those described for online searching, being based on the same text retrieval principles and employing similar search operators (for example, boolean operators) and search strategies. Accordingly, they share some of the advantages and disadvantages of online search facilities. The success of the search relies principally on the searcher's skilled use of search operators, field specification and choice of terms.

Given the problems of text retrieval in a large information source, however, it is worth considering hypertext as an alternative solution to text management problems. As discussed in Chapter 1, hypertext is an important component of Web publishing, as part of the markup language used to format Web documents (HTML) and as part of the retrieval method (HTTP). It provides users with the opportunity to follow associative links from document to document, or in other words surf the Net. Hypertext also has applications in the reference environment, since hypertext and hypermedia have been used in a number of CD-ROM products. Consider, for example, electronic encyclopedias, which consist of discrete nodes of text, linked not just to other nodes of text, but also to graphics, sound and video excerpts.

Obviously, not all forms of publication are well suited to the hypertext approach, but some reference sources are, for instance, encyclopedias, handbooks and guides.

Comparison of printed, online and CD-ROM resources

How do CD-ROM databases compare with the printed resources traditionally used by libraries and with the online information resources described earlier? Figure 2.9 provides a structured comparison of the three types of resource. It is worth noting, however, that the three media are not necessarily in competition with each other, and may in some ways complement each other. Surveys conducted in the late 1980s did suggest that the increased availability of databases on CD-ROM led to significant reductions in print subscriptions and online use. For a few years, the purchase of CD-ROMs grew dramatically, the reverse of a more general trend away from acquisition (of library resources) to access (to resources elsewhere) but there is anecdotal evidence to suggest that many librarians prefer to access online databases via the Internet. Print subscriptions continue to decline and there are even suggestions that CD-ROMs may disappear as information resources once the virtual library is fully established.

Many comparisons of the media focus on the costs. Because of the relatively high subscription costs of print and CD-ROM media, these need to be reasonably well used before they offer any cost benefits. Where a library consults a large range of sources on an occasional basis, online retrieval may be the most economical option. On the other hand, where certain sources are consulted frequently, it may pay to acquire these in print or CD-ROM format, and save online charges and communication costs (bear in mind, however, the added initial cost and maintenance of workstations in the case of CD-ROM).

One of the advantages of print and CD-ROM media is that they are easy to budget for, compared to online services which are notoriously difficult to predict. Not only does online searching incur high charges and telecommunications costs, but libraries (for those very reasons) often insist that librarians conduct online searches, which adds further to the costs and reduces end-user control of the results. One solution to the unexpected expenses associated with online searching is to charge for the service, which both discourages use and helps to recover costs. It is worth noting, however, that where a library charges for online searching, but not for the use of CD-ROM products, any savings due to decreased use of online databases may be picked up by the library user and not necessarily by the library.

One of the main advantages of online searching over use of CD-ROM resources is currency: issues of CD-ROM products are generally produced only three or four times a year. Where libraries can afford both facilities, CD-ROMs can be used for the bulk of searching, with online databases being used to check for the most current information. There are special gateways that allow users to move from an on-disk to an online search. Some vendors, for example, provide software that allows users to search their CD-ROM product first, then search for updates in the online file. The search strategy does not even have to be reformatted. The gateway acts as a front-end, connecting with the host database, uploading the search strategy, performing the search and downloading the results.

One of the other main advantages of online searching, particularly over print media, is the speed of search. The response time for CD-ROM (which is microcomputer-based) is generally slower than for online searching, where the searcher has the benefit of access to a powerful host computer. It is worth noting, however, that the speed of online searching is affected by other factors, such as the communication link between clients and servers and the type of user interface. The menu-driven and graphical user interfaces mentioned earlier may be more user-friendly than the older command-driven interfaces, but they are not as fast as a command-driven interface in the hands of an experienced searcher. In recent years, some library networks have bought their users greater access to electronic publications by uploading data from CD-ROMs (where licensed to do so) to network servers, but increased access is often achieved at the expense of speed, because of communication delays and the user-friendly interfaces.

	Print resources	Online resources	CD-ROM resources
Currency	Subscriptions typically frequent	Not necessarily better than print	Subscriptions typically infrequent
Ease of retrieval	Limited access points	Multiple access points; can reuse search strategies	Multiple access points
Speed of search	Slow, except for limited searches	Depends on communications link	Fairly fast
Use of staff time	Self-help encouraged	Staff online intermediaries; increasing self-help	Self-help encouraged but guidance required
Overall costs	High subscriptions and storage	Hardware, software, charges often by use, communication costs	Hardware, high subscriptions, licence (for multiple workstations)
Access	Unlimited	May be limited by terminals, staff and charges	May be limited by licences, availability of workstations
Non-text material	Available	Limited	Available
Number of sources	Large	Large	Not as many as print or online sources
Standardisation	(not applicable)	Some standardisation	Still problematic
File integrity	Material misfiled or mislaid	Misspelling a minor problem	Misspelling a minor problem
Presentation of results	(not applicable)	Variety of software products available	Variety of products available
End-user control of results	User in control	User unsure if all records retrieved	User generally feels in control
Ability to browse	Good	Poor	May be limited by demand for workstations

Figure 2.9: Print, online and CD-ROM resources compared

It was suggested above that, although librarians have tended to act as intermediaries between users and commercial online databases, there has been a shift in recent years to encourage users to conduct their own searches of those databases to which the library subscribes. Where users are empowered to conduct their own searches, they are able to become more self-sufficient. In theory, this gives them greater control over search results, although in practice, given the problems associated with boolean searching, the inexperienced user may retrieve less than an experienced intermediary and yet *believe* that a comprehensive search has been conducted, such is the power of boolean searching compared to manual searching. (This is not to suggest that in every situation reference librarians perform more effective searches than their end-users.) Another benefit of end-user searching, is that it has the potential to save librarians' time, although part of the time saved is eaten up in education and instruction – despite the popular view that information-literacy is greater than ever before.

Document delivery

Despite the substantial growth in the number of full-text databases over the last few years, a significant proportion of online databases used by libraries remain the bibliographic type. On occasion, these may give the user the information required, for example, through the provision of an abstract. More commonly, however, the answers sought by the user can only be found by obtaining the source material corresponding to the citations retrieved. The continuing growth in published information resources, combined with their rising costs and a general decline in acquisitions budgets in most countries, make it increasingly imperative that libraries look beyond their collections to provide access to the resources identified using information retrieval tools. The problem then turns from that of retrieval to one of delivery.

The retrieval of bibliographic citations, therefore, may be much faster using online services or CD-ROMs than using traditional print resources, but the user still has the frustration of waiting to receive the relevant material. The frustration may be all the greater if the speed and efficiency of the first part of the operation raises users' expectations unrealistically. The area of document delivery is one in which there have been considerable developments in recent years. This section looks at two areas in which there have been significant developments:

- document delivery services
- inter-library loans.

Document delivery services

Earlier it was mentioned that some online vendors provide document delivery services, that is, they will send copies of the information resources that have been identified on their bibliographic databases. Where a library does not anticipate heavy use of a particular set of source material (for example, a journal title), it is generally preferable if documents can be requested individually as required, in response to specific user needs. Dialog, for example, has an order service, which has a network of source locations that will supply copies of articles. Source locations include inhouse collections, large academic and government libraries, and specialised document suppliers.

Some of the major bibliographic networks (see below) also offer document delivery services. The largest document delivery service (known to these authors) is the service provided by the British Library Document Supply Centre (BLDSC) in Yorkshire, England, which handles millions of requests a year. One of the best-known document delivery services is the UnCover system, developed by a regional bibliographic network in the US, CARL (Colorado Alliance of Research Libraries). It is now available via the Web at Ingenta, which (currently) provides free access to information on over 25,000 journals and magazines and, for a fee, delivery by mail, by fax or electronically in HTML or PDF format (see Chapter 6 on file formats).

Commercial document delivery services often offer the benefit of speed. There is a perception that they are more expensive than use of inter-library loans cooperation (below), but library directors need to be careful with their costings because once staff time is factored in there may be no cost benefit in using inter-library loans in preference to commercial document delivery.

Inter-library loans

The term inter-library loans implies that something is lent between libraries (for example, books), but here it is assumed that inter-library loans also includes the sending of copies of resources (for example, copies of journal articles), which can generally be retained by the borrowing library's user. Traditionally, libraries have relied on inter-library loans to supplement their collections, but the speed at which they can trace bibliographic citations only serves to underline the slow pace of the inter-library loans process from the user's viewpoint. It takes time for staff to verify requests, find locations for them, send requests and wait for lending libraries to retrieve and dispatch requested items.

Technological developments have helped libraries to address some of the problems associated with inter-library loans. The main developments are:

- the formation of library networks, which facilitate and speed up the location of material
- electronic mail, which speeds up the request process
- CD-ROMs, which facilitate dissemination of large databases
- technologies that speed up the delivery process, for example, fax (facsimile transmission) or use of imaging technology – see below.

Library networks

In the introductory remarks about networks, in the last chapter, reference was made to bibliographic networks. A bibliographic network is a form of cooperative network that involves the sharing of bibliographic data and, typically, computer components such as a central server, on which to store the bibliographic data, and computer software (for example, retrieval software). Library networks of this kind are generally formed with two main purposes:

- sharing the costs and effort of cataloguing
- fostering library cooperation and resource sharing.

The goal of shared cataloguing is an important factor in the formation of bibliographic networks (see Chapter 3) but the opportunity for resource sharing is an increasingly important factor, given the growing amounts of published information resources which librarians have to access on behalf of their users and given the growing financial constraints, for many libraries, on the acquisition of such resources. Resource sharing generally predates the formation of formal bibliographic networks, but with the ability, using computer and communications technologies, to share union catalogues, there are strong reasons for libraries to formalise their cooperative agreements and to form networks. Where network administrations have been formed, their objectives have included acting as an agent in resource sharing and developing new information systems and services.

Cooperative networks of the kind described are a form of wide area network (WAN). Some are organised on a national basis, for example, Kinetica in Australia and New Zealand's Te Puna Interloan system, and enjoy the leadership of national libraries. Some include member libraries in different countries, for example, SABINET, based in South Africa, has members in Ghana, Namibia and Lesotho. Curriculum Corporation's SCIS (Schools Catalogue Information Service) could also be said to be supranational, because it provides a retrieval and cataloguing service for schools in Australia and New Zealand.

In the case of regionally based networks, it is most common for libraries of the same type, for example, public libraries or university libraries, to form networks, because their user communities tend to have similar information needs and there are therefore clear benefits in resource sharing. There are, however, examples of regional networks that bring together different kinds of library, for example, LINNET (Libraries in the Northern Territory Network), which includes public and community libraries, secondary school and college libraries and government department libraries, demonstrating the special benefits of resource sharing in sparsely populated regions like Australia's Northern Territory.

Shared cataloguing is one of the main topics of the next chapter, but it is necessary to say something here about network catalogues because of their impact on document delivery. Having access to network (or union) catalogues makes it easier for request or inter-library loans departments to check the bibliographic details of users' requests and to find locations. Moreover, with the ability to access libraries' or networks' catalogues via the Web, it becomes easier to identify information resources even if they are not held by any of the libraries in one's own network. One of the problems with internetworking like this is that different systems and networks provide different enquiry screens and search facilities, hence the development of the Z39.50 protocol (mentioned in the last chapter), which allows a web client to present information from different servers in a common format.

Inter-library loans systems and technology

Having identified a bibliographic item and found a location, it is often possible for a library to speed up the request process by the use of a networked inter-library loans system (see Chapter 4 for a discussion of systems). Once a library locates an item on the network, it is able, with most systems, to send a request by electronic mail (email) without rekeying bibliographic information, call numbers or locations. Information about the requesting library (for example, address, fax number) can be stored on the system and forwarded with each request without being keyed in every time. If the item is unavailable at the first location, the system should be able to send the request to the second library on the locations list, and so on until the request is satisfied.

Most networks will also provide a fast-track facility, which means that libraries with urgent requests can be assured of a faster inter-library loans service – provided they are willing to pay extra for the service. One of the main technologies for speeding document delivery, particularly relatively small information resources such as journal articles, is fax or facsimile transmission, which typically involves transmission between two fax machines or between a fax machine and a computer. At one site a fax machine scans a document using a photoelectric cell to convert the shades of black, white and grey into electrical signals which can be transmitted to a second machine using the telephone network. What is transmitted, therefore, is an image of the original document. The second machine decodes the signals, reconstructs the original image and duplicates it on paper. There are problems reproducing documents to the same standard as an original, but for purely textual material this may not matter. The main problem facing libraries is the need to balance speed of document delivery against the costs of fax (the costs of a machine and transmission).

Another technology, which is similar to fax and is finding increasing use in libraries, is image scanning. Image scanners are discussed in more detail in Chapter 6, as a form of computer input device, but it is worth noting their use here. A page is scanned in much the same way as above, except that the scanned shades of black, grey and white are converted into a computer readable format. This option allows libraries to deliver electronic copies of documents directly to the user's desktop – in other words, to the user's own computer. The use of *Ariel* software, developed by the Research Library Group in the US in 1990, involves the creation of a set of images of each page required, which can then be emailed directly to the user (note the reference in Chapter 1 to the Multipurpose Internet Mail Extension or MIME protocol, which enables people to send non-textual documents such as scanned images) or uploaded on to a website to which the user has access. In the latter case the library simply alerts the user to the document's availability.

Another development promoted by some libraries is the opportunity for user-driven inter-library loans. Earlier it was suggested that computerised catalogues can be searched not simply by users in the libraries to which the catalogues belong but also by users outside the library. The next step for some libraries has been to provide users with the means to place their own inter-library loan requests, for example, an electronic request form which, once complete, can be emailed to the lending library. One problem to be addressed is the fact that many paper inter-library loan request forms include a copyright declaration, to say, for example, that material is required for scholarly purposes, but electronic forms do not include legally valid signatures. A solution that has been developed by some libraries and networks is to require first-time users of the inter-library loan facility to download and print a generic copyright declaration, sign it and return it to the lending library. That signature is considered enough to cover subsequent requests. Where such user-driven systems are in place, it is possible to keep track of one's request.

It is also worth mentioning here the use of inter-library loans systems which enable libraries to track inter-library loan material, for example, books on loan to another library (see Chapter 4, which discusses library management systems).

Conspectus

Some library literature gives the impression that acquisitions and access are competing strategies (the phrase 'access versus acquisitions' has often been used). The two are actually complementary strategies, employed by libraries to support their overall aim of providing access to published information resources for their users. Nowhere is the complementary nature of these strategies more evident than in Conspectus, which is a means of describing library collections using standard descriptors, in order that others can tell what a collection's *subject* strengths are. There are two basic components in Conspectus:

- a set of standardised descriptors, used to identify the subject strengths of a collection
- a Conspectus database, used to store and disseminate information about libraries' collection strengths.

Several countries use Conspectus as a means of enhancing resource sharing, through increasing librarians' awareness of special collections elsewhere. Being aware of other libraries' collection strengths and collecting *intentions* may suggest to librarians where they can look for inter-library loans and even suggest areas in which collection development in their own libraries might be unnecessary. For some time, the Conspectus, in conjunction with the National Bibliographic Database, was seen in Australia as the means of developing a 'distributed national collection'. Currently there is little or no interest in this development, but it is probably worth being aware of the various attempts worldwide to establish Conspectus.

Automation of reference processes

So far, the focus has been electronic resources and the use of various technologies to assist sharing of resources, electronic and non-electronic. Here it is worth considering what aspects of reference work can be computerised – in particular, what aspects of reference processes, previously done manually, can be automated. Automation is not something associated with reference and information work, which is not generally characterised by the kind of 'routines' found, for example, in loans or circulation (see Chapter 4). There are obvious exceptions, of course, such as filing pages of tax law into loose-leaf binders. One area that has seen considerable development over the past few years is the management of information requests. Software products are available that provide:

- management of the response process for those information enquiries that cannot be answered immediately
- tracking of those requests that are referred to specialised staff in the organisation or to external agents
- maintenance of a database or 'knowledge-base' of answers that can save duplication of effort (equivalent of the loose-leaf or card 'ready-reference' file)
- provision of progress reports to end-users
- maintenance of statistics, such as response times, volume of enquiries and costs.

The key point to note about such systems is the extent to which knowledge and effort can be shared. Gone, one hopes, are the days when a user asked an information librarian about a previous request to hear, "Oh I don't know – who did you speak to?"

Development of inhouse resources

Prior to the preceding section, the resources discussed were published information resources – very much the bread and butter of library and information management. Some resources, however, are developed inhouse for the benefit of the library's specific user community. Two main activities are considered here: the digitisation of existing resources, and the creation of inhouse databases and other resources.

Digitisation of collections

Why digitise resources that already exist in another format? Deegan and Tanner, in their useful text on digital libraries, suggest the following benefits:

- fast access to high-demand and frequently used items
- easier access to individual resources within items, for example, articles within journals
- fast access to materials held remotely
- the chance to provide easy access to out-of-print materials

- the potential to display materials that are in formats difficult to access, such as maps
- 'virtual reunification' – meaning the 'bringing together' (in virtual terms) of physically dispersed collections
- the potential to enhance digital images
- the potential to provide virtual access to fragile and/or precious materials, making preservation of the originals easier
- the potential for the integration of virtual material into teaching resources
- enhanced searchability, including searching the full text of resources
- the potential integration of different media such as images and sounds
- the potential to reduce the burden or cost of delivery (2002, pp. 32-3).

Clearly, the reduction in cost of delivery has to be off-set against the costs of digitisation, which include the costs of hardware, including scanners, and software (see Chapter 6), possible copyright charges (although the library may opt to digitise only resources that are outside copyright) and, of course, staff time. Staff time does not include only the actual process of digitisation, which is time-consuming, but also the time expended in any project (see Chapter 8), assessment of resources for digitisation, seeking of copyright permissions (if appropriate) and provision for access. 'Access' is covered in the following chapter, and refers here to the provision of information that will enable users to find the resources – the so-called metadata, or structured data about data, that standardise the elements describing an information resource (such as creator or date created) and the actual content (for instance, thesauri to cover elements such as subject). Metadata will generally also include information such as unique identifiers for resources described, references to the original resources from which the virtual resources have been derived and rights management information: for example, copyright and reproduction rights (see Chapter 3).

The criteria used to assess resources for digitisation will resemble the benefits listed above – priorities will obviously depend on the type of library and information service. Preservation, for example, is likely to be more of an issue in, say, a national or state/provincial library than in the corporate sector. It is worth bearing in mind that use of resources will be affected by the digitisation process, so, for instance, the fact that materials are not currently used does not mean that there is no point digitising them, because fast and easy access to a digital surrogate may create demand for the resources, especially if libraries are dong a good job of marketing their digitisation projects to their user communities. Unfortunately, digitisation is sometimes a double-edged sword because, while it may increase demand for the surrogates – and so aid conservation – it does also have the potential on occasion to increase demand for the original.

Copyright and digitisation

As already indicated, copyright is an important issue in the development of digital collections. Scanning resources that are under copyright and disseminating them to users is legally a form of publishing, hence the need to seek copyright permissions. Sometimes this is granted, but it can be at a cost, and sometimes publishers see the digital library as a threat to their businesses and refuse to grant permissions. Chou & Zhou, in the digital reference services collection already mentioned (Lankes *et al.* 2003), point out that the vision of the digital library held by the library and information management community faces challenges, notably from the shrink-wrap licenses insisted upon by the software industry and legislation of the past few years that, they say, 'undermines the traditional fair use doctrine and the first sale doctrine', which have been used in the past to defend libraries' rights to reproduce material for educational use. Libraries, they suggest, should, first, 'strongly assert fair use and first-sale doctrine', second, expand 'their role as a Web provider and publisher in the digital environment, and ...further integrate themselves into the creation process' and, third; and 'unite to increase their bargaining power to force publishers and software developers to make concessions' (Chou & Zhou 2003, pp.55-6).

Inhouse databases

The databases used most commonly by reference libraries are remote online databases and, less frequently, CD-ROM databases. Some libraries, however, develop their own databases. These are generally available to library users as online products, although there is no reason why an inhouse database should not be stored on CD-ROM (or any other kind of optical disk). With the emphasis on providing remote access to users however, most new databases are likely to be offered via the Web. Sometimes inhouse databases have developed out of manual information files (typically recorded in card format) but the increasing use of microcomputers in the late 1980s saw some creation of small-scale databases. They are generally textual databases, falling into one of three categories:

- bibliographic databases, for example, bibliographies of local government information sources and indexes to special collections, such as local history collections
- full text databases, for example, to provide access to documents held in machine-readable format, and
- directories, such as community information services.

There are two main methods for creating an inhouse database:

- downloading records from a commercial database (online or ondisk database), that is, creating a subset of a commercial database, and
- creating and developing a database from scratch, that is, developing a new and (typically) local information resource.

Subsets of commercial databases

Why create a subset of a commercial database? Reasons may include:

- data from different providers and held in different formats can be merged for local use
- reduction in the costs of accessing the data, for example, a library network (mentioned above) may download subsets of commercial databases to its serverS

- the data can be filtered, for example, in the case of periodical indexes, only downloading data for those journals available in the library
- the library can add local information, such as location indicators
- data may be used for SDI (selective dissemination of information) services.

Obviously such databases lack the currency of the online sources and would need to be updated regularly, say, by downloading new records each month. Other problems include legal issues, such as copyright (a huge issue, as already indicated), and the high initial costs.

Locally developed databases

What are the reasons for developing a local database? The most immediate reason is that the information in the database may not be available anywhere else. This may be because the database is an index to material not indexed elsewhere, for example, local newspapers, or because it provides information of local interest only, for example, a community information file.

The following are examples of local inhouse databases:

- historical material such as original records
- special indexes, for example indexes to special collections, such as local newspapers, pre-1950 periodicals or a local photograph collection
- full text electronic resources, such as documents which have been word processed within the organisation that the library serves, for example, a research report, and
- information and referral services, such as a community information service, which is a type of directory database, in which the user is referred to a set of local organisations and services.

There is nothing new about special indexes or information and referral services (many libraries developed such resources long before the ubiquitous microcomputer), but the use of computers allows easy insertion, deletion and amendment of records, the kind of keyword access discussed earlier, and the ability to sort records and output them either as a screen display or in printed format. Where libraries have their computers linked in a network, it is possible to share such resources, for example, branches of a city or regional library service can access and maintain an up-to-date community information database.

Creating an inhouse database

Some commercial library management systems, still to be described (Chapter 4), provide modules which can be used to construct inhouse databases. Many, for example, include community information modules, which obviously require different fields from those used in bibliographic files (for example, names of organisations, descriptors, addresses, and contact names and numbers). The other common option is for libraries to develop databases using generic software (that is, software that is not library-specific), particularly text retrieval systems, which have been mentioned already, and database management systems. (The difference between the two types of system will be explored in Chapter 5.)

The decisions which need to be made when developing an inhouse database include:

- what kind of system is most suitable for the application, for example, a text retrieval system or a database management system

- what information to include, for example, whether or not to supply abstracts with an index (the decision will be affected by memory available on the computer system)

- whether or not the information can be organised in fields (a field structure might be suitable for an index but not necessarily for all applications)

- what length fields should be – may not be applicable for some software, for example, most text retrieval systems have variable-length fields

- what to do about repeating elements, such as subject descriptors, which may be given separate fields or may be listed together within the one field (see below) – another decision that may be determined by the choice of software

- which fields to use for retrieval – another decision affected by memory, since the indexes used for retrieval will use significant amounts of memory

- whether or not to use a thesaurus for controlled vocabulary, and if so, whether to use a commercial one or to construct an inhouse product.

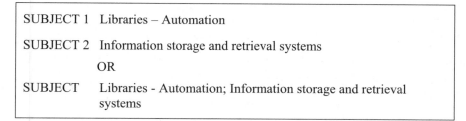

SUBJECT 1   Libraries – Automation

SUBJECT 2   Information storage and retrieval systems

OR

SUBJECT   Libraries - Automation; Information storage and retrieval systems

Figure 2.10: Treatment of repeating elements

Other inhouse resources

The inhouse resources discussed so far are local equivalents of the commercial databases described earlier. Libraries have developed other electronic resources which could not really be called databases. The most notable are:

- reference advisory systems (used to answer some of the questions normally answered by reference staff)
- computer-assisted instruction (CAI) packages, which formalise some of the user education programs normally conducted by librarians.

There has been some interest for several years in the use of computer systems to answer some of the questions normally answered by reference librarians. One reason for this may be that many reference services are often inadequately staffed and librarians do not have the time to answer large numbers of reference queries, particularly if they are also expected to cope with extra demands for instructional help (for instance, in the use of full-text databases). Computer systems may be used to answer some of the more straightforward directional questions, such as 'Where can I find the books on Australian Aboriginal mythology?' Benefits include:

- reference advice is available to users even when reference staff are not
- the facility can be made available throughout the library at different workstations, and
- there are savings in staff time which may offset the development costs.

Just as reference advisory systems are seen as a means of freeing reference librarians from simple questions, such as directional queries, computer-assisted instruction (CAI) packages can take some of the load of user education off reference staff. Like reference advisory systems, CAI packages can save staff time, be available when staff are not, and be accessible from various workstations. Other benefits include the fact that instruction can be standardised and that users can go at their own pace.

Initially, both types of package were developed on microcomputers, for use within the library, but recent years have seen the development of both as web products, especially CAI packages in the case of academic libraries. This latter development reflects in part the perception that academic institutions and their libraries can best encourage lifelong learning by teaching information literacy skills or at least encouraging students to develop these skills. It also reflects to some extent the growth in distance learning in many countries, which increases the importance of finding ways to make user education and instructional packages available to remote users. Such packages can, of course, be made available to internal students (from anywhere: computer centres, student residences, internet cafes), allowing them the opportunity for self-paced learning and, perhaps, taking some of the pressure of direct instruction off information librarians. Some educational material has been developed into full-blown information literacy programs which, at some institutions, have been integrated into academic courses.

During the early 1990s there was some interest from the library and information sector in the use of expert systems (a form of artificial intelligence) in the development of referral services and CAI packages. Expert systems were considered to be good at handling interactive sessions like a (simple) reference interview or an instructional session because they include a 'knowledge base' and an inference engine that could follow 'heuristic' lines of reasoning, as distinct from the more common and straightforward computer 'algorithm' (see Chapter 5).

Interest in expert systems receded in the latter half of the 1990s, partly, one suspects, because of the growing interest in development of web products and partly because the type of expert systems used then (rule- and frame-based systems) required a lot of time to develop. It is worthwhile to be aware of expert systems, however, because they have the potential on occasion to be effective tools. In a recent collection on virtual reference services, Kwan-Yau Lam, for example, puts the case for 'online pathfinder expert systems', which could be useful 'in situations where people keep coming and ask for information on the same topics.' Such a solution would require, not a system that relies on rules or frames, but a 'normative expert system', which relies on 'statistical data' – something that requires time and plenty of cases to build up (2003, pp.36-8).

Electronic publishing

If we had believed some of the literature of the late 1970s and early 1980s, the problem of document delivery should have become a thing of the past by now. Electronic publishing was seen by some as the answer. F.W. Lancaster was one of the foremost proponents of the electronic journal, which would release libraries from their reliance on print resources by making the full text of journals available for online searching and downloading. In a sense, electronic publishing is part of a logical progression, because print publishers already have their material in electronic format and can recycle it for non-print products. Indeed, as indicated earlier, many journals are already available as online products.

Online vendors and subscription agents provide access to thousands of full-text journals, particularly scientific, technical and medical publications and scholarly publications. Many bibliographic networks also store full-text, or even electronic journals on their servers for the benefit of member libraries. One of the most impressive collections is the *FirstSearch Electronic Collections Online* provided by OCLC, the largest of the US networks. At the time of writing (early 2003) it claims to have a collection of more than 3,680 journals from over sixty publishers, to present journals 'in their entirety,' to make most new issues available on or before the print publication dates and to offer archiving of all journal content, with libraries entitled to 'ongoing access to all of the journals it has subscribed to through *Electronic Collections Online*' (DA Electronic Media 2003).

There are clear advantages in being able to access journals (and indeed other material) online and download articles, papers and so on to a local client. The trend, according to the literature, is from acquisitions to access. Instead of purchasing a subset of available journals in print format, and therefore buying articles that will never be read, libraries will purchase articles for their users and organisations as they are required (although, as pointed out earlier, purchasing from aggregators means that libraries are buying access to whole journals that will never be read). The current level of electronic publishing is a substantial step towards the so-called virtual library, where the user has access to a much larger body of information resources than that which is available locally. Libraries and networks become gateways or switching centres to the virtual library (note the use of the singular noun) that is accessible via the Web. Note, however, the earlier discussion of aggregator services. It is easy, in a technology-focused work like this, to downplay economic factors and to ignore the oligopolistic nature of the information industry, which gives publishers considerable control over the costs of datasets and the conditions under which they are sold to libraries.

The experience of libraries and library networks with the electronic journal over the past few years suggests that there are benefits to users in terms of accessibility and to libraries in terms of economies of scale. There may also be benefits in terms of currency, particularly important in areas like science and technology, but the advantages of electronic journals should not be exaggerated because, in the case of refereed journals (both print and electronic), one of the greatest bottlenecks has been the refereeing process, not the printing process. Generally there is a delay of over a year between submission of an article to a print journal and its publication. The editors of the many new electronic journals are faced with the choice of waiting for referees' reports before making papers available (and perhaps facing further delay when papers are returned to authors with referees' comments) or making some papers available as unrefereed publications – in effect offering two forms of publication: works in progress and refereed articles.

It is also worth noting that only certain kinds of publication, such as the journal, have been developed as electronic products. Despite the advances of recent years, the e-book lags behind the e-journal. Why have aspects of electronic publishing been relatively slow to develop? Some authors resist electronic publishing because they need to see themselves in print, although the growing number of high quality, refereed electronic journals has broken down authorial resistance to a certain extent. Another area of resistance may have been the print publishers. Leaving aside issues like copyright, ownership and textual integrity, there are significant commercial pressures against the development of electronic publishing, for example, the loss of advertising revenue where circulation figures cannot be guaranteed. Nonetheless, there are signs that there may be a qualitative change in the next few years, with the demise, as some see it, of scholarly publishing, as university libraries spend a greater proportion of their declining budgets on database subscriptions and some university presses turn to electronic publishing of out-of-print and 'uneconomic' titles. Finally, while the e-book may not yet be to everyone's taste, it will be worth watching the progress of print-on-demand the next few years – a significant industry change in which local distributors (combining bookshop and print-shop) download electronic copies of books from the publishers and print single copies for individual customers.

The coming years will no doubt see a further shift from print publishing to electronic publishing, forcing information librarians to accept a shrinking physical collection. Areas of print publishing may continue to thrive (consider the number of books written about the Internet or computers in libraries!) but many of the information resources with which information librarians deal are well suited to electronic forms of publishing: for example, dictionaries, encyclopedias, directories, journals, newspapers, newswire services, legal information and government publications. There are librarians who argue that reference collections will disappear altogether but this does ignore the convenience, ease and speed of some high-usage print resources. Who was it who described books as 'portable databases that work without power cords' (other than Ferguson & Hebels, 2nd edition)? One of the problems facing information librarians is that they spend so much time mastering the electronic library and teaching users online information literacy skills that some forget their print collections. Print collections will shrink considerably more before librarians succeed in working out a new balance between access and acquisitions. This is part of a more general problem that requires an information management solution – something that is (sadly) beyond the remit of this book.

References

Arms, WY 2000, *Digital libraries*. MIT Press, Cambridge, MA.

Chou, M & Zhou, O 2003, 'Examining the impact of DMCA and UCITA on online reference service,' In *Implementing digital reference services: Setting standards and making it real*, RD Lankes *et al*. Facet Publishing, London, pp.47-57.

Deegan, M & Tanner, S 2002, *Digital futures: Strategies for the information age*. Library Association Publishing, London.

Hanson, A & Levin BL 2003, *Building a virtual library*. Information Science Publishing, Hershey, PA.

Lam, K 2003, 'Exploring virtual reference: What it is and what it may be,' In *Implementing digital reference services: Setting standards and making it real*, R.D. Lankes *et al*. Facet Publishing, London, pp.31-39.

Lankes, RD *et al*. 2003, *Implementing digital reference services: Setting standards and making it real*. Facet Publishing, London.

National Library of Medicine 2003, *Publications: Factsheets: Medline*, viewed 5 May 2003, < http://www.nlm.nih.gov/pubs/factsheets/medline.html>.

Pettijohn, P & Neville, T 2003, Collection development for virtual libraries. In *Building a virtual library*, A Hanson, Information Science Publishing, Hershey, PA, pp.20-36.

QuestionPoint Collaborative Reference Service. *What is QuestionPoint*, viewed 6 January 2003, <http://www.questionpoint.org/>.

Wells, AT 2003, 'E-Reference,' In *Building a virtual library*, A Hanson, Information Science Publishing, Hershey, PA, pp.95-120.

Review questions

1. Explain what a field is.
2. Name the main components in an online information retrieval system.
3. Identify the most common indexing parameters applied to text retrieval systems.
4. Name the main techniques for narrowing a database search.

5. Identify three kinds of help facility available to users of commercial databases.
6. Name two solutions to the limitations of boolean searching discussed in this chapter.
7. Name the main elements that make up a user profile in SDI.
8. Explain the difference between the index file in a commercial database and the subject index or descriptor field.
9. Outline the decisions to be made in the development of an inhouse database.
10. Outline the main technologies that contribute to the development of document delivery services.

Further resources

Chowdhury, GG & Chowdhury, S 2003, *Introduction to digital libraries*. Facet Publishing, London.
Not sighted, but the publisher describes it as a core text for students of digital librarianship and related courses, and essential reading for practitioners and researchers who need to get a good grasp of issues and developments in the field. International examples are used.

Google directory. *Digital libraries*,
<http://directory.google.com/Top/Reference/Libraries/Digital/>.
The Google directory contains a very useful set of links on digital libraries – follow Reference, on the top level of the directory, as per the URL.

Katz, WA 2002, *Introduction to reference work*. 8th ed. 2 vols. McGraw-Hill, Boston, MA.
William Katz's standard work on reference services and processes has been updated yet again, to take into account the impact on reference work of developments in the Internet, the World Wide Web and electronic publishing.

Kennedy, J 2002, *Collection management: A concise introduction*. Centre for Information Studies, Wagga Wagga, NSW.
A good overview of collection management issues, including some of the economic ones to which this chapter has referred.

Lankes, RD *et al.* 2003, *Implementing digital reference services: Setting standards and making it real*. Facet Publishing, London.
Reference has been made to this book already, but it is worth highlighting here as a useful resource. Collections are not always ideal for people who want to come up to speed on a topic, but this is an especially worthwhile read.

Mohlhenrich, J 2001, *Preservation and digitization in ARL libraries*. Association of Research Libraries, Washington, DC.

National Library of Australia, *PADI: Preserving Access to Digital Information,*
<http://www.nla.gov.au/padi/>
PADI is a subject gateway to digital preservation resources, such as events, policies,
strategies and guidelines, projects, organisations and websites, bibliographies,
discussion lists, glossaries, journals and newsletters, and news.

Pantry, S & Griffiths, P 2002, *Creating a successful e-information service.* Facet
Publishing, London.
Designed for those attempting to establish an electronic information service for the first
time or revamp an existing traditional service into an e-information service.

CHAPTER 3
Access to information resources

The main aim of libraries is to provide people with access to published information resources, whether these are printed monographs, videos on gardening or newspapers in electronic format at the other side of the planet. As long as libraries develop their own collections of information resources for potential users, borrow from the collections of other libraries on behalf of users or direct users to resources on the Internet, one of the key activities for the library and information sector remains providing users with the means of accessing these resources. Despite conference papers and journal articles that refer to the end of cataloguing, the catalogue remains one of their most important information retrieval tools in libraries. Cataloguing was one of the earliest library operations to be computerised and both catalogues and cataloguing have changed dramatically in the last thirty or so years. Given appropriate computer and telecommunications systems, one can sit at home and browse a library catalogue in another country, while the cataloguer in that country can make use of cataloguing effort that has taken place in a third country. Moreover, the enormous growth in the Internet, combined with a degree of dissatisfaction with web search engines, encouraged development of new standards for information access – the metadata standards to which reference has already been made. This chapter outlines the different forms of library catalogue in use, examines attempts by librarians to pool their cataloguing effort through a variety of networks and reviews the development of metadata. (The features that librarians can expect to find in a computerised cataloguing system are discussed in the following chapter on library management systems.)

Learning objectives

At the end of this chapter, you will be able to:

- describe the main types of catalogue in use today
- outline the main features of an online catalogue
- identify the main computer files associated with online catalogues
- explain MARC format
- outline the main technologies used to share bibliographic data
- discuss the costs and benefits of shared cataloguing
- outline the principal metadata standards that affect the library and information sector.

Keywords

Online catalogue
Authority control
Shared cataloguing
MARC format(s)
MARC tag
Data field
Control field

Bibliographic network
Copy cataloguing
Original cataloguing
Metadata
Dublin Core (DC)
Crosswalks
Document Type Definitions (DTDs)

Library catalogues

In the last chapter, three types of bibliographic database were mentioned: catalogues, bibliographies, and indexing and abstracting services. These were contrasted with other types of database, such as directory and full-text databases, which were described as source databases. Bibliographic databases are often described as a form of information retrieval tool, which is intended to denote the fact that they do not inform the people who use them, in the sense that they do not significantly change the knowledge of users (unless they are specifically looking for bibliographic information), but they do tell people whether or not an appropriate information resource exists and where to find it.

The library catalogue is a form of bibliographic database that describes information resources available in a specific library, or in a library network or, increasingly, on the Internet, and helps users to identify, select and locate either specific known resources (for example, works by a known author) or resources that contain information on a specified subject. The bibliographic file that is at the heart of the library catalogue consists of surrogate records (or entries, to use the term associated with traditional, print-based catalogues), like the brief record given in the last chapter to describe this book:

TI	Computers for librarians: an introduction to the electronic library
ED	3rd edition
AU	Ferguson, Stuart; Hebels, Rodney
PU	Wagga Wagga, NSW: Centre for Information Studies, 2003
SE	Topics in Australasian Library & Information Studies, no. 22
NU	1-876938-54-4
SU	Libraries - Automation; Information storage and retrieval systems

Figure 3.1: Sample bibliographic record (repeated)

This example contains two basic components:

- bibliographic description, which identifies the information resource or work, using attributes or elements of description such as author and title (in the example, the first six fields are familiar elements of bibliographic description),

- subject description, which represents the cataloguer's attempt to describe the subject content of works, similar to the subject indexing terms or descriptors assigned to periodical articles etc., as discussed in the last chapter – in the example, this is the seventh element, which contains two Library of Congress Subject Headings.

The library catalogue contains a third component:

- item-specific information relating to particular copies of an information resource or work, including call numbers and other location devices.

A library might, for example, purchase two copies of the book by Ferguson and Hebels and would require some way of distinguishing between the two copies: for instance, it would normally assign a unique number to each copy for purposes of circulation. There might be differences in loan conditions that could be indicated in the catalogue: for example, the book may be so popular with students that an academic library decides to put one copy in its short-loan collection at the counter and uses some location device to indicate its availability. A public library might put a copy in its teenage collection and might assign a slightly different call number to it: for example, precede the classification number with a 'T' or 'YA'. There might also be differences in copy status: for example, one copy may have been mislaid (for instance, by someone putting it among the books on viticulture) and it might be described as 'missing'. These item-specific data elements would not normally be stored in a bibliographic file, but in a separate holdings file (see Chapter 4).

A cataloguing system, of the kind discussed in the next chapter, might also include authority files, such as an author authority file. The way in which records like the one above are displayed may seem to imply that the bibliographic data are stored together on the database in a neat package, but the name 'Rodney Hebels', to take an example, may appear only once in the database, regardless of how many works by that author appear in it. The name may be stored in an authority file and linked in some way to all records that represent works of his authorship. In this way, space is saved, because data do not have to be unnecessarily repeated, but more important, from the user's perspective, consistency is introduced, so that if a user searches under the name 'Hebels, Rodney', the catalogue will display all works associated with the name in the authority file. Without such authority control, users might miss those records which did not contain the authoritative version of the name (for example, where publisher and/or cataloguer use variant forms such as 'Hebels, R.' or 'Hebels, Rod'). In cataloguing terms, the use of authority files acts to *collocate* works by a specific author, that is, bring them together for the benefit of the user.

Library catalogues have taken a variety of physical forms. There are, however, five main forms of catalogue:

- online catalogues
- CD-ROM catalogues
- card catalogues
- book-form catalogues
- microfiche catalogues.

Online catalogues

In many countries the most common form of catalogue is the online catalogue. The term online indicates merely that there is a communications link between the device used to search the catalogue and to display search results, and the computer on which the cataloguing data are stored. Online catalogues, for some reason, continue to be referred to as OPACs, or Online Public Access Catalogues (sometimes further shortened to PACs – another acronym that could easily be dropped), perhaps reflecting the fact that the earliest computer-based catalogues could not be accessed by library users and that it was some years before public access could be properly developed. Library users often had to make do with one of the 'output' versions described below. Librarians tend to use the term OPAC to refer to the actual device by which the bibliographic database is accessed, typically a terminal or microcomputer acting as a terminal.

The advantages of online catalogues are readily apparent. Older forms of catalogue, particularly book-form and microfiche catalogues, are not updated as often as online catalogues. A new bibliographic record is generally available in an online catalogue as soon as a cataloguer or technician adds it to the bibliographic file (although some of the systems considered in the next two chapters may add new records only in a batch, say, at the end of the day). Book-form and microfiche catalogues, however, are not updated on a record-by-record basis, but are generally reproduced as a whole at regular intervals, hence they go out-of-date in the periods between productions.

Moreover, it is not just cataloguing information (bibliographic and subject descriptions and item-specific information) that is available to users through an online catalogue. They can often see the status of items. Provided the online catalogue is linked to the computerised circulations and acquisitions functions (discussed in the next chapter), then users can see if an item is on loan, when it is due back, if it is on order or even whether it is 'in process' in the cataloguing department. Another advantage is that users do not even have to be in the library to check its holdings – they can access the catalogue from another site, even from overseas. This is clearly an attractive feature for some types of user, for example, students studying distance learning (correspondence) courses.

The main advantage of online catalogues, compared to earlier forms of catalogue, however, is the search facilities provided. Those who have used a card or book-form catalogue, for example, will be aware of the limited choice of access points – one could search under author, title and, perhaps, subject heading or classification number. It was simply uneconomical for libraries to provide a large number of extra catalogue entries (the so-called 'added entries' of traditional cataloguing). The problem of which bibliographic elements to use as access points becomes an academic one in an online catalogue. Users can typically search in a variety of significant fields, such as author (personal and corporate), title, series title and subject heading, as well as search for specific words (keywords) across these fields. The more recently developed library management systems (see next chapter) allow users to search in fields which it was generally not possible to search in manually produced catalogues, for instance, Notes (for example, for individual titles in a sound recording) and GMD or General Material Designation (for example, if the user specifically wants videos).

Many of the early online catalogues did not have such a range of retrieval facilities. Indeed, one of the criticisms levelled at early versions is that they tended to imitate existing forms of catalogue, such as the card catalogue, instead of presenting something qualitatively different from them. Many of them relied on phrase indexing, so that as a user, for example, one could search for the title of the book, *Computers for librarians*, as a phrase or character string. It is worth noting, by the way, that the term indexing is used here to refer to indexing automatically conducted by the computer, as discussed in the last chapter. Keyword searching and the boolean features discussed in the last two chapter were not features of the so-called first-generation of online catalogues. For several years, however, free-text searching across fields and use of boolean operators have been a feature of online catalogues, as for online databases.

Other features of online catalogues

Other features might include:

- giving users the option of checking their own borrower data using their borrower numbers: for example, to check what items they have already borrowed
- allowing users to renew their own loans via the online catalogue
- allowing users to reserve library resources via the online catalogue
- offering users navigational facilities based on hypertext principles, for example, if a record retrieved by the user displays an useful-looking subject heading, other records with that subject heading can be explored without starting a new search
- allowing users to see the reference structure linking subject headings, in order to help them broaden or narrow their searches through the exploration of relationships within the structure

- acting as a gateway to other databases (for example, other catalogues) or electronic information resources owned by the parent organisation or available elsewhere via the Internet (for example, in a parliamentary library it may be possible to access legislation stored elsewhere in electronic format)
- providing a helpful user interface.

The term user interface refers to the computer hardware and software that allows users to communicate with a computer system. Chapter 1 mentioned use of terminals to communicate with computers, consisting of two main hardware components: keyboards and monitors or screens. The first is used to input data and the second is used to display both the data being input and the responses of the computer system (for example, search results). A further software component determines how human-computer interaction takes place. It determines, for instance, what screen documentation the user sees: for example, it may offer a choice of screen documentation, each option geared to a particular level of user expertise (such as a beginners' option), or the screen documentation may include a help option which, if selected, presents the user with specific information on the activity currently being undertaken by the user (such as telling the user what search operators can be used and offering advice on appropriate use of each operator).

The importance of a helpful user interface should be emphasised. In the case of some online catalogues, the interface is not user-friendly and discourages some people (although those who use their public libraries on a Saturday and have to fight schoolchildren for an online catalogue may find that a strange idea). There have been considerable changes in recent years in the user interface. Gone, one hopes, are those command-driven systems which required users to know the correct commands with which to communicate an enquiry: for example, to search for a particular author you had to know how to precede the author's name (for example, 'au Hebels, R'), otherwise one was made to feel stupid by being told that one had entered an incorrect command.

The early command-driven interfaces were replaced by menu-driven ones (see Chapter 6), which present the user with a choice of actions or options from which to select – like a choice of food dishes – with some prompts and, sometimes, use of special 'function keys' at the top of the keyboard. Many online catalogues have since gone a stage further, with the use of graphical user interfaces (the GUIs mentioned in previous chapters), which allow users to select actions, commands or options that are displayed on the computer screen as icons. With an increasingly 'Web-literate' user population GUIs are very much a mandatory feature of the current generation of online catalogues.

Even if an online catalogue does use a graphical user interface, however, not all users are going to understand the screen documentation, and there should an easy way for users to obtain on-screen help: for example, a key or, more commonly, an on-screen option marked 'help' or '?'), with help screen documentation relating specifically to what the user is trying to do at the time. Of course, even help options can be misunderstood. Some years ago, Bob Walton, a systems expert from the US, told a library automation conference the story of an elderly person who believed that pressing the red help key summoned a 'nice young man' from the information desk. Given the developments in virtual reference services discussed in the last chapter, however, the idea is perhaps not so far-fetched.

Earlier it was suggested that online catalogues offer retrieval opportunities that print-based catalogues did not provide, for example, the ability to search fields which were not previously used for access (for example, the notes area) or, in the case of some systems, to see the reference structure linking subject headings. Linked to that second facility is the use of classification schemes as a means of navigating online catalogues. In some countries, for example, the UK, there is some research into use of the hierarchical arrangement of concepts in a classification scheme to guide users, for example, from specific to less specific concepts. Some research examines the potential use of specific classification schemes: for example, OCLC, not surprisingly, has looked specifically at the use of the Dewey Decimal Classification as a navigational tool. A related area of research is the use of concept mapping techniques to create visual displays for textual information (such as bibliographic information) stored in a computer.

Another issue to excite some interest is the question of subject enhancement, which some libraries have explored. Options include describing sections of a book or reproducing contents pages and/or book indexes. Obviously, the reason that most libraries do not provide detailed subject enhancement of this kind is that it is time-consuming and would add further to the costs of cataloguing, but the information could be obtained from publishers, since they have data such as contents page information in electronic form anyway. For an example of a catalogue that uses subject enhancement, see the Australian Defence Force Academy (ADFA) Library catalogue. Another constraint to the use of subject enhancement is the fact that it requires extra computer memory, but given the continuing developments in computer storage, this is perhaps a factor that is of diminishing significance.

Other forms of catalogue

Given the fact that online catalogues are so common in many countries it may seem strange to consider any other type of catalogue. In some countries, however, the costs of computerisation may be prohibitive for many libraries and catalogues may continue to be manually produced. Historically, as mentioned earlier, the use of computers to store bibliographic databases predated the development of online catalogues, hence the use of computers to generate catalogue cards, book-form catalogues and microfiche catalogues. Even once libraries developed or purchased online catalogues, however, they often continued to produce these older forms of catalogue. One reason was that there may have been limited numbers of online catalogue terminals (or OPACs). Another reason for producing other forms of catalogue is that the library director feels the need to have a backup catalogue in case the online version is unavailable, either because the computer on which the catalogue is stored is 'down' (not operational) or because the communications link is down, in the case of a library network that shares an online catalogue.

CD-ROM catalogues

Because CD-ROMs can store enormous amounts of data, they are well suited to the production of large catalogues, such as shared, or union, catalogues. CD-ROM production is not cheap, which means that it is generally not an option for small libraries, but the process has become relatively less expensive in recent years. CD-ROM catalogues offer similar search facilities to online catalogues – in fact, many CD-ROM catalogues provide search facilities that older generations of online catalogue fail to provide. In the case of shared online catalogues (see below), copies of the catalogue can be customised so that individual libraries have their holdings indicated for the benefit of their users. CD-ROM catalogues, however, are not as up-to-date as online catalogues – it would be uneconomical to update them as frequently – and they also lack some of the attractive features of online catalogues: for example, they cannot tell the user the status of an item (whether it is out on loan, on order or in process).

Non-electronic catalogues

The card catalogue is the information retrieval tool that many people still associate with libraries. Even in those countries that have automated widely, demand for catalogue cards persisted for some years, reflected in the fact that many vendors of library management systems have for years provided the ability to produce computer-generated catalogue cards. This may have been due both to the relatively late development of online (public access) catalogues and to the fact that early microcomputer-based systems did not provide the multi-user, multi-tasking facilities required to run library management systems of the kind described in the next chapter (and therefore could not offer online catalogue access). In general, however, it is only in very small libraries that one is ever likely to see a card catalogue or in countries that do not have the money or the ICT infrastructure.

For a short time, the book-form catalogue made a return, in a computer-generated format. Many of the problems of card catalogue maintenance were overcome (for example, time-consuming filing), but one of the major problems of the printed book-form catalogues returned, that of keeping them up-to-date, given the expense of producing regular updates. The microfiche catalogue is essentially a type of book-form catalogue, reproduced on microfiche instead of on paper. Microfiche (or fiche) are sheets of transparent film containing small images which can be enlarged and displayed using a microfiche reader. The catalogue is reproduced on microfiche using a COM (Computer Output on Microform) recorder. Although production is expensive, individual fiche are not (unlike book-form catalogues), which means that microfiche is a format well suited to production of multiple copies, for example, union or shared catalogues. Microfiche catalogues are in many respects the least user-friendly of the catalogues described here and are quickly disappearing in the most highly computerised countries.

Shared cataloguing

Several references have been made in this and the previous chapter to shared cataloguing – something that has been enormously facilitated by developments in computer and communication technologies and that has greatly enhanced access to library-based information resources. In this section, shared cataloguing, MARC format (which underpins shared cataloguing) and bibliographic networks are considered in more detail. Before they are discussed, however, it may be helpful to make a distinction between two types of cataloguing: original cataloguing and copy cataloguing. Perhaps it would make most sense to start with copy cataloguing. This refers to the copying of existing catalogue records, for example, downloading an electronic copy of a record from a library network's bibliographic database to a local computerised catalogue. Original cataloguing, on the other hand, refers to the creation of cataloguing records from scratch by examining the information resources themselves and providing bibliographic descriptions that are consistent with an established set of cataloguing standards – whether inhouse, network-wide, national or international.

While original cataloguing may be seen as a valuable activity, in terms of facilitating access to library resources, it is also a costly one. It takes time both to make the required intellectual decisions and to create and check the catalogue records. Moreover, most libraries have employed cataloguing and support staff to catalogue resources that have been catalogued elsewhere in countless other libraries. Unless a library's cataloguing requirements are radically different from those of other libraries, there are significant gains to be made in sharing cataloguing data. Undoubtedly, the greatest impact of computers in the area of cataloguing has been to facilitate networking and the consequent pooling of cataloguing effort.

There is nothing new in the concept of shared cataloguing, of course. As long ago as 1901, the Library of Congress had a Card Distribution Service which provided American libraries with catalogue cards, thus saving them considerable cataloguing effort. Subscribing libraries could then adapt cards for local use: for example, add classification numbers or indicate items held in a special collection (the kind of item-specific holdings information mentioned earlier). They could also take advantage of the Library of Congress authority structure for names and subject headings, although again these could be adapted to local needs. Obviously, the existence of a service like this does not remove the need for local libraries to create some records themselves, that is, perform original cataloguing. Nonetheless, much duplication of cataloguing effort can be eliminated through the agency of a centralised cataloguing service. Given that the cost of cataloguing a single item (for example, a paperback book) can exceed the cost of the item itself, this is a considerable benefit – bearing in mind, of course, that shared cataloguing carries substantial costs.

Computerisation makes the sharing of cataloguing effort even more attractive because it is relatively easy to copy bibliographic data when they are in electronic format. There are two main ways in which libraries share electronic catalogue records:

 obtain copies of records in machine-readable form, using one of the storage media discussed later in this book, for example, magnetic tape or diskette (floppy disk)

download (copy) records in electronic format over a communication medium, such as the telephone network.

Both methods are used, but the first, earlier method has steadily been replaced by the second. Both require a standard for the packaging of bibliographic data – if bibliographic data are to be transferred from one computerised system to another, there must be some way in which the computer receiving the data can interpret them: for instance, it needs to be able to identify both individual records and the fields or data elements within the records. MARC format is the principal means of packaging electronic bibliographic records for exchange.

MARC formats

The acronym MARC stands for machine readable cataloguing (occasionally also referred to as machine readable code). It is a standard originally designed for the exchange of bibliographic data using magnetic tape. One of the recurrent misconceptions about MARC is that it is a cataloguing standard, rather like the Anglo-American Cataloguing Rules. Although it reflects cataloguing standards such as AACR and International Standard Bibliographic Description (some would argue that its links to AACR2 and, for instance, the concept of 'main entry' is a drawback), it is in fact an exchange format, or more accurately a group of exchange formats, used to identify and organise elements of bibliographic data, and thereby transfer bibliographic records electronically. Since Library of Congress began its MARC Distribution Service in 1969 using its own LCMARC (later USMARC), over twenty other formats were developed, mostly by national libraries or national bibliographic agencies. All adhere to a particular record structure developed by the International Standards Organisation (ISO 2709; although there are some MARC-like standards that do not conform to ISO2709).

At one point, too, a standard intended for the international exchange of data – UNIMARC or Universal MARC format – was developed. The intention was that it would enable accurate exchange of data from one MARC format to another, but, despite its development under the sponsorship of IFLA (International Federation of Library Associations), it has not become the *lingua franca* for the international exchange of bibliographic data. For many countries, however, the *de facto* standard has become MARC 21, which was the name established in 1998 when differences between USMARC and CANMARC (the Canadian version) were resolved. (The 21 label reflects the fact that it was seen as a standard for the twenty-first century.) Even before the establishment of MARC21, an Australian MARC 'dialect', AUSMARC (based in part on UKMARC), had been abandoned in favour of adopting USMARC.

Another common misconception about MARC is that it is a standard used for storage and processing of bibliographic records in computerised systems, such as library management systems. The internal formats used in computerised library systems do not *have* to conform to an exchange format such as MARC, and in some cases there may indeed be good reasons why they should not. For libraries and information agencies wishing to subscribe to MARC services, the important point is to establish if their computer systems can *import* MARC records, regardless of whether the records are actually stored in MARC format or are converted into internal formats. In view of the fact that many libraries have migrated to second or even third library management systems, the ability to *export* records in MARC format, and so be able to upload them to a new system, is also important (see Chapter 4).

What a MARC format did then was to provide a standard for organising bibliographic data so that they could be stored on magnetic tape and then retrieved from the tape as a set of meaningful bibliographic records. Like the records discussed in the previous chapter, MARC records are divided into fields. The main elements in a MARC record are:

- the leader (twenty-four characters), which identifies the record, and provides information such as length of record and type of material being described
- the directory, which is a computer-generated index to the location of data within a record, consisting of a sequence of data elements, each referring to a data field in the record and identifying its tag, length and starting location – this makes it easier to update and search records, since it becomes possible to locate particular fields without searching all the data fields that precede it in a record
- control fields (tags 001-009), which provide additional information about the record: for example, 005, the date and time of the last transaction; 008, which contains coded

information about the record as a whole; and 009 which is for local use – these are variable fields, with the exception of 008, which is fixed

- data fields (tags 0X0-9XX) , which contain the kind of bibliographic data found in any traditional catalogue record: for example, 020 ISBN; 092 Dewey Decimal Classification number; 100 personal name main entry; 245 title; 250 edition; 260 imprint; 650 topical subject heading; and 700 personal name added entry.

In order to demonstrate some other elements in a MARC record it might be worth considering an example. Earlier in the chapter, there was a sample bibliographic record, based on the data for this book. This can be packaged in MARC21 as follows:

```
020  ƀƀ   ‡a 1876938544
100  1ƀ   ‡aFerguson, Stuart, ‡d1953-
245  10   ‡aComputers for librarians‡h[text] : ‡ban introduction to the electronic
            library /‡cby Stuart Ferguson and Rodney Hebels.
250  ƀƀ   ‡a3rd ed.
260  ƀƀ   ‡aWagga Wagga, NSW : ‡bCentre for Information Studies, ‡c2003.
440  ƀ0   ‡a Topics in Australasian library & information studies ; ‡vno. 22
650  ƀ0   ‡aLibraries‡xAutomation.
650  ƀ0   ‡aInformation storage and retrieval systems.
700  1ƀ   ‡aHebels, Rodney, ‡d1969-
```

Figure 3.2: Sample MARC record (data elements)

This is not a complete MARC record and shows only those data fields that were listed in the earlier sample. It excludes, for instance, common data fields such as Physical description area (300) and Notes (500). Each of the bibliographic elements, such as author, title or subject, is identified by a three-digit number, called a MARC tag. Each of the fields identified by a tag is referred to as a tagged field. The tagged field 245 is always used for the main title, that is, the tag '245' indicates that the main title is the next bibliographic element, and is a mandatory field (all information resources have a title field). Some tagged fields are repeatable. For obvious reasons 245 is not a repeatable field – although there are tagged fields for other title elements, such as uniform title – but field 650, Subject added entry - topical term, can be repeated.

It is worth noting that within the tagged fields there are *subfields*. Field 260, Imprint, for instance, contains the common bibliographic elements: place of publication, publisher and date of publication. Just as the field needs to be identified by a MARC tag, the subfields also need to be identified. This is done with a *subfield code* which consists of a delimiter

here the ‡ symbol used in MARC21

and a further character (a lower case letter), for example:

$\ddagger$c in the 260 field

always indicates that publication date follows. Similarly,

$\ddagger$c in the 245 field

indicates (in MARC21) that a statement of responsibility is to follow. As with some tagged fields, some subfields are repeatable: for instance:

the general subdivision ($\ddagger$x) in field 650.

The other MARC feature shown in the sample above is the use of indicators, the two numerical characters that come between the tags and the data elements. These provide information about the field, for example, the '1' after the 245 tag indicates that a title added entry is required (some argue, of course, that in a computerised environment the concept of main entry and added entry is irrelevant), while the following zero indicates that there are no non-filing characters present. (Were the title to start with 'The', there would be four non-filing elements, 'T', 'h', 'e' plus the space, and the indicators would therefore be '14'.)

For the sake of legibility, the sample has been shown as a MARC record might appear if displayed on an online catalogue. On magnetic tape, the data would appear sequentially as follows (using the alphabetical characters represented, obviously, and not the magnetically charged particles that would appear on magnetic tape!):

...Ferguson, Stuart, $\ddagger$d1953- 245 10 $\ddagger$aComputers for librarians$\ddagger$h[text] : $\ddagger$ban intro...

Figure 3.3: Sequential recording of data on magnetic tape

This should indicate the critical importance of being able to package the bibliographic data, so that the computer to which they are downloaded or uploaded can know at what point one field has ended and another has begun, and at what point one record has ended and another has begun.

It is worth noting one increasingly important MARC21 tag: tag 856, reserved for a URL and used to link Internet resources to a MARC record. This is a repeatable field, which means that more than one URL can be added to a single record.

Finally, the example above shows sample data fields for a bibliographical record, but it should be noted that MARC21 formats also cover holdings data, authorities data and classification data.

Bibliographic networks

The last chapter introduced library networks which, it suggested, are formed for two principal reasons: in order to share the costs and effort of cataloguing and in order to foster library cooperation and resource sharing. While resource sharing tends to predate the formation of formal networks, developments in computer technology and telecommunications over the past thirty or more years have generated considerable growth in networking. This section looks in more detail at some of the developments, with a few examples. The term network is used here, but it is worth knowing that some of the networks described below (for instance, OCLC) are also referred to as 'bibliographic utilities': non-profit organisations that use telecommunications to share bibliographic data in machine-readable form.

Bibliographic networks correspond, approximately, to one of two models:

- centralised networks, where a central agency is responsible for provision of cataloguing and other services, and

- cooperative networks, in which member libraries contribute original cataloguing to a joint bibliographic database.

The MARC distribution services of the kind supplied by the US Library of Congress are typical of a centralised network. The British Library is a notable example of a national library that performs a centralised cataloguing function. BLAISE (British Library Automated Information Service) offers a variety of services, including cataloguing support. Where libraries have legal deposit rights (that is, they receive one copy of every book published in a country), their catalogues are fairly comprehensive as far as that country's publications are concerned. The decision by many national libraries to computerise production of national bibliographies facilitated the development of authoritative and computer readable bibliographic databases and, as a result, national libraries are a major source of copy cataloguing.

Many libraries rely on MARC distribution services for copy cataloguing on a regular basis. It is also possible for libraries to use national cataloguing agencies when computerising for the first time. MARC records can be ordered by supplying ISBNs, or other control numbers for earlier material (British Library, for example, uses the serial numbers from British National Bibliography, the so-called BNB number). Initially, MARC files were limited to records for items catalogued since the beginning of MARC programs. Since then, however, some institutions have undertaken retrospective conversion programs. Central agencies are a source of other cataloguing products, for example, Library of Congress provides its Library of Congress Subject Headings in machine-readable form and many national libraries distribute authority files, such as name authority lists (see Chapter 4).

There are some library networks, generally at the regional level, that centralise all technical services functions, such as acquisitions, cataloguing, end-processing and database administration and development, but this is usually only typical of groups of libraries that are answerable to the same political or administrative authority, for example, small college or school libraries that fall under the control of a particular government department. In such circumstances, there may be significant economies of scale, including discounts from library suppliers for bulk orders.

Cooperative bibliographic networks grew out of attempts to share cataloguing resources through the collective development of a union catalogue. This offers the same savings in terms of cataloguing effort as subscription to a centralised agency. Moreover, as Chapter 2 mentioned, the development of a union catalogue may be a worthwhile end in itself since it facilitates the sharing not only of cataloguing resources but also of the actual information resources. Cooperative networks are more proactive than centralised networks, in the sense that member libraries are generally expected to contribute original cataloguing to the shared database, as well as simply copy cataloguing from records that are already on it. There may well be a central agency to administer the database itself and provide technical support and advice (which may provide an extra incentive for some libraries to join a network), but member libraries provide the cataloguing input.

This can give rise to the perception on the part of the more active members that they contribute more to the network than they get back. One solution is to establish the value added to a network by cataloguing input, in order to recompense the contributing library. There may also be a perception that a cooperative network lacks the high bibliographical standards of a centralised network, especially a centralised network directed by a leading institution such as a national library. The database will reflect the standards of the contributing libraries, and these standards may not be uniform. This raises another issue, whether or not to build into the network some means of quality control. If there is a central database administration then this may fall under its operational provisions.

In practice, most networks are a mixture of both centralised and cooperative models, with a central agency, such as a national library, providing a leadership role, and some (but not all) member libraries contributing original cataloguing. A few examples of bibliographic networks are considered in the remainder of this section.

Kinetica (Australia)

Kinetica began life as the Australian Bibliographic Network (ABN), when the National Library of Australia began using the latter to catalogue monographs. ABN became publicly available in November 1981. Previous NLA developments included a card distribution service for Australian publications (1967), computerised production of the *Australian National Bibliography* (1972), a CIP (Cataloguing-in-Publication) program (1974) and the Australian MARC record service (1974). During the late 1970s, a number of software packages were examined and it was decided to implement the proposed national network using the system operated by the Western Library Network, a large regional network in the US. The original National Bibliographic Database (NBD) consisted of the WLN database, as it stood in 1980, Library of Congress files and the *Australian National Bibliography* file. Over the next few years, it was enlarged with the addition of records from British National Bibliography, Canadiana, New Zealand National Bibliography, retrospective records from the large university libraries and original cataloguing from participating libraries, including regional networks such as CAVAL in Victoria.

Although the National Library directed development, ABN was seen essentially as a cooperative network. The original members were expected to contribute original cataloguing. Participating libraries can access the National Bibliographic Database online, create cataloguing records, modify existing records or perform authority control work. Where records already exist, members can add holdings information (the database supports resource sharing as well as cataloguing services) and retrieve the records for copy cataloguing, either by downloading or by requesting copies on portable media such as magnetic diskette. Not all members of the network, however, are full participating members, although originally that was the only form of membership. Currently, there are four categories of membership:

- full service users, who can perform the functions just mentioned
- products only users, who can order, for example, MARC records, using identifying elements such as ISBN or ISSN
- search only users, who can search the database for purposes of inter-library loans and in order to check classification numbers or authorised forms of headings (for example, personal names), and
- search and products users, who have the search only facilities, plus the ability to add holdings data, purchase copy cataloguing and make use of the inter-library loan subsystem.

All users of the service, except the search only users, can purchase copy cataloguing, but full service users receive what is in effect a discount, on the basis of the number of records added by them to the database. The network also provides a retrospective conversion service, which allows libraries to convert existing manual catalogues into electronic format or to upgrade existing electronic records. (Retrospective conversion is discussed in Chapter 8.)

At the beginning of 1998, the National Library announced the completion of the tendering process for the new service, to be called *Kinetica*. For some time, the national libraries of Australia and New Zealand cooperated in an ambitious joint project, the end-result of which was to be World 1, a service that would unify and replace ABN, the New Zealand Bibliographic Network and the national libraries' own online information services, then Ozline and Kiwinet. For reasons which cannot be explored here, the World 1 project did not eventuate, and both libraries returned to developing separate services and systems. The contract for the new Australian system went to IBM Australia and IBM Global Services Australia. It was a six year contract and was operational by the first quarter of 1999.

The library software selected for the new system was AMICUS (IBM), an integrated library management system (see Chapter 4 for a discussion of library management systems). AMICUS is already in use in the National Library of Canada (in fact it was developed in association with the NLC) and was also purchased by the British Library and the National Library of Hungary. Features of the service include:

- the ability to support up to a thousand users simultaneously and to handle up to fifteen million bibliographic and authority records

- Web search interfaces
- Z39.50 compliance (see Chapter 7)
- superior duplicate detection capabilities (a significant problem, given the way in which large numbers of bibliographic records from a variety of sources have been batch uploaded to the bibliographic database over the years).

It is worth noting the National Library's decision that libraries would require an Internet connection. (At the time of the decision, the library noted that 78% of networked traffic with ABN was via the Internet.) The AMICUS software is based on the client/server model. Client software is needed only by those libraries which contribute original cataloguing online to the National Bibliographic Database. Alternative methods of adding bibliographic records are to send records to the NBD by FTP (File Transfer Protocol) or to use portable magnetic media. Holdings can be added and maintained via the web interface. Not all of the NBD was migrated to the new system. Priority was given to records with holdings and subsets of those without holdings, such as files of regional interest and records from overseas sources not easily accessible otherwise via the Internet.

The AMICUS software does not include support for inter-library loans and the National Library selected separate ILL software to replace ABN's ILL subsystem: Fretwell-Downing's OLIB VDX ILL software. OLIB, or Open Library Systems, is a library management system, which includes an ILL subsystem called VDX (Virtual Document eXchange). VDX is compliant with the International Standards Organisation's ILL Protocol (mentioned in the previous chapter) and is already used by LASER, a large bibliographic network in England (London & South Eastern Library Region). Features include integration with the AMICUS system (giving access to the NBD) and support for creation of requests, selection of suppliers, tracking and management of requests and the ILL payments scheme.

Kinetica is run by a central office based at the National Library. Questions of quality and development are overseen by the Kinetica Advisory Committee, which reports to the Director General of the National Library, who is responsible for appointing members of the committee. In keeping with the belief that Kinetica is a national resource, however, some representatives are nominated by CAUL (Council of Australian University Librarians), public libraries and special libraries. Kinetica users continue to have input via annual users meetings and state-based user groups.

See the case studies, at the end of the book, for further information on Kinetica and Kinetica development.

Te Puna (New Zealand)

Like the NLA, the National Library of New Zealand, Te Puna Mātauranga o Aotearoa, has provided considerable leadership in the development of shared cataloguing and the sharing of resources. The National Bibliographic Network (NZBN) was introduced in 1984, since when it has acted as a National Union Catalogue. The database serves both as a source of copy cataloguing and a means of locating items for inter-library loans. The NZBN Interloan service began in early 1989.

After the demise of World 1 (see above), the National Library of New Zealand went ahead with its own New Systems Project (NSP), which examined replacement of the NZBN, Interloan and Kiwinet systems (the latter was the online information service mentioned in Chapter 2). In 1998, the Library completed the tender process and announced that its proposed BIBU (Bibliographic Utility) and IR (Information Resource) systems would be supplied by Endeavor Information Systems of Illinois, US, and that the new ILL system would be supplied by Fretwell-Downing, the same English company supplying the Australian ILL system.

Currently, Te Puna offers the following subscription services:

- Te Puna search – access to the National Bibliographic Database, National Union Catalogue, Index New Zealand and gateways to international library databases
- descriptions of databases available through Te Puna search
- Te Puna Interloan – a 'standards-based electronic document supply system'
- Te Puna Cataloguing, which allows subscribers to download records for local catalogues and to upload records and holdings for resource sharing
- Te Puna reports, to support cataloguing and inter-library loan activities (National Library of New Zealand 2003).

Schools Catalogue Information Service (SCIS)

Schools in Australia and New Zealand could make use of their respective national bibliographic networks for purposes of shared cataloguing, but there are many reasons why schools have in fact developed their own shared cataloguing service, not least because the cataloguing standards adopted by Kinetica and Te Puna (for example, level of cataloguing and use of Library of Congress Subject Headings) are not particularly helpful in the Australasian school environment. SCIS is a database which contains approximately 780,000 records of educational materials (books), audio-visual materials, computer programs and websites, with around 3,500 being added every month (Curriculum Corporation 2003).

It has been managed by the Curriculum Corporation since 1990, but dates from 1984 as a cooperative venture involving state and territory government schools authorities and independent education authorities. It was originally called the Australian Schools' Catalogue and Information Service, or ASCIS, but in 1991 New Zealand joined the Board of Curriculum Corporation and, since early 1992, the database has been known as SCIS. It is worth considering a rationale for its development:

- SCIS adheres to a specific standard of catalogue record creation. This standard is nationally endorsed and accepted. Use of SCIS output products by schools ensures that this standard is maintained;
- The use of SCIS reduces time spent by teacher librarians in original cataloguing of resources and enables greater involvement in other curriculum and educative duties. This is a more cost effective use of a teacher librarian's time;
- Duplication of time and effort across many schools is eliminated by the use of SCIS and its output products;

- More effective organisation and utilisation of resources in school resource centres is facilitated by the use of accurately catalogued, nationally consistent, quality controlled records (Maddick 1997, p. 86).

Each catalogue record on SCIS includes title, authors/editors, ISBN, publisher, place of publication, publication date, a brief physical description, SCIS order number, Dewey classification numbers (DDC Edition 21 and Abridged DDC Edition 13) and SCIS Subject Headings. Most of the educational authorities involved in SCIS have agencies responsible for the input of original cataloguing into the database. These evaluate new material for its suitability in supporting curriculum programs before cataloguing it. The agencies are consulted by Curriculum Corporation on policy issues, such as the decision to use a new edition of Dewey. They meet to make amendments to the SCIS Subject Headings, which can be suggested by agencies or individual schools via the agencies.

The system that manages the database is the Voyager library management system. SCISWeb, introduced in 1998, provides users with access to SCIS via Curriculum Corporation's home page on the Web and with the ability to download selected records in MARC 21. Two other important products are SCIS Subject Headings on Disk and the Update Disk, which enable librarians to download cross-references into online catalogues.

OCLC (Online Computer Library Center)

No discussion of library networks would be complete without some mention of OCLC. Some of the largest bibliographic networks are in the US, and the largest is OCLC (Online Computer Library Center), which started life in 1967 as the Ohio College Library Center. Its union catalogue of MARC records, WorldCat, contains more than forty million records, with around two million being added every year, and the network as a whole handles more than fifty million inter-library loan requests. Although the majority of OCLC's large membership is in the US and Canada, it also has members in more than fifty other countries (hence the auspicious name, WorldCat, for its union catalogue).

Cataloguing services include:

- Internet access to WorldCat (the OCLC Union Catalogue)
- the PromptCat service, which automatically provides copy cataloguing for books delivered through vendors
- retrospective conversion from catalogue cards to full MARC records
- an authorities service, which provides Library of Congress name and subject authority files
- support for Chinese, Japanese and Korean scripts (OCLC CJK software).

OCLC's CD-ROM products include subsets of the main database, covering areas such as medicine, music, pre-1900 books, and visual materials and computer files, as well as Library of Congress Authorities (name and subject authority records). These offer libraries outside North America the opportunity to rely on OCLC for their specialised data requirements while using regional or national networks to help organise their general collections.

Users can access WorldCat, OCLC Authority File and so on via OCLC Connexion, for which access and support fees apply. Features include:

- access to WorldCat
- record editing in either MARC or Dublin Core view (discussed later in the chapter)
- addition of original records
- larger bibliographic records
- export of records in OCLC MARC, Dublin Core HTML, or Dublin Core RDF/XML format (see below).

It is worth noting that one of the previously separate services now subsumed under OCLC Connexion is the so-called CORC service – Cooperative Online Resource Catalog – which started out as a research project into the cooperative development of a catalogue of Internet resources. The idea was to save individual libraries from reinventing the wheel and from attempting to provide their own access to the huge amount of Internet resources that are of interest to their user communities.

It is worth remembering that OCLC also provides considerable support for information librarians through its *FirstSearch* service (mentioned in the previous chapter).

RLIN (Research Libraries Information Network)

If OCLC is the Jupiter of bibliographic networks (or utilities), RLIN has to be the Saturn. It is owned and managed by the Research Libraries Group (RLG) in the US. Its database contains over thirty million bibliographic records, with especially good coverage in areas such as non-book materials, archival materials and older material. It has an international membership, which includes a considerable number of research libraries (not surprisingly), special libraries, national libraries and archives. It is a good example of a network organised around a specific type of library, but it also has considerable significance for the wider library and information management community because of its subject and material strengths. Another feature that is of special interest to some libraries is the inclusion in the RLG Union Catalogue Arabic, Chinese, Cyrillic, Hebrew, Japanese and Korean scripts – bibliographic records contain both original and Roman-alphabetic scripts, which, according to the RLG supports precise searching and cataloguing, and makes the database 'the largest and richest resource online for Middle Eastern, Hebraic, and East Asian materials (Research Libraries Group 2003).

RLIN databases include:

- the bibliographic database, which includes discrete files covering books, serials, maps, computer files, visual materials, sound recording, musical scores, and archival and manuscripts control
- English Short Title Catalogue (ESTC), which describes publications printed in Great Britain and its colonies from 1473 to 1800, plus material printed in English during that period anywhere else in the world
- name and subject authority files

- special databases, such as the Hand Press Book database (European printing from the 15th Century to the 1830s), SCIPIO (Art and Rare Book Sales Catalogs) and RLG Conspectus Online (conspectus was discussed briefly in the previous chapter).

Costs of shared cataloguing

It is widely assumed that shared cataloguing is a cost-cutting exercise. Looked at logically, it makes sense to cut down on staff time by replacing original cataloguing with copy cataloguing. Moreover, not only is copy cataloguing quicker to perform than original cataloguing, but it is frequently performed by library technicians who (sadly for them) are generally not paid as much as librarians, leaving cataloguers to perform original cataloguing, catalogue maintenance and authority control. In fact there is some evidence to suggest that while librarians find themselves being replaced in the cataloguing department by library technicians, the latter find themselves being replaced by unqualified clerical staff. Although this raises fears among staff – for example, the fear that newly qualified librarians may find it difficult to obtain base level cataloguing positions – there are financial benefits for employers. There may also be savings that have nothing to do with cataloguing, such as the sharing of software costs in a network.

There is little evidence so far, however, that library networks have benefited their member libraries financially. Indeed, the costs of network membership may be prohibitive for many libraries. Major costs include:

- financial support for network administration
- maintenance of a central bibliographic database
- extra equipment, for example, communications hardware
- high telecommunications costs.

For many libraries, membership of a network is not a cost-cutting exercise and, indeed, belonging to a network may be more expensive than not belonging to one. There is some evidence that librarians join networks with a view to enhancing resource sharing among libraries. Most library directors take the view that membership of networks, including the large bibliographic utilities, is not a cost-cutting exercise, but view it as a means of improving users' access to resources and gaining benefits in terms of access to other collections. The benefits of shared cataloguing (which is not a new phenomenon), therefore, are not to be expressed purely in dollar terms but, as in so many areas of library activity, in terms of improved service. Finally, while the idea of a distributed national collection may not excite great interest, at least in Australia, there is the thought that by enhancing resource sharing it may even be possible to promote efficiencies in terms of the rationalisation of collection development activities, as suggested in the last chapter.

Metadata and other standards

So far this chapter has focused on the means by which library and information services provide access to 'traditional' information resources. Although MARC formats can be used to provide access to Internet resources through use of the 856 tag to record URLs, it is not regarded universally as an ideal standard. Internet resources are notoriously difficult to describe for a number of reasons. Quite apart from the fact that digital objects cannot be 'examined' like a physical resource, there are issues associated with the development of digital libraries that simply do not arise in traditional collection development: for instance:

- digital objects mutate – librarians are used to describing what they call 'ongoing' publications such as multi-part works and serials, but there are real problems keeping track of the different electronic versions of the same work
- different versions of digital objects are sometimes deliberately created: for example, low-resolution copies of images that can be quickly transferred over the Internet
- there are issues associated with the preservation of the 'original' or principal versions
- there is typically a need to map the complex relationships among digital objects
- legal aspects, such as the copyright and reproduction rights mentioned in the last chapter, need to be recorded and disseminated
- aspects of technical functionality are significant.

Before looking at an example and making the discussion a bit more concrete, it would be worth recalling the point mentioned earlier, that in the early to mid 1990s there was some disappointment with the ability of web search engines to act as effective search tools – a situation that did become somewhat less critical with the search engine improvements that Google pioneered. This, combined with issues such as those listed above, prompted interest in the development of new 'metadata' standards that would be better suited to the Internet environment.

Metadata have been mentioned in previous chapters. They are often described as 'structured data about data'. That is itself is especially helpful, but the main point to note about metadata is that they are structured data that are used to describe information resources, and that they resemble 'traditional' standards developed by the library and information community such as the Anglo-American Cataloguing Rules (AACR) and International Bibliographic Description (ISBD). This is not to suggest that metadata are purely descriptive – as suggested above there is a need, for instance, to include information about legal rights, and that is something that has been taken up by the many bodies developing metadata standards. Nonetheless, they are primarily seen – like accurate bibliographic records – as a means of improving resource discovery by users. Indeed, although the term metadata was first used in computing to refer to datasets, some librarians have been quick to suggest that the catalogue records they have been creating for a long time constitute a form of metadata.

Like other words throughout this book that begin with 'meta', the term metadata incorporates the Greek word meta, meaning beyond or above. 'Meta', therefore, denotes 'of a higher or second-order kind' (Deegan & Tanner 2002, p. 112). Consider the word 'metalanguage', which is a language or a system of symbols used to discuss another language or symbolic system. The best way in which to understand metadata, however, is to consider an example: the so-called Dublin Core Metadata Element Set, which is the standard used most widely by the library and information management community and was in large part developed by that sector.

Dublin Core (DC)

Dublin Core or DC is so called because it originates from a workshop held in Dublin, Ohio, in 1995. The Dublin Core Metadata Element Set is the key part of the standard, and consists of fifteen sections or elements – the term element is preferred here, but it is essentially the same as the term field, used already in this book, and the term attribute. The fifteen elements are:

1. Title: the name given to the resource – an element 'recommended' in DC, although more commonly a mandatory one (see, for instance, AGLS, below).
2. Creator: an entity primarily responsible for making the content of the resource, for instance, a person, an organisation, or a service (usually the name of that entity).
3. Subject: the topic of the content of the resource, most commonly a keyword, key phrase or classification code.
4. Description: an account of the content of the resource, for example, an abstract or table of contents.
5. Publisher: an entity responsible for making the resource available – again, a person, organisation or service (as for Creator, normally a name).
6. Contributor: an entity responsible for making contributions to the content of the resource – as above, normally the name of a person, organisation or service.
7. Date: a date associated with an event in the life cycle of the resource, for instance, the date on which the resource was created or made available.
8. Type: in other words, the type of resource – generally described in terms that relate to factors such as function or genre.
9. Format: the physical or digital manifestation of the resource, including, for instance, media type, dimensions of the resource or technical requirements, hardware and software required to operate the resource.
10. Identifier: an unambiguous reference to the resource within a given context, for example, a Web address (typically a URL), an International Standard Book Number (ISBN) or a Digital Object Identifier (DOI).
11. Source: reference to a resource from which the present resource is derived (recommended to use a number or other character string that conforms to a formal identification system).
12. Language: language of the intellectual content of the resource.

13. Relation: reference to a related resource (again, using a number or character string conforming to a formal identification system).

14. Coverage: the extent or scope of the content of the resource, generally including location, jurisdiction (such as a named administrative entity) or temporal coverage (for example, a date range).

15. Rights: management information about rights concerning the resource – typically covers such rights as intellectual property rights (IPR), copyright and various property rights.

Although the actual DC Metadata Element Set is relatively simple (relative, that is, to 'traditional' standards such as AACR2), there is more to it than the fifteen basic elements. As the brief overview above illustrates, DC does more than provide consistency in terms of structure – it also attempts to standardise the actual content through use of further tools, such as formal identification systems and thesauri. Similarly, in traditional cataloguing consistency of data elements helps to provide effective resource location but if the form of personal names, for instance, is not controlled by established authority files then resource location is certainly not as effective or as efficient as it might otherwise be.

What is covered in the fifteen DC metadata elements is descriptive metadata. They obviously do not cover all the issues covered in the opening of this section on metadata standards. Other *types* of metadata exist, principally:

- structural metadata, which describe 'the associations within or among related individual information objects' (Sun Microsystems 2002, p. 19): for instance, individual images, stored as separate files, may have to be related to the larger works to which they belong such as a specific webpage

- administrative metadata, which deal with issues such as access, management and preservation of the digital resource: for instance, they 'can provide a record of how and when an object was created as well as archival and rights management information' (Sun Microsystems 2002, p. 19).

Preservation does not seem like an obvious issue in the development of digital libraries, but there are a number of problems that complicate the long-term maintenance of digital objects: namely, the deterioration of digital media; the evolution of media type and format (for instance, the evolution of magnetic disks – see Chapter 6); developments in applications and operating systems (also discussed in Chapter 6), which means that information stored in a contemporary system may one day become inaccessible; and the need to preserve processing results, because some digital objects 'exist only fleetingly as a program runs' (Sun Microsystems 2002, p. 21).

Where to find metadata

Metadata can be found in one of three main places:

- embedded as meta tags in the head of HTML web pages

- included in separate HTML files that contain the metadata and act as 'pointers' to the web resources they describe
- listed in a separate web metadata repository (not unlike a library catalogue).

Metadata creators

Ideally the creators of the resources to which the metadata refer should also be the creators of the metadata. This is one of the reasons, perhaps the primary reason, why DC was developed as a relatively simple standard – one that steered a middle course between Internet anarchy, to which Chapter 1 referred, and the incredibly complex standards developed by the library and information management sector. Given the sheer volume of Internet resources, it clearly makes sense to put the onus of metadata creation on the original resource creators. Of course, this raises the perennial problem of quality – one only need recall the quality management issues that beset leading bibliographic networks such as Kinetica and OCLC and then consider the impact of entrusting metadata to every creator of web-based resources. Considerable research and development has gone into the automation of metadata creation, but despite some products being available, there is currently nothing that guarantees quality output for all metadata elements – subject is a notoriously difficult element for which to provide consistency, and it would be fair to say that the general community is not as concerned with such issues as the library and information management sector.

Other metadata standards

There are many metadata standards other than DC, some of them based on DC, having been developed for specific applications or by specific sectors of government, industry and the professions. Those most applicable to the library and information management sector include (the list is indicative only, since the purpose of this section is not to discuss metadata standards in their own right):

- AGLS (Australian Government Locator Service), which was developed with a view to making the information and services it disseminates via the Internet more accessible – it based on DC, but has nineteen elements and other differences (for instance, it makes Title a compulsory element)
- TEI (Text Encoding Initiative), a DTD (Document Type Definition) of SGML, like HTML (see Chapter 1), which was developed initially in 1987 to enable electronic textual material in the humanities to be represented in electronic form through development of a header – the TEI header – containing the required information about the electronic document
- EAD (Encoded Archival Description), which was adopted by Society of American Archivists (SAA) in 1999, and allows archival metadata to be distributed electronically: for instance, via RLIN's Archival and Mixed Collections file (AMC) – EAD is actually a DTD (Document Type Definition), used to encode electronic versions of archival finding aids (something that addresses much more complex relationships than the library catalogue)

- METS (Metadata Encoding and Transmission Standard), which 'provides a format for encoding metadata necessary for both management of digital library objects within a repository and exchange of such objects between repositories (or between repositories and their users)', and has provoked considerable interest from leading academic and research libraries (Sun Microsystems 2002, p. 19)

- ONIX, which is the international standard for representing and communicating book industry product information in electronic format – developed and maintained by EDItEUR in conjunction with Book Industry Communication and the Book Industry Study Group (EDItEUR 2003).

DTDs or Document Type Definitions were discussed briefly in Chapter 1, in the introduction to HTML – itself a DTD of SGML, specifically designed for web documents. Basically, a DTD is that part of SGML that defines a framework for a specific type of document: for instance EAD provides the framework for the structure of an archival finding aid. Other than the DTD-defined structure, there are another two layers in an SGML document: the actual content, with the added extra tags required, and the style, which determines how the document will be presented, for example, on a computer screen or on a printed page (Kochtanek & Matthews 2002, p. 103).

SGML has had an enormous effect on electronic publishing because of its system independence (a result of its use of ASCII, an industry standard for data representation, which is discussed in Chapter 6). The way in which SGML encodes the parts of a document means that the document can be transferred between different computer systems with its structure unchanged. In other words, SGML and its many DTDs offer a degree of interoperability. Where there is a proliferation of standards, however, there are clearly barriers to the extent to which metadata can be shared across different systems and different networks. To take an obvious example, library and information services have made a huge investment over the years in MARC – is the result different and incompatible metadata standards for Internet resources and 'traditional' resources? How do library and information managers ensure the kind of universal resource discovery that they want for their users: for instance, search across a variety of information retrieval tools (catalogues, databases and digital collections)?

Crosswalks

Considerable effort has gone into the development of 'crosswalks' over the past few years. Rather than trying to develop a universal metadata standard – which would hardly be workable, let alone feasible – various groups, including the library and information management sector, have developed, and are in the process of developing, crosswalks between specific standards: for instance, a crosswalk between Dublin Core and MARC21. What is involved, basically, is mapping specific elements in a metadata standard to those in another standard. There can be problems, however, when mapping a 'rich' standard such as MARC21 to a 'less rich one' such as DC (which has less elements than MARC21), but it is argued that mapping is nonetheless worthwhile from the perspective of resource discovery (Deegan & Tanner 2002, p. 143).

Specific standards, such as DC, are suggested as 'filters' or 'switching languages' that could be used for mapping between two other standards: in other words, instead of developing crosswalks for every standard that needs to be mapped to another, each standard might be mapped only to the 'filter'. Clearly the problem of 'rich' and 'less than rich' standards looms large – although DC has been suggested as a filter, it is not ideal because of its simplicity. It seems likely (at the time of writing!) that any solution is likely to involve XML or similar markup language.

Resource Description Framework (RDF)

One proposed solution is the use of 'Resource Description Framework' or RDF, which is an XML application, developed by the World-Wide Web Consortium (W3C) and designed to facilitate the exchange of metadata. RDF provides the framework to describe any web resource (in other words, any resource that has a URI or Uniform Resource Identifier), by means of a group of 'properties', called an RDF Description. RDF, according to Renato Iannella's readable introduction (1998),

> provides interoperability between applications that exchange metadata and is targeted for many application areas including: resource description, site-maps, content rating, electronic commerce, collaborative services, and privacy preferences. RDF is the result of members of these communities reaching consensus on their syntactical needs and deployment efforts (1998).

At the time of writing, there is an attempt to represent the Dublin Core in RDF. Whether RDF ends up as a kind of 'MARC format' for metadata still remains to be seen, but it is safe to say that the next few years will see continued research and development in the provision of metadata interoperability.

Open Archives Initiative (OAI)

The Open Archives Initiative (OAI) is an attempt to develop standards that will allow interoperability between digital collections, such as exchange of metadata. Its main thrust has been the development of protocols – protocols are discussed in Chapter 7, but here they can be taken to refer to the sets of conventions or rules governing the transfer of data between separate computer systems. An important starting-point was the implementation in 2001 of the first version of the OAI Protocol for Metadata Harvesting. Harvesting refers to the gathering of metadata from repositories or, in other words, network accessible servers that can process the PMH requests defined in the protocol. (Consider the way in which search engines 'harvest' index terms and links from the Web.) The record that is harvested from the repository is transferred in XML format. By facilitating interoperability and the ability of digital libraries to gather metadata from other repositories, OAI offers considerable enhancement of resource discovery.

OpenURL Framework

Before leaving standards, it is probably worthwhile mentioning OpenURL, which is an attempt by the National Information Standards Organization in the US (NISO) to develop a standardised format for transporting metadata in a URL.

> The proposed OpenURL is a syntax to create web-transportable packages of metadata and/or identifiers about an information object. Such packages are at the core of context-sensitive or open link technology. By standardizing this syntax, the OpenURL will enable many other innovative user-specific services (National Information Standards Organization, 2003).

The metadata referred to include some of the standards discussed earlier, such as MARC, Dublin Core, ONIX and OAI, while identifier standards include familiar library and book trade standards such as International Standard Book Number (ISBN), International Standard Serial Number (ISSN), Serial Item and Contribution Identifier (SICI) and Book Item and Component Identifier (BICI) – the last two being unique identifier standards for journals & books created or stored in digital format. Another example of an identifier is the Digital Object Identifier (DOI), an attempt to manage items of intellectual property on the Internet and in fairly common use in the scholarly publishing sector.

Like the Web's URI (Uniform Resource Identifier) specification, the OpenURL Framework recognises the importance of having a uniform public naming system, but it also represents a recognition of the reality that there are a number of public naming systems in everyday use that are not integrated under any registered URI scheme, not to mention many private naming systems, and that a standard cannot be imposed from 'above'. The OpenURL Framework, therefore, provides a common syntax that will permit the many user communities on the Internet to promote their existing systems to public recognition.

This, as one may gather, is an acronym-rich area of research and development. The next chapter steps into the more 'traditional' area of library and information management – that of library management systems – which is somewhat easier for the electronic library novice in terms of readability.

References

Curriculum Corporation 2003, *SCIS: Contents of the SCIS database*, updated 18 November 2002, viewed 26 April 2003, <http://www.curriculum.edu.au/scis/contents.htm>.

Deegan, M & Tanner, S 2002, *Digital futures: Strategies for the information age*. Library Association Publishing, London.

EDItEUR 2003, *ONIX product information standards*, viewed 26 April 2003, <http://www.editeur.org/onix.html>.

Iannella, R 1998, *An idiot's guide to the Resource Description Framework*, updated 25 January 1999, DSTC Pty Ltd, viewed 25 April 2003, <http://archive.dstc.edu.au/RDU/reports/RDF-Idiot/>.

Kochtanek, TR & Matthews, JR 2002, *Library information systems: From library automation to distributed information access solutions*. Libraries Unlimited, Westport, CT.

Maddick, P 1997, 'The role of SCIS cataloguing agencies: The NCEC,' in *School library automation in Australia*, K Dillon (ed.), 2nd ed., Centre for Information Studies, Wagga Wagga, NSW.

National Information Standards Organization 2003, *The OpenURL framework for context-sensitive services*, viewed 16 April 2003, <www.niso.org/committees/committee_ax.html>.

National Library of New Zealand 2003, *Te Puna subscriber services: About subscriber services*, viewed 26 April 2003, <http://subscribers.natlib.govt.nz/about.htm>.

Research Libraries Group 2003, *RLG library resources* (online). [Accessed 26 Jan. 2003] http://www.rlg.org/libres.html

Sun Microsystems 2002, *Digital library technology trends*, August 2002, viewed 26 April 2003, <http://www.sun.com/products-n-solutions/edu/whitepapers/pdf/digital_library_trends.pdf>.

Review questions

1. Name three files associated with online catalogues.
2. Suggest two distinct uses of the term 'OPAC'.
3. Identify the main disadvantages of CD-ROM catalogues.
4. Explain what MARC is.
5. Explain the difference between data fields and control fields in MARC.
6. Identify some of the cataloguing services provided by national libraries.
7. Explain how libraries can be recompensed for the addition of catalogue records to a cooperative bibliographic network.
8. Identify things that might be shared by libraries in a bibliographic network, other than bibliographic data.
9. Suggest three technologies used to copy catalogue records from a bibliographic network to a local system.
10. Identify the main costs of shared cataloguing.

Further resources

Caplan, P 2003, *Metadata fundamentals for all librarians*. American Library Association, Chicago.
Not sighted; but according to the ALA this book defines both descriptive and non-descriptive forms of metadata, including the TEI Header, the Dublin Core, EAD, GILS, ONIX and the Data Documentation Initiative, and applies them to actual library functions.

Harvey, DR & Hider, P 2003, *Organising knowledge in a global society*. 2nd ed. Centre for Information Studies: Wagga Wagga, NSW.
An excellent overview of the provision of access to information resources and the development of standards, written from an Australasian perspective but with an international readership in mind. It is specifically geared to students but also to practitioners who are interested in keeping up-to-date on principles and practice.

International Federation of Library Associations. *Digital libraries: Cataloging and indexing of electronic resources*, <http://www.ifla.org/II/catalog.htm>.
An excellent place to look for resources (electronic and print-based) on the description of electronic resources. It includes: Internet sources, periodicals, bibliography, mailing lists, spiders and robots, and selection of electronic resources.

Jones, W, Ahronheim, JR & Crawford, J (eds.) 2002, *Cataloging the Web: Metadata, AACR2 and MARC 21*. Scarecrow Press, Lanham, MD.
Papers from the ALCTS Preconference on Metadata for Web Resources, July 2000, by a virtual who's who of the digital world (no pun intended).

National Library of Australia, *Standards*,
<http://www.nla.gov.au/initiatives/standards.html>.
Portal includes areas such as Australian Committee on Cataloguing, ensuring best practice in cataloguing and classification, Kinetica Expert Advisory Groups, standards for libraries and the NLA's guide to standards for libraries.

Tennant, R (ed.) 2002, *XML in libraries*. Neal-Schuman, New York.
Covers topics such as the use of XML in library catalogue records, for interlibrary loans, for cataloguing and indexing, for building collections, in databases and for systems interoperability.

CHAPTER 4
Library management systems

Unlike previous chapters, this one refers principally to the traditional library environment, in which an important strategy in the provision of users with access to published information resources is the acquisition of resources such as print and audiovisual material. For years, libraries have made use of computerised information systems in the acquisition, cataloguing and circulation of information resources. These three functions involve control and record-keeping activities and readily lend themselves to automation. An acquisition system is used to generate orders for information resources and thereafter to keep track of orders, financial commitments, the receipt of resources, and expenditures. A cataloguing system, as suggested in the last chapter, is a means of recording what resources are held by a library and thereby aiding resource discovery. Circulation systems are a means of recording and controlling the movement of library resources once they are received and processed. These three functions are at the heart of any library management system (or integrated library system, to use another common name) and form the main focus of this chapter, along with a fourth main function, the generation of management reports, based on acquisition, cataloguing and circulation operations. Even here, however – the area of the automated library – the wider issues of access to digital resources discussed in the preceding chapters are of great importance, because increasingly the library management system is not merely a tool for the control of physical information resources – it is an integral part of the broader electronic library and is increasingly expected to conform to the standards that support that wider information environment.

Learning objectives

At the end of this chapter, you will be able to:

- explain the purpose of library management systems
- explain parameterisation
- outline the main features of a library management system, and
- describe different kinds of information system used in library operations and management.

Keywords

System
Information System
Parameters
Copy cataloguing
Authority control
Output

Default
Data processing system
Barcode
Down-time
Management information system
Decision support system

Systems

Before discussing library management systems, it might help to talk about systems. A system is something formed of parts, each of which interacts with the other parts to achieve some common purpose. In the case of a library management system, the parts work together to support the management of library information resources: their acquisition, representation and circulation. Each of these parts constitutes a subsystem which in turn comprises a set of interconnected parts. In other words, each of these subsystems can be broken down into yet smaller subsystems, for example, a subsystem to control the catalogue display options. It is worth noting that vendors of library management systems often refer to the main subsystems, such as acquisitions and circulations, as modules. Some modules can be added on to a basic system: for example, a special module to manage serials collections or (as mentioned in Chapter 2) an inter-library loans module.

A library management system is an example of an information system. An information system, whether it is computerised or not, is a system that represents objects in a physical system, for example, information resources in a library collection. The catalogue discussed in the last chapter is a system that represents the actual information resources of a library, whether that representation consists of marks on a card, marks on a microfiche sheet or data stored in a computer.

Text retrieval system

Textual data → Store (input) → Bibliographic database → Retrieve (output) → Textual data

Figure 4.1: The catalogue as an information system

It is worth noting, however, that the objects represented need not themselves be physical entities such as books. They may be abstract entities, such as the sums of money committed to the purchase of information resources in an acquisition system or, as the last chapter demonstrated, a digital object. Moreover, an information system does more than merely record the existence of an object: it also represents the status and movement of objects. A circulation system, for example, records the movement of information resources such as books and, if the circulation system is linked to the online catalogue, library users can see the status of the item (for example, date due or missing).

Before specific subsystems are discussed, there are three general points worth making. First, the term 'library management system' is the one most commonly used by librarians and system vendors to describe the systems that perform acquisition, cataloguing and circulation functions. It has generally replaced earlier terms, such as 'library housekeeping system' which used to be in common use in the British literature and indicated that this kind of system is used to handle a library's day-to-day transactions. The change in terminology perhaps reflects the fact that these systems also perform management reporting, thus supporting higher levels of library management than the transactional subsystems.

The other term in common use is integrated library system – this and the following data management chapter should explain the level of integration expected. It is worth bearing in mind, however, that, although most libraries have developed or migrated towards integrated systems, some subsystems are available as separate systems in their own right: for instance, systems for the management of serials or media collections. It is easy to assume that all libraries will migrate, or have migrated to integrated systems, but there are small libraries, typically small special libraries that cannot afford to purchase a complete library management system.

Second, most library management systems are prewritten by commercial companies and are not written for specific libraries. For this reason, it is in the interest of vendors to write some flexibility into their systems so that they can be customised for individual libraries. This is done by the use of *parameterisation*. A parameter, in this context, is a variable value that can be left to the library manager or systems librarian to define. A circulations subsystem, for instance, requires values such as loans period to be defined. These must be variable values, because they are determined by the loans policies of individual libraries and not by vendors. They must, nonetheless, be defined if the system is to operate. Hence when a library system is implemented, parameters like loan period must be established by those in charge of implementation.

As far as commercial library management systems are concerned, each of the subsystems discussed in this chapter would be expected to offer a degree of parameterisation. There are also parameters that affect more than one subsystem. It may be considered desirable, for example, to have security parameters that can be defined by individual libraries. These are values that can either determine password access to certain applications (for instance, acquisitions) or define a range of applications to which an individual staff member has access. (In the latter case, the staff member would have to be identified by the system, for example, through use of a staff identification code.) The reason for this is that access to some applications may be inappropriate: for example, library managers may decide that there is no reason for circulations counter staff to be able to access the acquisition function or for them to be able to waive fines owed by library users. Other common parameters include:

- online help: it may be possible for libraries to tailor online documentation (help messages, etc.) to local needs
- output control, that is, define the types of document to be generated by the system, such as messages to library users or to library suppliers.

Parameters specific to particular functions are discussed below, under the appropriate subsystems.

Finally, it is worth bearing in mind that the library management systems discussed in this chapter are continually being adapted to the changing library and information service environment and that, as librarians cope with the current 'hybrid' library, they are increasingly demanding in terms of the features that they expect library management systems to exhibit.

Cataloguing systems

It was suggested earlier that a system comprises a set of interconnected subsystems. One of the reasons for discussing cataloguing subsystems before the others is that what typically connects the subsystems in a library management system is the bibliographic file, which contains the records representing the information resources in a library collection (whether that collection is purely physical or includes digital resources). The acquisitions and circulations subsystems must either duplicate some of the descriptive data in the bibliographic file or use these data directly, since the first system manages the acquisition of information resources and the second records their movement. This is one of the reasons why library system vendors have developed integrated systems in which bibliographic data are shared among the three main functions. This is not to say that all such products are integrated systems, because a survey of available library systems will find some which handle only specific functions.

As the last chapter indicated, library catalogues include bibliographic descriptions, subject descriptions and item-specific information. A library may have more than one copy of a particular work, in which case it is important to be able to identify not just the work but also the individual item or copy. Many commercial library management systems will record such data in a holdings file, separate from the main bibliographic file. Holdings data are required for the circulation of library resources (see below).

What are the features to expect in a cataloguing subsystem?

It will generally support the following activities:

- original cataloguing, that is, the local creation of catalogue records
- importation of records from external sources (for example, bibliographic networks)

- catalogue enquiry, using boolean search techniques
- editing of catalogue records
- deletion of catalogue records
- authority control
- output of stationery, such as catalogue cards and book labels.

Original cataloguing

The primary requirement of any cataloguing subsystem is that it allows for the creation of catalogue records. Although a library may be able to minimise cataloguing effort by importing records from a bibliographic network, it is unlikely that a library will be able to derive all its cataloguing requirements from external sources.

The most common means of entering original cataloguing data is by using a computer keyboard to enter data character by character. The operator who enters the data can see what is being entered on a computer screen. What the operator sees on the screen varies according to computer system, but in original cataloguing, there are two main approaches to data entry:

- formatted screens or form filling
- question and answer (a series of prompts).

Use of a formatted screen is the computer equivalent of paper form filling, and for that reason is popular. What the operator sees on the screen resembles a form, with labels indicating particular fields or data elements to be entered and spaces in which to enter the appropriate data. This has the merit of being familiar, and operators have the option of moving quickly through fields and subfields that are not required using the tab key on the computer keyboard. Moreover, in some libraries the cataloguer will not perform all the data entry (perhaps for reasons of health and safety, perhaps for financial reasons, perhaps for reasons of workflow), leaving the bulk of data entry to support staff. Where support staff work from worksheets manually prepared by cataloguing staff, it is obviously convenient for the screen to resemble a worksheet.

In the question and answer approach, the system leads the operator through a series of prompts for data relating to specific bibliographic fields. Again, the operator can bypass unwanted fields, ideally with a single keystroke. Some prompts may be dynamic in that the system may recognise certain character strings and give an apparently intelligent prompt. For example, when an operator enters an International Standard Book Number and then a publisher's name into a record, the system may create a link between the publisher's code in the ISBN (the bundle of figures after the first figure) and the publisher's name. Future entry of an ISBN with that publisher's code will generate a display of the publisher's name and a prompt giving the operator the chance to select that name for the record or to insert a different imprint.

Regardless of which approach is taken, the screen should be as uncluttered and unambiguous as possible. Many library management systems will allow for a degree of parameterisation such as the following:

- choice of fields to be entered, appropriate to the material being catalogued: for instance, monographs, audiovisual or cartographic material (cataloguing departments can then organise their work flow according to material type)

- choice of level of cataloguing – even material with common fields, such as fiction and non-fiction books, may not need to be described in the same detail: for example, brief records may be created for fiction in a public library.

In general, verification of bibliographic data is left to human review. Nonetheless, some automatic verification can be expected. The ISBN, for example, has a check digit (the tenth), and many systems will run through the set of rules (algorithm) used to determine the check digit. If the system's solution of the algorithm does not match the check digit entered, it will inform the operator that there is a problem.

When a catalogue record is being created, there should be a facility whereby the cataloguer is alerted to the fact that duplicate records exist. Where there is a unique identifier, such as ISBN, the system can be expected to recognise the record. Even where there is no unique identifier, a system should alert cataloguers to the existence of possible duplicates; for example, it may recognise the title entered and give the cataloguer the chance to add the new item to an existing record.

Finally, cataloguing subsystems vary according to their acceptance of character types (for example, Chinese characters) and diacritics (for example, the ^ symbol used in French). The main standard to refer to is the ALA Extended Character Set, developed by the American Library Association. It is also worth noting the so-called CJK codes, which specify how Chinese, Japanese and Korean characters are handled (recall the earlier reference to Unicode, which is discussed in Chapter 6).

Copy cataloguing

Copy cataloguing is the copying of existing catalogue records, a process made comparatively easy once records are stored in electronic format. The main ways in which catalogue records are imported into cataloguing systems are:

- records are sent on magnetic tape or diskette by a central agency (for example, with new acquisitions)

- records are selected from an external bibliographic database and downloaded via the Internet to the local system

- records are selected from an external bibliographic database, ordered and received on magnetic tape or diskette

- records are downloaded from a CD-ROM source, such as a trade bibliography (see also 'Acquisitions systems', below).

If catalogue records are to be *imported*, the local system should be able to accept external records in the given format (for instance, MARC21) and be able to handle them. Some commercial library management systems will not store bibliographic records in a MARC format, but will use an internal, proprietorial format, especially for purposes of transactions, such as circulation. It is worth bearing in mind, too, that full MARC records may not be required for the local system, and it should be possible to specify which fields and subfields are to be accepted (this is a parameter which may be defined by the library in consultation with the system vendor or designer).

It may also be necessary to consider the *export* of records from the local system, for example, if the local system is to upload records to an external database. Export of records may also be an issue in the long term, since a library will at some point migrate to another library management system, as many have, and will need to move data files from one system to another (see Chapter 8). Finally, it is worth bearing in mind the 'hybrid' library environment and the need to consider new standards, such as XML, which may be used in web-based access tools. Is there, for instance, software available for conversion of bibliographic records from MARC to XML?

To download catalogue records from an external source, such as a bibliographic network, requires special computer software and specific hardware. Increasingly, librarians and library technicians make use of sophisticated workstations to ensure flexibility in downloading bibliographic records from remote servers, such as those belonging to the networks described in the last chapter.

Editing catalogue records

One of the advantages of computerised cataloguing over manual systems is the ease with which records can be amended or deleted. It should be possible for cataloguing staff to add, amend or delete specific fields, subfields or character strings within a record, or to delete a record entirely (see below).

Where records have been imported from external sources, item-specific holdings data will need to be added. Moreover, local systems may use fields not used by external agencies, for example, a local classification code. With the increased use of integrated systems, original bibliographic records can be created in the acquisitions function (typically in brief form) or even downloaded from the supplier's database, and edited on receipt of the corresponding material: for example, with the addition of subject headings, classification number and holdings data. Another reason for editing records may be that there is a facility that allows the cataloguer to copy an existing record (for example, where a record exists for an earlier edition of a work), edit the new record and add new holdings data. It should also be possible to edit while performing original cataloguing (for example, to correct errors).

Deletion of catalogue records

Catalogue records may need to be deleted when the last copy of a work is withdrawn from a library's collection. When the last copy is withdrawn (deleted from the holdings or item file), the system may automatically delete the bibliographic record to which the holding is attached, along with any related authority file data (see below). Ideally, however, since the copy of the work may be replaced, deletion of a bibliographic record should be a separate process from deletion of holdings data. The deletion of bibliographic records may even involve different staff (for example, librarians with collection development responsibilities), which may be reflected in staff privilege levels (a set of parameters).

Authority control

Authority control is maintained by means of authority files which record the correct form of headings (for example, personal name headings). The point of authority control is that if catalogues are to help users identify information resources, there needs to be consistency, particularly in the case of popular access points such as author, title and subject description. If cataloguers are to provide an effective service, they must ensure, for example, that if users search for resources by a particular, known author, the system will retrieve all records relating to the author's work and not just some of them. Authority files, therefore, have a function similar to thesauri. A thesaurus is in fact a form of authority file which provides a list of preferred and non-preferred *subject* terms, with linkages between preferred and non-preferred terms, between broader and narrower terms and between related terms. Where authority files differ from thesauri is that they are a guide to preferred and non-preferred vocabulary for a range of fields, whereas thesauri specifically control vocabulary in subject fields. As the last chapter mentioned, national libraries are often a source of authority files: for example, personal name and corporate name file listings.

Authority files may function in much the same way as thesauri, that is, as listings to which cataloguers refer, but in library management systems they may be more than this. As the last chapter suggested, certain types of data, such as authors' names, may be stored only once in a system, in an authority file separate from the main bibliographic file. In fact, some data elements in the bibliographic file, for example, personal names, corporate names, titles, series titles and subject headings may be drawn from discrete authority files in order to construct and present a bibliographic record. Each authority file (for example, author authority file) would in that case list preferred terms, along with relations (for example, non-preferred terms) and pointers to those bibliographic records which 'contain' the terms. The pointers are often system-generated bibliographic record numbers which appear in both files. (This point may become clearer, after the discussion of relational database management systems in the next chapter.) As well as using authority files for access elements, such as author and title, the cataloguing system may also maintain an authority file for other data elements, such as publishers' names.

Features of authority control include:

- automatic creation of an authority file entry when a new heading is created or imported with a new catalogue record
- automatic deletion of references when the last catalogue record with which they are linked is deleted
- ability to import authority file terms from an external source, for example, the integration of Library of Congress Subject Headings with local systems
- ability to establish a reference structure among authority file headings
- global change facility, so that, for example, when country's name changes all instances in the subject authority file of the old name can be changed to the new one, with an appropriate reference from the disused name
- ability to merge authority file headings, for example, where two entries in the author authority file are for the same author
- easy navigation between cataloguing procedures and authority files
- listing of new and dropped authority file terms, for cataloguers to review (see 'Output from cataloguing systems', below).

The ease with which cataloguers can move between catalogue creation and authority files has not always been satisfactory, but the use of windows (see Chapter 6 on the user interface) presents cataloguers with the opportunity to check authority files while in the middle of entering catalogue data. Inspired by the development of the Apple Macintosh microcomputer (which is window-orientated), many software packages now allow the operator to split the screen into a number of boxed areas or windows and run more than one application simultaneously (or at least display more than one application and run one of them). For the cataloguer this means being able to access authority files while creating records, instead of having to leave the record creation application. A similar facility should be available if the cataloguer is editing records. It must be said, however, that cataloguers are not always happy with the way in which library management systems handle authority control.

Output from cataloguing systems

Finally, cataloguing subsystems offer a range of output options:

- stationery, such as spine labels for books (with call numbers), item labels to identify individual items, barcode labels (see 'Circulations systems' below)
- printed reports listing all new catalogue records (facilitating control of bibliographic standards)
- printed reports listing new and dropped authority file terms
- catalogues in other formats (an increasingly unlikely option).

Some systems will also allow the cataloguer to check classification numbers already in use, and even report subject headings used in conjunction with particular classification numbers and vice versa. Not all of these options may be required: for example, stationery may not be produced by the local system, as such material is very often provided with information resources by library suppliers.

Acquisition systems

Acquisition systems, like circulation systems (below), are transaction-based information systems, concerned with the everyday operational aspects of the library: for example, the ordering of library resources, their receipt, and the management of financial data. Both acquisition and circulation systems are examples of *data processing systems*. Data processing systems transform well-defined data, according to well-defined rules, to some 'normal form', for example, an acquisition system transforms data on an order (such as order date, supplier, number of items ordered and receipt) into a completed order transaction. The information resources that the library orders are represented in the information system as 'on order', while the funds necessary to cover the purchase are committed, in the system, to be 'moved' from a library fund to the supplier. Once the information resources have been moved from the supplier to the library, they are receipted, their status changes to 'in stock' or 'in process' (the latter indicates that the item is now being catalogued) and the funds committed for their purchase are 'moved' into expenditure. The process can be represented as follows:

Figure 4.2: Acquisitions system as data processing system

Data processing of this kind is well-suited to automation. Many of the procedures involved are routine, predictable, time-consuming and labour-intensive. Accounting procedures are relatively complex and, as with maintaining card catalogues, there is considerable filing involved in manual systems.

Basic features of acquisitions systems can be summarised as follows:

- bibliographic checking
- creation and dispatch of orders
- receipt of orders and fund accounting
- claiming for or cancellation of outstanding orders.

Bibliographic checking

Before ordering an item, the acquisitions department would normally check if any copies of the item are in stock, if it has already been ordered, whether it is in print and whether the bibliographic details are correct. An integrated system will make it an easy matter to check if items are in stock, on order or in process. (Under manual systems, separate bibliographic and order files would have to be checked, and in-process items could be a problem area.) As well as traditional sources of in-print and bibliographic information, acquisitions librarians have access to external electronic sources:

- bibliographic networks such as those described in the last chapter
- CD-ROM bibliographic products, such as trade listings
- suppliers' databases: for example, some library suppliers will provide electronic records for resources sent in library approval plans.

These can also be used as sources of copy cataloguing and, in fact, one of the phenomena noted in much of the library literature is the merging of cataloguing and acquisitions sections in many libraries.

Creation and dispatch of orders

It should, of course, also be possible to create a new order. Data entry is generally achieved via a formatted screen (form filling). As with cataloguing systems, different levels of entry are desirable, so that acquisitions staff can, for example, create brief bibliographic records for later enhancement (such as addition of subject headings and holdings data). As with cataloguing systems, with a fully integrated system, the operator should be prompted for possible duplicates on entry of fields such as ISBN and title. Where a field is not used, it should be possible to move past it using the tab key. Some values can usually be assumed (for instance, the currency of the country in which the order is raised), and tabbing past that field will cause the assumed value to be automatically entered. Such a value is called a *default*. Should an alternative value be required (such as a sum in another currency), it is simply entered in the normal way.

When an acquisition system is implemented, supplier and fund files can be set up as local parameters. A supplier file, separate from the order file, will contain data such as names and addresses of suppliers and supplier codes. The supplier code identifies the supplier record (in the supplier file) and enables the operator to link an order (in the order file) to a particular supplier by entering the code and not the full name and address. The library should also have the option of setting up separate fund files: for instance, if each branch library or department has a budget of its own. A separate file would be established in advance, and operators creating an order need only enter the appropriate fund codes against particular items. (Again, this is clearer with an understanding of relational database management systems – see the following chapter.) They should be alerted if a fund is going to be over-committed. In some systems a *desiderata* file may also be created, so that, if there are excess funds at the end of the financial year, these can be quickly committed to purchasing material recorded on file.

Most acquisition systems are parameterised, so that the library can determine standardised text to go on the order, with an option to add specific instructions when required. Generally, orders are sent as a batch, either as a printout or, more commonly now, as an online order. The major suppliers of library information resources offer online ordering facilities.

Receipt and accounting

When items are received, it is necessary to be able to retrieve the order record through a choice of bibliographic fields, order number or supplier code (in the case of a batch). Normally, the system can be expected to change the status of an item from 'on order' to 'in process' (a change that should be documented in the online catalogue), and record the date of receipt automatically. It should also be able to handle receipt of part of an order, where there were multiple copies or multi-volume items.

The acquisitions system will also be expected to update fund details from money committed to money expended, and to provide financial reports summarising fund allocations, commitments, expenditures and balances (either as figures or as graphics). When a significant proportion of information resources is published in other countries, the ability of a system to cope with currency conversion is a useful feature. Finally, once material is receipted, the operator should be able to process invoices and payments. As in other fields of business, the development of communications standards has enabled libraries to pay suppliers electronically – it is especially worth noting the support among vendors for EDI or Electronic Data Interface for online acquisitions.

Claiming

Systems should be able to generate claims for items not received within specified periods. Ideally, there should be sufficient flexibility to allow acquisitions staff to define acceptable delivery periods for specific orders or for batches of orders dispatched to specific vendors. In the case of non-receipt of items within specified periods, options include automatic generation of claims notices or the generation of an overdue report. In the latter case, the acquisitions librarian may either produce a claim letter or cancel the order. Again, the library should be free to create standardised text for its claims notices.

Impact of ICTs on acquisitions

Computers have already had considerable impact. In the short term, the greatest impact is organisational. The increasing use of integrated systems in collection management (or technical services) departments, as previously noted, has led to some integration of library functions. The most obvious area of convergence is that between acquisitions and copy cataloguing, since both functions make increasing use of external sources of bibliographic data, and both often establish interim bibliographic records which can, if necessary, be brought into line with local cataloguing practice by cataloguers. In some libraries, copy cataloguing is the responsibility of acquisitions staff.

In the longer term, electronic publishing can be expected to have considerable impact on the acquisitions department. Over the years, there has been considerable comment in the library literature about the focus of library operations moving from acquisitions to access (see Chapter 2). At present, electronic publications are most often handled by information services or reference departments, but as electronic publications grow as a proportion of library budgets, so library managers will need to take a more holistic approach to the ways in which they provide access to information resources. At present (a dangerous phrase), electronic access does not look like supplanting acquisitions in many sectors, but the process by which librarians evaluate their information delivery strategies has become more complex and dynamic than it used to be in the days of print-only publication.

Circulations control systems (loans systems)

In circulations control, librarians attempt to record and control the movement of library resources between a library and its users, between libraries, or between a library and another agent, such as a binder. Users are generally individual people, but they can also be corporate bodies, such as schools or playgroups.

Like manual acquisitions systems, manual systems of circulations control are time-consuming and labour-intensive, involving considerable filing, problems in the preparation of overdue notices and queues at the loans desk in busy libraries (especially with systems that expect borrowers to complete transaction slips or cards). Most systems involve repetitious, boring work and are error-prone, leading to poor staff morale and occasional public relations problems. Non-computer technologies, such as photocharging, were developed to alleviate some of these problems, but none was a complete solution. The first libraries to automate circulations control were often large academic libraries with a high rate of transactions.

The main activities associated with circulations control systems are:

- issue, renewal and discharge of loans
- management of overdue resources
- reservation of resources
- maintenance of borrower files
- enquiry, for example, material, borrower, loans and reservations data
- stocktaking
- output of lists and notices.

Loans of library resources

Much of the circulations control function is driven by loans policies and procedures, and it is important that library and system managers should be able to establish parameters (values) for the circulations system in advance. For example, they will want to determine loan periods, which may vary according to type of resource, and loan entitlements (quotas), which may vary according to category of borrower (staff and students of a university may be able to borrow more than community borrowers). Calendars constitute another set of parameters that would need to be determined by an individual library (recording public holidays, days of the week when the library is closed, etc.). When items are issued to borrowers (checked out), the system should automatically determine the loan period for each item, using loan period and calendar parameters.

The circulations control system will also be expected to provide checks (or traps) on transactions, for example, blocking loans of certain resources (for example, reservations), or categories of resource (for example, 'reference only' material), or alerting staff to problems, such as borrowers exceeding their loan entitlement or having 'defaulted' on an earlier loan.

During the issuing process, the system will create a link between the items and the borrower's record. Transaction data will be recorded in a loans file. Data will include:

- borrower identifier (generally a number unique to an individual borrower)
- item identifier (also a unique number)
- date of issue
- date due (system generated), and
- number of renewals (if these are restricted).

Note that, because of the use of unique identifiers, the loans file need not contain detailed borrower and bibliographic data. The identifiers make it possible to draw on data in other files as and when they are required: for example, from a borrower file (below), if borrowers need to be sent overdue reminders. (Once again, see Chapter 5 on database management systems.)

Renewals procedures (the extension of loans) are similar to issues, except that there should be provision for remote renewal, involving keying in of borrower and item numbers by staff, in the case of telephone renewals, or by users themselves communicating electronically from remote computers, with the library management system. Again, the system should alert staff and users to loans policies, such as renewal restrictions.

When an item is discharged (checked in), the system will cancel the link between the borrower and the item: although some library management systems will keep a record of the link in an archive file. It should also alert staff to reserved items (trap them) and calculate any overdue fines.

Barcodes

The unique numbers that identify items and borrowers are often represented by barcodes. A barcode is a set of parallel lines (bars), which represents data using factors such as width of the lines and distance between them. In this application, the data represented are numerical, either an item identification number or a borrower identification number.

Figure 4.3: Example of a barcode

Barcode labels can be affixed to each loan item and to each borrower identification card. The number encoded on the label can be read by a computer system via a light-pen, a light-sensitive device which is 'wanded' over the label (sometimes the light-pen is referred to as a wand), and a barcode reader, which interprets the signal from the light-pen and sends it to the circulations control system in a format that the system can handle.

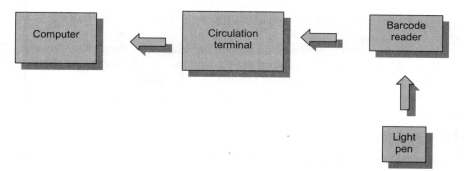

Figure 4.4: Circulations workstation

When the system is ready to issue resources, it will expect first a number that corresponds to a borrower's number in the borrower file (see below). Subsequent item identification numbers sent to the system via the light-pen and barcode reader will be linked to the borrower number as loans transactions. Entry of another borrower number will indicate to the system that a new loans transaction has started. The main advantage of barcodes is the speed of transaction. An additional benefit is that if operators were to enter numbers using a keyboard, there would be errors. Sometimes numbers have to be keyed in, if a barcode label is unreadable. A successful transaction should be indicated on a computer screen, but some systems also indicate the success or failure of a transaction with an audible signal – a useful feature at a busy loans counter.

Some barcodes are so-called smart barcodes. When a smart barcode is produced, the number encoded on the barcode label already appears in the holdings file as an item identifier. Some data relating to the item (for example, call number and short title) may be printed on the label to enable staff to match the label to the correct item. There are instances, however, where use of generic (dumb) barcode labels is preferable, in other words, items are barcoded first and then the barcode number is linked to the bibliographic record that represents the actual information resource.

Data files

Three types of data file have already been mentioned:

- the loans (or transaction) file
- the bibliographic file
- the borrower file, which records membership details such as full name, address(es), telephone number(s) and category of membership.

Many library management systems also use a holdings or item file for circulations control. This will contain only brief bibliographic data and item-specific data, such as barcode numbers, volume numbers (in the case of multi-volume works) and the status of items (for example, missing items or items that are not for loan). The loans transaction will link borrowers with items in the holdings file and not the much more detailed bibliographic file. It is still possible to link a loans transaction to data in the main bibliographic file, because there will be links between the holdings file and the bibliographic file. (The way in which files can be related is discussed in the next chapter in the section on database management systems.)

Self-charging

In recent years there has been considerable interest in self-charging, that is, library users checking out or issuing loans for themselves. The objective is to save staff time (either releasing staff for other useful duties or allowing the library to make staff cuts, depending on the ruling philosophy of the day). Unless a library has an honour system in operation, self-charging relies on integration with a theft-detection (security) system. The self-charging unit should desensitise an item as soon as the circulation system has approved a loan (desensitisation allows an item to pass through electronic security gates). Basic features to look for in a self-charging system include:

- compatibility with the library's circulations control system
- a good optical scanner, to read barcodes
- a small printer, to provide the user with the due date
- PIN numbers (as for banks) so that lost cards cannot be used by other people.

Although not currently a basic feature, it is worth noting the use of RFID (Radio Frequency Identification) technology for the identification of library resources. This requires special RF tags to be embedded in resources, which are then detected by a transceiver with decoder, via an antenna. The antenna can be placed in a variety of places: for instance, in a doorway or a library security gate (or, of course, in a shop doorway or gate). When the radio wave from the tag is detected, it is decoded and the data encoded in the tag is sent to the computer for processing. The transceiver/decoder can also be packaged with the antenna, which can then become a handheld reader.

Management of overdue resources

Circulations control systems do not merely represent loans transactions, but also assist library staff in the enforcement of loans policies. Some of the ways in which they assist library staff have already been mentioned: for instance, automatic generation of loans periods or alerting staff to borrowers who are 'defaulting' on previous loans. Another two ways in which they assist staff are:

- generation of overdue lists and notices
- calculation of fines due (if applicable).

Again, the subsystem is driven by parameters, such as loans periods, calendars and fines schedules (penalties). Once a set of items is overdue by a specified amount the system will alert library staff. One means of doing so is the generation of a printed list of overdue items sorted into call number order – this enables staff to check the shelves before contacting users. The next step would normally be to produce overdue notices for individual users, listing overdue items.

When an overdue item is checked in and the loan discharged, the system should calculate any fines due, based on the parameters determined for the relevant categories of borrower and resource. Where borrowers have defaulted, staff may be free to override loan restrictions, but some libraries prefer to nominate staff authorised to do so (staff privilege levels are parameters that are left to individual libraries to determine).

Reservation of library resources

Reservations (holds) should be identifiable by searching on a variety of fields, preferably without leaving the reservations process. Normally, one would expect to be able to reserve all copies of a work, or specific copies only, such as copies at a particular branch library or campus. Where only one copy is required, the system should automatically cancel the trap once one loan has been discharged and the trap has been acknowledged. Libraries would also expect to be able to cancel reservations, fix expiry dates, maintain queues for heavily demanded material, and shorten loan periods to accommodate demand. Systems should also generate notices recalling material on loan and alerting borrowers when reservations are available. Some systems will alert staff if reservations are not collected within a specified period.

Maintenance of borrower files

Entry of borrower data is normally via a formatted screen (form filling), and should allow for amendments of specific fields or deletion of records. Normally data are keyed in manually, but some libraries have been able to obtain user files in machine-readable format: for instance, some academic libraries can access and transfer student data from the information systems of parent institutions. Here, as in much of this book, the importance of standards and protocols should be emphasised. In order to preserve the integrity and accuracy of the data that are to be transferred, a communication protocol called an Application Programming Interface (API) is often used (Kiochtanek & Matthews 2002, p. 48).

Given an appropriate level of parameterisation, libraries should be able to define their own borrower fields, because fields established by a vendor for one type of library may not be appropriate for another type of library. Most libraries require the ability to define borrower categories. This allows libraries to maintain different loans policies for different categories of user: for example, academic libraries may permit institutional users to borrow more items than community borrowers, and public libraries may have a policy not to charge overdue fines to junior members. There should be online access to borrower files, for example, via name or borrower number. Access to borrower data may be limited to certain staff by the use of passwords or staff privilege levels.

Some systems will provide reports on expired registrations (borrowers may be registered for specified periods, so that borrower files do not become full of inactive borrowers) or lists of inactive borrowers (those who have not borrowed material for a specified period).

Stocktaking

Some automated systems facilitate stocktaking. Staff can check what material is on the shelves, using a light-pen, a barcode reader and a portable unit to record the barcode numbers. Missing items can be found by loading these barcode numbers onto the main library management system and comparing them (something a computer is good at) against the barcode numbers for all items that are not on loan. A list of missing items will then be available for collection development purposes. Items may be recorded as missing until the library can assume that they are not going to turn up. After a specified period, missing items may be deleted from the holdings file and, in the case of last copies which are not to be replaced, the bibliographic file. If a dollar value can be put on missing items, regular stocktaking may provide library managers with justification for purchasing theft detection systems.

It is worth considering too the application of RFID technologies, discussed briefly above, for stocktaking purposes, because if individual items can be tagged then it is possible using a handheld device (incorporating a transceiver/decoder and antenna) to speed up the checking of stock on library shelves.

Down-time

Down-time is any period when the computer on which a system is based is not operating. This may be because of a serious hardware or software problem or simply because of power failure. For such cases, libraries require a back-up system. This may be manual, for example, the provision of transaction sheets on which staff write details of loans and returns (that is, borrower and item numbers), for later keying into the system. Many library management systems, however, provide automated back-up: for example, a portable unit that can store transaction data in machine-readable form until the main system is operating again. The data can then be uploaded to the main circulations control system in the correct sequence.

This should not be confused with another kind of back-up, which is the copying of data and software in case these are lost: for instance, from a magnetic hard disk to magnetic tape. This kind of back-up is not peculiar to circulations control subsystems and is discussed in more general terms in Chapter 5.

Management of special resources

Some library resources have special characteristics not catered for by the generic cataloguing, acquisition and circulation systems discussed so far. The following examples are described below:

- serial publications
- media collections
- inter-library loans
- reserve collections
- pictorial collections
- records or documentary material.

Serials control systems

Serials control is not much different from the three main library management subsystems described so far, since it incorporates the three functions of acquisitions, cataloguing and circulations. Nonetheless, it presents particular problems, which require unique features. Problems include the receipt of individual issues which may not arrive at regular intervals, the publication of irregular issues (for example, indexes), changes of publisher and even title, the need for extensive holdings data, binding requirements, and the need to renew subscriptions. Libraries have generally been slower to automate serials control than the preceding functions, which may seem strange given the importance of serials to academic and special libraries. This may be partly due to the relative complexity of serials control. Nevertheless, serials automation can save considerable clerical effort, particularly in the area of claims.

The main activities to be addressed by an automated serials control system are:

- record creation
- ordering and renewal of subscriptions
- receipt of issues and fund accounting
- claiming overdue or missing issues
- routing and circulation of issues
- administration of binding
- output of reports, letters, lists, etc.

Many of the features required of an automated serials control system duplicate features already mentioned. Systems will be expected to enable librarians to create original records. As with monographs, there are also opportunities to copy existing data. Some of the networks mentioned earlier can be used for copy cataloguing, and there are CD-ROM products to use for bibliographic checking, such as *Ulrich's Plus*. Where libraries use large subscription agents, such as EBSCO Subscription Services, Hills Library and Information Service or DA Information Services, there is also the option of accessing the agent's database.

Ordering procedures are similar to those for other kinds of material. Serials control systems are expected to generate orders in paper format, if necessary, or in electronic format. Supplier and fund files should be available, as for book ordering. The automatic generation of claims for late or missing issues, although problematic, can save a lot of time from the librarian's point of view. For the agents and publishers, however, it has meant increased workloads. It is desirable for library staff to record the frequency of issues, so that delivery patterns can be predicted. Systems are expected to enable library staff to identify late or missing issues and to add special issues (not necessarily predictable) to the holdings.

Serials control systems may also be expected to advise librarians when subscription renewals are due. Some systems can generate useful information to assist renewal decisions: for example, lists of titles arranged by subject or in decreasing order of price. Serials holdings data are extensive and complicated.

Where libraries lend serials, it will be necessary for systems to handle circulations. This generally involves the barcoding of items when required by users and creating a link between a barcode number and the appropriate holding. Another method of distributing serials is to create a routing list, that is, a list of people, departments and so on, to which they are to sent in order. Routing is used especially in commercial and industrial libraries and in the case of trade literature, such as publications of the book trade. In an automated system, the librarian/technician should be able to enter a routing list into a serial record.

When an issue of that serial is receipted, a routing slip will be generated, for attachment to the serial.

Another peculiarity of serials control systems is the need to bind some serials. Once frequency and number of issues per volume are entered into the system, it should prompt library staff once they have a run of serials ready for binding. Instructions to the binder (for example, colour of binding, spine lettering) may also be held on file and generated by the system when required.

Like acquisitions, serials control systems are expected to produce financial reports, summarising fund allocations, commitments, expenditures and balances. Automated systems produce a wealth of information compared to manual systems. The latter make production of information, increasingly required by library managers, a laborious process (see 'Management information systems', below).

Serials control systems are available both as stand-alone systems and as modules within generic library management systems.

Media management systems

Media management systems are designed specifically for media centres, which provide a high proportion of non-book materials and equipment, such as computers and videoplayers. Often media centre managers are responsible for presentation space, such as rooms adjoining the centre. Many of the functions of a media centre can be met using a generic library management system, but there are special needs, such as the ability to book rooms and equipment in advance. Like serials control systems, media management systems can be stand-alone systems or modules within generic library management systems. Features include:

- ability to describe items not generally described in generic cataloguing systems, such as equipment and presentation space
- bookings facility (not the same as reservations, because its purpose is to link borrowers and resources at a future specified date)
- ability to track equipment and items requiring repair and maintenance (similar to recording the fact that books are at binding)
- management of production projects, where the centre is involved in the creation of new items (for example, videos).

Inter-library loans systems

As mentioned in Chapter 2, library management systems can be expected to include a facility for control of inter-library loans, although many libraries continue to use manual inter-library loan systems long after automation of circulation systems. One of the reasons for not automating is that, for borrowing libraries, there is no bibliographic description of the loan items and it is time-consuming for staff to create a temporary record for a single loan. There is not the same problem for lending libraries, because they do have a bibliographic record to which to link a loans transaction, but, they do have to create a record for the borrowing library in the borrower file (as a corporate member). In addition, policies and procedures are also quite distinct from other loans (for example, requests for renewal may need to be made several days before the due date). Basic facilities of an inter-library loan system include:

- production of requests, increasingly in electronic form
- issue, renewal and discharge of inter-library loans (including items not on the bibliographic file)
- generation of overdue notices (perhaps at different intervals from those established for other loans and, typically, worded differently from notices sent to library members), and
- reporting of unsatisfied requests, prompting librarians to enquire about their status or to seek alternative sources.

One of the other features that might be looked for, or even required, in an inter-library loans system is the ability of users to request articles or books that they find during an online search via their libraries' inter-library loans departments, or even to send their own requests to the borrowing library (as distinct from filling in an online form for their own library). Whichever facility is provided, it would normally be expected that users would be able to keep track of their requests. Other features would include management of statistics and of copyright issues. Compliance with the International Standard Organisation's ILL Protocol (mentioned in the previous chapter) would generally be considered a mandatory feature.

Reserve collection systems

A reserve or short-loan collection in an academic library has special needs that may not be satisfied by any circulations control systems, most notably the varying loan periods. Other special needs include differing fines policies, the proportion of non-book and non-library resources circulated (for example, lecturers' photocopied articles) and the continually changing nature of the collection.

Generally, these needs are most effectively handled by a separate reserve collection module. Such a module can either operate as a stand-alone system or as a subsystem of an existing integrated library management system. As items are added to a reserve collection, staff enter into the system the course for which each item is reserved, the lecturer's name and the loan period.

Bear in mind, however, that many of the resources put in a reserve collection is part-work material such as journal articles and chapters out of books, and it is common practice for university libraries to develop e-reserve collections. Further, as more and more journals take the form of electronic subscriptions, the need for even e-reserve does tend to diminish (and, indeed, copyright restrictions may discourage further development of e-reserve collections).

Management of pictorial collections

Pictorial collections fall outside the kind of library material discussed up to this point, because so far the focus has been *published* information resources, which does not generally encompass pictorial collections (nor the organisational records discussed below). It is interesting, however, that the technological developments mentioned below, combined with web publishing, mean that the pictorial collections of national, state and other major libraries are effectively becoming published resources.

Pictorial collections present particular problems to librarians, principally providing physical access to collections that present storage and conservation problems and providing catalogue access to the collections. For many years, librarians have attempted to use computers to index pictorial collections using a variety of generic data management systems. Computers offer distinct advantages because descriptions of pictorial items are typically complex and a variety of access points is required, quite distinct from those available for published information resources. In describing pictorial items, librarians are performing a similar function to that performed by records managers, in that they typically have to create titles for items and in that their standard tools for subject description, such as Library of Congress Subject Headings, are not appropriate.

In recent years, it has been possible to go a step further and store images of pictorial items in electronic format. This has happened because of improvements in:

- imaging technologies – imaging refers to the scanning of documents and pictorial items and the conversion of the scanned image into a format that can be manipulated and stored using a computer-based system (a process discussed in Chapter 6.)
- compression techniques, which allow images to be stored in smaller files than before, and decompressed again with little loss of clarity
- storage media, particularly optical disks, such as compact disks.

With images available in electronic form, it becomes possible to link records in the computerised index to an image of the item to which the record refers. As suggested previously, this makes problems of user access and conservation of items more manageable. What is more, provided telecommunications systems can cope with the sheer volume of data, users need not even be in the library where the pictures are stored. It becomes possible for users, including other libraries, to access the pictorial collections of the major libraries.

So far, what has been discussed is the 'traditional' text-based approach to image retrieval. It is worth also being aware of 'content-based' approaches, which involve the use of special software and a computer algorithm to extract information about the colours, the textures and shapes used in an image and to store this information in an index. While this approach is currently limited (Lee 2001, pp.104-5), it is an area worth watching.

Records management systems

Why should library managers be interested in records management? This is a function traditionally conducted by a set of information professionals quite distinct from librarians. There are two reasons. First, there is the convergence of librarianship and records management within the information management function of some organisations, particularly in the corporate sector. Directors of organisations do not care where information comes from as long as it meets the criteria of timeliness, relevance, accuracy and so on. Second, library and information managers, like any other manager, need to manage their own documentary material: for example, manuals, publishers' and trade catalogues, bibliographies and correspondence.

Whereas a library management system controls the acquisition, organisation, retrieval, circulation and disposal of published information resources, a records management system is expected to control the creation, storage, retrieval, dissemination and disposal of the records created or received by an organisation in the course of its business. Like published information resources in a library, these records or documents may be in a variety of formats: print, audiovisual and electronic. The main functions of electronic records management systems are:

- storage and retrieval of files/documents in electronic format, for example, word processed material produced internally and electronic correspondence, and

- the indexing of records not held in electronic format, for example, paper or microform files.

The latter function is similar to the cataloguing of library resources, in that a surrogate record is created on computer file. The surrogate record will contain fields similar to those in a library catalogue, such as title, subject descriptors and classification number (the last is used to locate the item to which the surrogate record refers). One difference is that the records manager will generally have to give the item a title, whereas titles are normally already given in the library environment (except for resources such as images). As in librarianship, subject descriptors are often taken from a controlled indexing language in the form of a thesaurus – as distinct from a subject heading list – ensuring vocabulary control.

Many commercial records management systems include as part of the system an image scanner, of the kind previously mentioned. As imaging, storage and optical disk technologies improve, it becomes increasingly viable for an organisation to scan those records not held in computer-readable form and store them as a series of images. Like the original documents, these images will need to be indexed, since a page of text stored as an image is not in itself retrievable.

Like library management systems, records management systems are available as prewritten, commercial packages, which can be parameterised for local use: for example, records managers can establish disposal schedules which determine the periods that certain classes of record are retained. Some of the text retrieval systems discussed in the next chapter, particularly those designed for the corporate sector, provide library management systems and records management systems as add-on modules.

Management information systems (MIS)

Many of the systems and subsystems described so far in this chapter are examples of data processing systems. They are sources of large amounts of transaction data, much of these data providing useful operational information for library staff: for instance, data on expired registrations, overdue items, missing items, items on recall, outstanding requests, orders not received within specified periods, desiderata files, subscriptions due for renewal, titles ready for binding, and missing serials issues. Data processing systems also generate *management information*, which is quite distinct from the above operational information. Operational information is used in day-to-day library work, whereas management information can be used to help evaluate library performance. The place of management information in the management process can be seen by considering the following breakdown of the management function:

- planning, that is, the establishment of the main goals of an organisation, analysis of means of achieving them and making decisions that facilitate their achievement
- organisation, which is the acquisition and use of resources such as people, finance, buildings, stock and equipment
- direction, which is concerned with winning staff commitment to organisational goals and encouraging a motivated workforce
- control, which is the measurement of performance, the comparison of performance with organisational objectives, and the modification of work practices in order to ensure future achievement of objectives – this should not be confused with controls, plural, such as circulation controls.

Management information systems support the control function. There are many definitions of management information system in the literature, but here it is taken to be a system that provides regular, predefined information that helps a manager to measure organisational performance. It may be helpful to think in terms of a feedback loop in which data generated by a management information system are compared to performance measures to become management information. The data provided may be routine summary reports, such as totals and averages of predetermined sets of transactions (for example, loans figures over a specified period), or exception reports on individual transactions that exceed specified standards (for example, items issued more than a specified number of times in a specified period).

Management information systems have generally been developed as a by-product of the development of data processing systems. Indeed, one of the complaints about them is that they have been technology-driven (in other words, so-called management information is supplied simply because it *can* be supplied) rather than management-driven. That particular issue is beyond the scope of this chapter, but it is worth bearing in mind.

Most of the management information generated by library management systems is of a statistical nature. It is obtained by cumulating numerical data relating to stock and borrowers. The data can be a straightforward count of loans made in a specified period, or they can be more complex, for example, loans analysed by category of borrower or by classification number. Here it is worth noting, however, that statistics, as such, are raw data which are of no value unless they can be analysed in some way: for example,

- as a ratio, such as the ratio of loans figures to figures for loanable stock, which could be used to compare different parts of a collection
- as part of a time series comparison, such as a comparison of this year's loans figures with previous years' loans figures
- as part of a comparison with external standards, such as loans figures for libraries of a similar size (bearing in mind that this is a crude comparison, which does not take into account different user communities and information needs).

Not all management information consists of statistical reports. Other kinds include:

- lists: for example, the lists of new catalogue and authority file records mentioned in the last chapter constitute a means by which head cataloguers can check work that has been performed against standards such as the Anglo-American Cataloguing Rules
- exception reports: for example, generating a report on reservations queues longer than a specified figure may tell the collection manager something about the adequacy of collection development.

Collection evaluation

Most of the data generated by library management information systems are used for collection evaluation. This is not surprising since most of the data comes from the circulations control subsystem, which records and controls movement of a library's collection. The library manager can use a range of statistical and other information to help evaluate the effectiveness of a collection development policy and procedures. Measures and indicators include:

- loans figures for new stock, which may indicate problems in recent purchasing policies
- loans figures by call number ranges or by user's main field of study/research
- loans figures by borrower category
- loans figures by material types (here time series comparisons would be instructive)
- loans figures as a ratio of stock figures (as above)
- loans figures by call number ranges as a ratio of stock figures for the same call number ranges
- reservations and inter-library loans requests figures (high figures implying inadequate acquisitions)
- reservations and inter-library loans requests figures by call number or by user's main field of study/research (subject areas with high requests would seem to require special development)

- lists of reservations queues that are longer than a specified figure (may suggest that not enough copies have been purchased)
- items issued more than a specified number of times in a specified period (again, this may imply inadequate acquisition of these titles).

One of the advantages of computerised management information over non-computerised systems is that they can generate analysed information of the kind above (for example, loans figures analysed by call number range). Analysed statistics can often tell collection managers more than raw figures, for instance, loans figures analysed by call number range and user's main area of study/research may tell a collection manager something about cross-disciplinary use of library material and may prompt a future reallocation of funds. Raw loans figures, on the other hand, can indicate little unless they form part of a time series or an inter-library comparison, and even in those cases their value is limited.

Deselection of information resources ('weeding' collections)

Although the final decision to discard or otherwise dispose of an item is normally made by a librarian, computers can assist the decision-making process. The reports required to assist weeding are generally on-demand reports and consist of lists or analysed statistics. These include:

- lists of items never issued on the automated system or not circulating in a specified period ('dusty book' lists)
- lists of items loaned less than a specified number of times in a specified period
- lists of items by date of publication (or those items with publication dates earlier than a specified year)
- lists of items by call number range and by date of publication
- loans figures by date of publication or by call number range and by date of publication.

The reason for wanting to know about call number ranges is that some subjects (for example, science and technology) may date more quickly than others. Obviously there is no substitute for knowing the library's user groups and their needs, but having a quantitative method for assessing collection activity can assist collection managers not just to weed collections, but also to evaluate policies and procedures.

Other management information

Other than collection evaluation, the areas addressed by library management information systems include:

- effectiveness of management decisions, for example, policies and procedures
- staff performance
- vendor performance, and
- effectiveness of specific services, for example, user education programs.

Figure 4.5 (Ferguson & Whitelaw 1992, pp.188-9) summarises some of the management information that can be obtained from a library management information system. It shows, in the left hand column, a set of management objectives and, on the right, some corresponding performance measures and performance indicators. It is worth pointing out that the proper approach to management information would be to define management information needs first and then examine means of satisfying these needs. In practice, library managers generally investigate what information can be obtained from a commercial management information system and then ask what use this might be. This experimental approach has been the one taken here.

Objectives	Performance measures/indicators
Effective staffing levels	Acceptable number of transactions by time period or by terminal
Efficient work flows	Acceptable number of transactions (for example, serials check-ins) by terminal or staff i.d.
Effective loans policy and procedures	No renewals or overdues Average period items are on loan is the same as the library's loan period
Effective user education program	Acceptable level of use of particular facilities (for example, reservations) by specified categories of users No unsuccessful keyword searches or syntax errors in use of OPAC
Effective inter-library loans service	All inter-library loans requests satisfied
Efficient and competitive service from vendors	Comparison of claims and discounts

Figure 4.5: Library management information systems: performance measures and indicators

The distinction between measures and indicators is taken to be that a measure is precise and quantifiable whereas an indicator is merely suggestive. If all inter-library loans requests are satisfied, that is an unambiguous measure of the effectiveness of the inter-library loans service. If, however, students make little use of the reservations service, does this mean that the level of stock is adequate or that the library should put more emphasis on the reservations service in its user education program? The management information generated by the automated system (for example, low number of reservations from student users) is *indicative* of something, but it is not a clear performance measure. It merely suggests an area for possible management action.

It is also worth noting that even although information is available, the library manager may elect not to use it. Monitoring staff performance, for example, could arouse fears of an electronic sweatshop and have a demotivating effect on staff. The management paradigm outlined earlier included, *as a key management function*, winning staff commitment to organisational goals.

Finally, there is evidence to suggest that, in terms of automation objectives, management information systems are not regarded as particularly important by library managers. This is despite the increased demand for accountability over the years, which has prompted many library managers to make use of performance measures. The lack of priority given to management information systems may be partly because the management information generated by an automated system offers managers only part of the story. It is no substitute for other, less convenient ways of gathering management information, for example, user surveys. Another reason for the lack of priority given to management information systems may be that, in older library management systems, much of the information is difficult to extract without the requisite level of technical knowledge. Commercial library management systems have been transaction-orientated and geared towards finding data on particular borrowers and particular items. Nonetheless, in the case of the newer systems, management information systems, like online catalogues, have grown much more user-friendly in the recent years.

Decision support systems (DSS)

Decision support systems are sometimes confused with management information systems, but they are quite distinct. Whereas the latter provide predefined information to the manager, decision support systems (DSS) are used by the manager to predict actions based on a formal model of the organisation. There are various definitions in the literature. Indeed, the literature of the mid-1980s tended to use the terms 'management information system' and 'decision support system' interchangeably. Here the distinction between the terms is taken to be that whereas management information systems provide information, the manager uses a decision support system to manipulate information. Spreadsheet packages are typical decision support tools in a library environment, used to explore 'what if' scenarios, for example, 'If the library cuts its printed serials budget by 10% over the next year, what would be the likely effect on document delivery services?'

Decision support systems are less structured than management information systems, and are based on a more or less formal model of the organisation and its relationship with its environment. The model may be a simple 'what if' spreadsheet analysis of a budget or a more sophisticated model such as resource scheduling. Whereas data for a management information system are drawn mainly from internal sources (typically a data processing or 'transaction-oriented' system), a decision support system will draw its data from internal sources, such as data processing systems or management information systems, but also from external sources, such as user surveys.

Executive information systems

There is a further computer-based information system worth mentioning here: executive information systems. These are often mentioned in the literature on information management in the business and financial sectors. In the business environment a distinction is made between management information systems, which provide routine feedback on current policies, and executive information systems, which provide less structured, irregular information to help senior management to formulate new policy. Executive information systems answer such questions as: 'What are our competitors doing?' and 'What should we be doing?' In the library environment, marketing information might be said to fall into this category. (In the broader information management environment this kind of enquiry is closely related to environmental scanning.)

Another example is the deliberate varying of system parameters to see if a change of policy or procedures could result in the more effective achievement of objectives. Earlier it was stated that many commercial vendors of library management systems leave parameters (variable values, such as loan periods) for library managers to define. This does give managers the opportunity to change parameters and so test existing policies and procedures: for example, the periods at which overdue notices are sent could be varied. Delaying the dispatch of overdue notices might produce the same end result with lower postal charges (because more loans might be returned before notices are generated). Similarly, loan entitlements (quotas) could be varied and the results monitored. Arguably, this testing of policies and procedures could be seen as the application of an executive information system in the library environment.

Library management systems and the electronic library

This chapter focused on the basic functions of any library management system, such as cataloguing, acquisitions and circulations control. What is defined as a basic function, however, changes as the vendors of computerised library management systems vie with each other for market share. Serials control subsystems, once regarded by many systems librarians and software developers as too problematic, are now a common feature; management information systems provide a range of management reports; and several systems now include media management modules. The fact that many library management systems are modular makes it possible for librarians to add modules to their systems either as they become available or as funds become available. Whether the additional modules come from the same vendor or whether some 'mixing and matching' is possible depends on the degree to which 'open systems' are provided for (see Chapter 6). Some vendors, for instance, provide a module that offers full-text indexing of documents, but at the present time it is not a common feature.

In a library management systems conference in 2000, Marshall Breeding characterised the LMS market as follows:

- It is generally mature.
- It exhibits rich features for basic operations (e.g., cataloging, circulation control, online catalogs).
- The majority of installed systems are older "legacy systems."
- Newer installations are based on distributed network technologies and are predominantly Web-based in their approach to user-interface design.
- Serials and acquisitions subsystems are the most complex and the last to be completed (Kochtanek & Matthews 2002, pp. 15-16).

It is worth recalling the point made in the last chapter, that online catalogues are increasingly seen as gateways to electronic information resources and information retrieval tools beyond the library. At library technology exhibitions, vendors are keen to claim that their library management systems can provide 'seamless' access to these external resources. Although this chapter has concentrated on everyday library operations, it is worth remembering that library management systems are part of an increasingly interconnected electronic library environment that also includes commercial databases, web-based resources, digital collections and electronic publications. Issues such as Z39.50 compliance (mentioned in passing in the previous chapter, and to be discussed in Chapter 7) have been addressed by the vendors of LMS. It would be fair to say that Z39.50 has been implemented in most of their systems, but librarians need to be aware that not all systems keep pace with developments in the standard.

Vendors will talk about open systems interconnection, portability of systems, interoperability and Z39.50 compliance. The next three chapters are intended to introduce the systems, technologies, networks and standards underlying the applications that have been discussed up to here.

References

Ferguson, S & Whitelaw, M 1992, 'Computerised management information systems in libraries', *Australian Library Journal*, vol. 41, pp.184-198.

Kochtanek, TR & Matthews, JR 2002, *Library information systems: From library automation to distributed information access solutions*. Libraries Unlimited, Westport, CT.

Lee, SD 2001, *Digital imaging: A practical handbook*. Library Association Publishing, London.

Review questions

1. Explain the point of parameters in library management systems.
2. Outline the main features of a cataloguing subsystem.
3. Give examples of parameterisation available in cataloguing subsystems.
4. Describe two meanings of authority file in the context of library management systems.
5. Outline the main features of an acquisitions subsystem.
6. Explain a default in data entry and give an example from acquisitions.
7. List the data files that need to be set up before a basic library management system becomes operational.
8. Give examples of the parameters that need to be established for a circulation control subsystem.
9. Suggest the provisions that can be made for down-time in a circulations department.
10. Distinguish between transaction information used for operational purposes and management information.

Further resources

Computers in libraries (annual conference). Proceedings published by Information Today: Medford, NJ.
   These conferences are held in the US and therefore reflect the North American market. Nonetheless, those interested in keeping up to date with developments in library management systems should make a point of seeing the conference proceedings (if not attending the conferences). The 1997 conference focused on the World Wide Web and the Internet, and provided examples of how library management systems are becoming gateways to the Web.

Kochtanek, T R & Matthews, J R 2002, *Library information systems: From library automation to distributed information access solutions*. Libraries Unlimited, Westport, CT, 2002.
   This is referred to several times in this book – not without reason, because it is very much worth reading.

Osborne, A, *Library Automation pages: List of library automated systems and vendors*, <http://www.libinfo.com/vendors-systems.html>.
   Andrew Osborne's *Library Automation* pages contain a (generally) useful set of links to system vendors. His website contains other relevant pages, including knowledge management, Internet marketing, search tools and useful books for librarians.

Victorian Association for Library Automation (http://www.vala.org.au/).
   VALA runs a biennial conference, each of which focuses on a specific aspect of library automation. Again, if you can't attend, the proceedings are well worth obtaining. If you can attend, there is a large exhibition with leading library management systems on display.

CHAPTER 5
Generic data management software

The last chapter focused on library management systems, which automate the everyday work of librarians, such as cataloguing, circulations and acquisitions. In this chapter, the focus is on generic computer software that is used for data management. The two main types of software discussed are text retrieval systems and database management systems. Text retrieval systems have been mentioned already as a means of searching online hosts such as Dialog and CD-ROMs. Database management systems represent a radically different approach to data management and, since they form the basis of some leading commercial library management systems, are discussed in some detail. The chapter also includes an examination of two special solutions to text retrieval problems (both referred to in earlier chapters), hypertext and expert systems, and a brief discussion of personal bibliographic software. It concludes with an outline of the main facilities of spreadsheet software, which is used primarily for the management of numerical data.

Learning objectives

At the end of this chapter, you will be able to:

- outline the main generic software packages used to manage data in libraries
- contrast the features of text retrieval systems with those of database management systems, and
- describe the main features of expert systems, hypertext, personal bibliographic and spreadsheet software.

Keywords

Text retrieval system
Inverted file index
Postings file
Database management system
Relational model
Query language
Data dictionary
Back-up
Normalisation

Hypertext
Node
Stack
Expert system
Knowledge base
Inference engine
Personal bibliographic software
Spreadsheet
Macro programming

Text retrieval systems

The term 'text retrieval system' is used here in preference to a number of other terms, such as 'information retrieval system' (a term often used in reference work to describe commercial host systems) or 'information management system' (often used in the organisational context to describe an inhouse system). 'Text retrieval system' is used, first, because it is a more generic term (describing both host and inhouse systems) and, second, because text retrieval is a most apt description of what this type of system actually does. Its main function is to enable the user to locate occurrences of specified text within a document or a file, such as the keywords input in a boolean search of an online database or a web resource.

It is worth noting that text retrieval systems focus on retrieval rather than on the manipulation of data. The latter is an important feature of database management systems and is a requirement of the library management systems described in Chapter 4: for example, circulation and acquisitions functions. Libraries generally require systems that will both retrieve text and manipulate data. Once both text retrieval and database management systems have been examined, the distinction between the two will be discussed.

Types of text retrieval system

The main text retrieval systems to consider fall into one of three main categories:

- structured text retrieval systems, such as the system used to search online hosts like Dialog
- unstructured text retrieval systems
- image retrieval systems, that store images of documents in machine-readable form and link these to index files containing surrogate records.

Structured text retrieval systems

The 'structure' referred to here is the file structure discussed in earlier chapters, in which computer files (such as files stored on online hosts or reference-type CD-ROMs) are organised into individual records, each record describing an information resource (for example, a monograph or a journal article) and each record consisting of fields, in this case, specific elements of bibliographic data, such as author, title and abstract. Such records are sometimes described as surrogates, because they only represent the resources to which they refer. It is worth remembering, however, that the full-text commercial databases described in Chapter 2 will also be structured, and differ from bibliographic files only in having fields containing the text of the documents to which the bibliographic data refer.

Structured text retrieval systems are well known to librarians through the use of large-scale commercial products, but they are also used by many small libraries to store and retrieve their bibliographic data. Some inhouse systems use essentially the same retrieval software as the large-scale systems, for example, the BRS/Search software package used in some special libraries. Some of these systems are also used in archives and records management.

Unstructured text retrieval systems

As the name suggests, unstructured text retrieval systems are those which, unlike the systems just described, do not organise data into records and fields. These are used to search the full text of documents that have been stored in electronic format, such as word processed documents that have been created internally by an organisation or that have been transmitted electronically from another organisation. Typical applications fall into the records management area in the corporate sector: for example, the storage and retrieval of medical, legal, personnel and financial records.

Image retrieval systems

Like both systems above, these can store the full text of documents, but the documents in this case are stored as images, not as retrievable text. Pages from documents are scanned using special image scanning equipment (see the next chapter) and are stored in exactly the same way as, say, a page of graphics. This means that documents cannot be retrieved by searching for text in the documents (unless a further process is undertaken – see the account of optical character recognition in the following chapter). When the documents are scanned, they must also be indexed in the same way that paper-based or microform documents are indexed. In other words, a surrogate record is created for each document. The surrogate record may contain data elements such as titles, names, dates, classification codes and subject descriptors, similar to the data elements that appear in a library catalogue.

Like the unstructured text retrieval systems, applications are generally of more interest to the records manager than to the library manager. Nonetheless, image retrieval may be of interest to libraries that need to store specific kinds of document on a computer system: for example, a press clippings file, original manuscripts, departmental and organisational memos or (in the case of an academic library) educational and research documents. Note also that, following records management practice, 'document' may also refer to non-textual resources: for example, large pictorial collections, such as those in national and state libraries, may be scanned and stored on a high-capacity storage medium, typically an optical disk of some kind (see Chapter 6).

File structure

Since most of the text retrieval systems used by librarians are structured, they form the focus of the following sections. First, what are the main features of a structured text retrieval system? It was suggested above that in a structured system, computer files are organised into discrete (separate) records, each of which in turn can be subdivided into fields. In an earlier chapter, the relationship among files, records and fields was represented by a matrix, in which each row represented a record (for example, a bibliographic record), each column represented a field or data element (for example, author) and each cell in the matrix contained a single datum (for example, 1998). Contrast this with an unstructured system, in which a document may be stored as a single field.

The size of fields can vary considerably. There are two basic ways that systems can handle fields of variable lengths:

- force data into fields of fixed length
- allow for variable length fields.

Fixed length fields have two main disadvantages: (1) what to do with data that do not fit into a field of specified length, and (2) the waste of space, when data do not fill the space allocated to them in a fixed length field. As a general rule (for which one can always find exceptions), text retrieval systems allow for variable length fields, while fixed length fields are more typical of the database management systems discussed later.

Where fields are not of a fixed length, the system must have some way of knowing when a field finishes. There are two main strategies for indicating where a field begins and ends:

- use a field terminator, or
- indicate the length of each field, for example, at the start of each field or in a directory at the start of the record.

A significant feature of bibliographic files is that some bibliographic elements, such as author and subject, are repeated. Does this necessitate repeating fields? In the case of database management systems, where there is more emphasis on manipulation of data and greater use of fixed length fields, fields may be repeated, for example:

> SU 1   Libraries - Automation
> SU 2   Information storage and retrieval systems

In a text retrieval system, which generally uses variable length fields, however, the repeating elements are generally contained in the one field, for example:

> SU   Libraries - Automation; Information storage and retrieval systems

The repeating elements are separated by use of a terminator (in this case a semicolon has been used).

Features of a structured text retrieval system

The structured text retrieval systems described in Chapter 2 were expected to provide the following search and retrieval facilities:

For the user:

- free text search across all or most fields
- search under specific fields, such as title, author, subject or notes
- search for words (keywords) or phrases (for example, author's names)
- use of Boolean search operators (AND, OR, NOT) to narrow or broaden a search
- use of proximity operators to narrow a search (by paragraph, sentence, and so on)

- building of sets of records, for further search refinement (for instance, searching for the 'overlap' between two sets of search results, resulting in a third and, one hopes, smaller set of results)
- truncation of search terms
- display of index terms
- use of a thesaurus to explore controlled vocabulary.

For the database creator:

- specification of words that are not to be retrievable (stop words)
- specification of fields not required for retrieval
- specification of fields that are to be word-indexed or phrase-indexed or both.

The text retrieval engine

How then does a text retrieval system retrieve text? The text retrieval software generally arranges records in the order in which they are added to the file, that is, in a sequential arrangement. To retrieve records, the system could search sequentially through the entire file for the text entered by the user. For a small file this might be tolerable, but for the files required by most libraries, retrieval speeds would be too slow. Users would not have the patience to wait for the results of a search.

In Chapter 2, it was suggested that a text retrieval system will generate an *index* to the main file or bibliographic file. The index will consist of a list of terms from the main file (words and phrases) that are considered worthwhile for retrieval (including all separate terms with the exception of the stop words). The system automatically amends the index as new terms are added to the main file. It is up to the person(s) creating the database to establish the parameters within which the system extracts terms: for example, which fields or subfields are to be indexed. The establishment of these parameters represents an important set of editorial decisions to be made by the database creator. When a library is implementing a text retrieval system to handle its bibliographic needs, it needs to consider carefully not just what fields to include in its bibliographic records, but which fields will contain retrievable text. The more terms that are indexed, the more storage capacity that is required of the system. Some libraries may need to take this into account when planning their hardware needs. It is worth noting, however, that as computer hardware improves in speed, storage and processing capabilities, questions of storage become less significant.

The most common type of index used in text retrieval systems in libraries – at present – is the inverted file index (also sometimes called a dictionary file or alphabetic index). In an inverted file index, the index terms are linked to the records in which they occur, so that when a match is made (that is, the user's search term matches a term in the index), the user is led to the corresponding records.

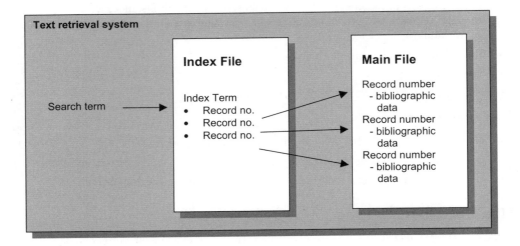

Figure 5.1: Inverted file index

In practice, the system might use an intermediate file (sometimes referred to as a postings file) to link the index file and the main file. As above, the system would first search the index file to find a match with the user's search term. The index file will contain links to the postings file, in the form of postings file numbers. The postings file will alert the user to how many postings (that is, matches) there are, and in turn will contain links to the main file, in the form of record numbers. Should the user want to view the set of records that has been identified, the system displays the required bibliographic data from the main file. The relationships can be represented like this:

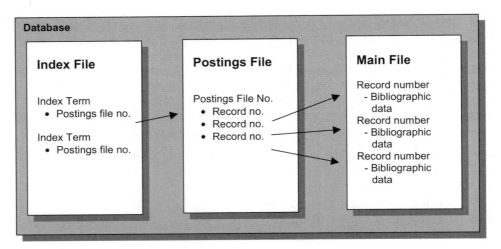

Figure 5.2: Use of a postings file

The way in which the index file is organised determines how fast the system will match the search terms entered by a user with the terms in the index. One technique is to sort the index terms in alphabetical order and conduct a binary search. In a binary search, the system compares the search term with a term in the middle of the index list. The comparison will tell it which half of the file contains the term for which it is searching. It then finds a term halfway through that sequence and compares it with the search term. Clearly, binary searching will find a match more quickly than a sequential search, but there are problems:

- the need to access the index file several times in the case of a large file
- the expense of keeping a file sorted, and
- the need to re-sort files periodically, which is time-consuming for large files.

Other means of improving search times include dividing indexes into pages and the design of so-called B-trees.

Database management systems (DBMS) *Relational*

The other main computerised system used in libraries is the database management system. Earlier it was suggested that libraries which place a high priority on data manipulation will tend to use database management systems. What does this mean? How does a database management system differ from a text retrieval system?

What is a database management system?

A database, it was suggested earlier, is a collection of related computer files. In reference libraries, the term 'database' describes the host system on which one or more computer files are mounted. In the case of a library management system, 'database' refers to a collection of related files, such as bibliographic file, borrower file, order file and supplier file. A database management system is a type of computer software that manages not just the database itself, but also handles enquiries from users and the computer hardware on which the software and data are mounted.

Database management systems were developed out of the file management systems (file managers) of the 1960s. To facilitate understanding of the strengths of database management systems, it would help to consider the features and limitations of a simple file management system.

A file management system or file manager is used to process only one file. The facilities provided by file management systems include: file creation (for example, determination of field names and field sizes); data input; amendment of data; retrieval of records, using the search techniques discussed already (for example, keyword and phrase searching, Boolean and proximity operators, truncation); sorting of records, for example, into alphabetical order; display of search results; and printing of search results.

What are the limitations of a simple file management system? From the library viewpoint, the main limitation is the duplication of data common to separate files. The most obvious example is bibliographic data, which may be common to cataloguing, acquisitions and circulations subsystems. Where manual systems are used, duplication of data is inevitable. When an order for material is created, bibliographic data are likely to be used at least twice: once in the order sent to the supplier and once in the record retained by the acquisitions department. When the material arrives, another record is made by the cataloguing department. For circulations purposes, another record is made: for example, a book-card. (In some manual systems, even the long-suffering user was required to create a short bibliographic record at the point of issue.) With a computerised system, there is little point in reproducing this data duplication by creating separate files for each of these library functions. Disadvantages of discrete files include:

- time spent entering the data (for example, bibliographic data) is multiplied, which adds to costs
- there is unnecessary and undesirable duplication of storage
- when data are amended, there is further duplication of effort
- if data have to be amended in different files, there is an increased chance of errors
- information cannot be shared across separate files: for example, a user cannot tell whether a book is on the shelves by accessing the catalogue, and it is difficult for the library manager to combine data from different files to obtain management information.

Database management systems were developed to overcome the perceived limitations of file management systems. Before considering the features of a database management system in more detail, it might be instructive to summarise the main ones:

- data are stored only once instead of being repeated in different files, thus reducing data redundancy
- records in different files are related, so that all data on a particular item or topic can be retrieved: for example, the status of a bibliographic item (on loan, on order) can be displayed on an online catalogue as well as the bibliographic description
- library managers can retrieve data from one or more files using a *relatively* simple query language
- the user does not have to worry about how data are stored and accessed by the system (see below)
- retrieval speeds are adequate for online user enquiries
- the system can allow for fast insertion, amendment and deletion of records and changes in data structure
- access can be limited to authorised users: where computer files are being shared by different types of user (for example, staff and end-users), the question of security and privacy becomes important, and
- the integrity of data files will be protected in the event of problems such as power failure.

Features of a database management system

The main components in a database management system are:

- the database itself, the hardware component that contains all the data elements
- the applications software, which allows the user to retrieve and manipulate data from the database
- a further software component that acts as an interface between the applications software and the actual database
- a data dictionary, which stores definitions of data elements and data characteristics.

The database is the component that physically stores the data. The data in their physical form are stored on a hardware device, such as a magnetic hard disk (see the next chapter). For the user to be able to retrieve and manipulate data, applications software is required: that is, a kind of software that allows the user to carry out a specific function, such as retrieval. (The library management systems described in the last chapter represent another kind of applications software.) The second software component is an example of systems software (also discussed in the next chapter). This interprets instructions from the applications software and controls the hardware, such as the storage device. Finally, the data dictionary records the parameters within which the system operates (see below).

Logical and physical schema

The user need not worry how the data are stored on the database (the actual storage device) or how they are accessed. What the user sees is a logical schema quite distinct from the physical schema that defines the physical organisation of data on the storage device. The physical organisation of the data on the database is handled by the system software mentioned above. The system software insulates the user from the physical schema. In a library management system, for example, it appears to the user as if there are separate bibliographic, order and loans records. In the physical schema, however, these data are not held on the storage device as three separate packages. The data that appear to the user to form a record may be stored all over the database and are assembled by the database management system as required (see 'Types of database management system' below). While the physical schema is concerned with how the data are physically organised, the logical schema is concerned with what the database looks like from the user's perspective.

Moreover, many users will only need to see part of the database: for instance, a library user should see the bibliographic file and certain other data such as order dates for items on order and due dates for items on loan, but should not see the names of the people to whom items have been loaned. For this reason, subschemas are written into a database management system, limiting certain users to specific types of data.

Query languages

One of the characteristic features of database management system is a query language, used to access, manipulate and retrieve data from the database. Computer languages are discussed in the following chapter. Here it is worth noting that query languages look a bit like natural language. Take, for example, the following query written in a language called ACCESS (offered by system software called PICK, which supports library management software such as URICA and Dynix):

SORT STAFF BY DEPT BY NAME DEPT DEPTDESC NAME

The instruction is to some extent self-explanatory. It asks the system to sort staff by two elements (by department and by name) and then specifies the data that are to be displayed in the report (that is, department, department description and name). Note the significance for the production of management information. The library manager need not rely solely on regular predefined reports (such as loans statistics) for management support, but can generate customised management reports on demand.

Query languages are generally system-specific, but there is some industry standardisation; for example, a large number of database management systems support SQL (Structured Query Language), which is a standard of the International Standards Organisation (ISO).

Data dictionaries

A data dictionary is at the heart of any database management system. The data dictionary contains important information, such as what files are in the database and descriptions (called attributes) of the data contained in the files. This information is used by the system to assess whether or not a particular process can be accomplished and whether or not a particular user is authorised to carry it out. Information stored in the data dictionary could normally be expected to include:

- what data are available
- where on the storage device they are located
- data attributes (for instance, data type numerical or alphanumerical)
- how the data are used
- definitions of data security requirements (who is allowed to access the data, who is allowed to update/amend them)
- relationships to other pieces of data
- definitions of data integrity requirements.

Security

Note the need to define data security requirements. It is necessary to protect data from unauthorised use. In the library environment, it is generally considered unsatisfactory if library users cannot conduct their own searches. It is important, however, that users can access data and generate reports (for example, printed lists of bibliographic references) without being able to amend data or delete records. The need for security is increased in a database management system, because of the sharing of data and the added risk of unauthorised use (for example, one library user accessing another member's borrower or loans data). Note too the need to define different levels of staff 'privilege', because not all staff will be authorised to amend data (for example, fines data) or delete records.

Back-up facility

Creation of a database is a considerable investment, not only in terms of the hardware and the software required but also in terms of data input: for example, purchase or keying-in of bibliographic data or the keying-in of unique data such as community information. Most libraries also hold large amounts of transaction data: for instance, circulations data. It is important, therefore, to protect data from accidental loss. Copies of data files must be kept regularly. These copies or back-ups are generally made on a magnetic storage medium (see the next chapter), such as tape or diskette. Ideally, they should be stored in a location separate from the computer system itself (for example, in a fire-proof safe or a separate building) along with a copy of the system software, so that if the computer system is destroyed (for example, by fire) data and programs can be recovered.

Two of the key features of database management systems mentioned earlier were:

- the ability to store data only once, reducing data redundancy, and
- the linking of related data.

How are these achieved? The next section attempts to answer this.

Types of database management system

The logical schema that the user sees depends on the type of database management system. The basic models are:

- hierarchical
- network
- relational
- object-oriented.

The object-oriented model is the newest of the four. A fifth model, worth adding for the sake of completeness, is one that combines object-oriented and relational principles. What are the features of these models?

The hierarchical and network models are the oldest and have all but disappeared, so there is no point in considering them in any detail. The problems associated with these models, however, throw some light on the relational model, which is (currently!) the most common one in the library environment.

In a hierarchical model, the user sees data displayed in a tree-like structure. Data elements are organised into record segments, with segments linked to other segments in a parent-child, one-to-many relationship. There are problems with this model where a user wishes to manipulate or retrieve data in a way not allowed for when the database was established: for example, it takes considerable effort to relate record segments in different branches of the structure.

The network model overcame some of the limitations of the hierarchical model by establishing relations between record segments in different branches of the hierarchy. It is a more flexible model than the hierarchical one, but the user is still limited to retrieving data that can be accessed using established links. Note that these hierarchical and network structures are *logical* ones (see 'Logical and physical schema' above) – data are not physically stored in this way. Linkage of record segments to their related segments is achieved by the use of *embedded pointers*. An embedded pointer is a data element that is part of each record segment in the physical storage device, directing the system from one record segment to related segments. The fact that these models are limited to those relationships determined by previously established pointers means that data manipulation is correspondingly limited. Consider the implications for the management information systems discussed in the last chapter.

Relational database management systems

Relational database management systems are much more flexible then the two earlier models. Two important features are that:

- data are organised in small data structures called relations or tables
- relations or tables are linked using the data themselves (not embedded pointers).

Consider first the data structures. In the relational model, data are organised in small data structures called tables or relations. In a circulations control subsystem, for example, the following relations might be formed:

Borrower relation:	Borrower number, borrower name, borrower address and so on
Bibliographic relation:	Bibliographic record number, title, author, ISBN and so on
Holdings relation:	Bibliographic record number, item (copy) number, call number and so on
Loans relation:	Borrower number, item number, transaction data (for example, due date).

Figure 5.3: Sample data structures in the relational model

Note that in a non-relational database these relations might be called files. These particular relations are given simply for illustration. In practice, they may be broken down into still smaller data structures (for example, the bibliographic relation may be considered too large). The process of producing these data structures is called *normalisation*. The main purpose of normalisation is to reduce data redundancy. The process of normalisation should ensure that data insertions, amendments and deletions can be made without undesirable consequences, such as losing borrower and bibliographic data when a loan transaction is deleted.

The relational model differs from the other two models in not making use of embedded pointers. The links between two relations are found in the data themselves: for example, the bibliographic relation (above) is linked to the holdings relation through a common data element, a system generated bibliographic record number. Similarly, the loans relation has data elements linking it to the holdings and borrower relations (item and borrower numbers). These common, linking elements are referred to as *identifiers* or *keys*. This makes the relational model more flexible than the earlier models. From the management point of view, the advantages are significant. Because of the ability to link relations through the data themselves, the user (here the library manager, not the library user) can construct and manipulate a wide variety of data sets and extract the data as useful management information: for instance, link the accession dates of books with transaction data for the same books to tell what percentage of new books are actually being borrowed.

The point discussed earlier about the avoidance of data redundancy should be clearer. Even though there are multiple copies of a resource, that copy-specific information will be recorded separately from the bibliographic information, in the holdings relation – the bibliographic information common to all copies appears once in a separate, bibliographic, relation, with links between the two relations via a unique identifier, such as ISBN or a system-generated bibliographic record number. What the library user sees on the online catalogue (bibliographic and holdings information) looks as if it is all stored together as one record but, again, that is the logical schema that the user is seeing. Similarly, there are likely to be separate authority relations for the storage of authoritative versions of specific data elements such as personal and corporate names. These authoritative versions are therefore stored only once, with links to the bibliographic records in which they occur.

Another feature of relational systems, worth mentioning here, is the near-English fourth-generation languages, 4GLs, used to develop new applications by users with some knowledge of computer systems development. Computer languages are discussed in Chapter 6.

For many library applications, the power of a fully relational system may not be required. Contrary to the claims of some advertisers, databases may not be truly relational. There are, however, some well known library management systems are that are relational or, at least, semi-relational, for example, Dynix, Geac ADVANCE, LIBS100, URiCA 2000 and BOOK PLUS.

Relational systems do have disadvantages. The next section gives a brief comparison of text retrieval and database management systems (after object-oriented systems have been mentioned).

Object-oriented database systems

There has been considerable interest in recent years in the development of object-oriented database systems, encouraged to a large extent by the use of object-oriented programming languages. It is beyond the scope of this book to examine such a complex topic as object-oriented systems, but it is worth noting that relational systems are not the final word in the development of database management systems. It is suggested that applications that involve highly interrelated data, such as product definitions, multimedia or bills of materials, are not well handled by relational systems. Object-oriented database systems are seen as 'Database systems that can implement conceptual models directly and can represent complexities that are beyond the capabilities of relational systems.' (Hansen & Hansen 1996, pp.443 & 448).

The authors are unaware of any concrete applications of object-oriented database systems in libraries but there are library applications for which the object-oriented approach might offer advantages: for instance, the proposed 'manifestation entry' which, stated very briefly, is an attempt to replace the traditional edition-specific catalogue record with a 'super record' that would include all manifestations of a work, such as different editions, translations, versions (by physical format) and even works about the work. It is also worth noting the view that, because object-oriented databases store not just data, but also instructions on how to manipulate the data, they are well suited to handling 'unstructured data such as photographs, graphics, audio and video' (O'Leary & O'Leary 2002, p. 298).

Integrated library management systems

There are many generic database management systems and text retrieval systems that can be used to manage textual data in libraries. When it comes to library management systems, however, most libraries opt to purchase commercial packages that are designed specifically for libraries (see Chapter 8). Most of these are *integrated* library management systems, although there are also stand-alone products, such as media management systems. What is meant by an integrated library management system? A narrow definition might be that an integrated library management system is one in which data are held only once (as in the case of a relational system), but it might be more realistic to say that an integrated system is one that *behaves* in an integrated manner. A library management system based on a text retrieval system, for example, may have the following features:

- the operator who keys in data only needs to do so once: for example, bibliographic data entered in one function (such as acquisitions) can be copied into other files

- amendments to data are made in one file (for example, the bibliographic file) and are updated in other files

- the library user can see from the online catalogue if an item is on loan or on order (that is, the catalogue is linked to the circulations and acquisitions functions).

Such an arrangement overcomes some of the problems associated with file managers, such as duplication of effort (keyboarding data more than once) and the increased likelihood of making mistakes. It does not solve the problem of data redundancy, since some data may be stored more than once in different files. Vendors of text retrieval systems may, of course, claim that the problem of data redundancy is exaggerated, and with continuing improvements in computer storage there is some truth in the claim.

One of the other disadvantages of a text retrieval system is the speed of updating files, which generally will not match the update speed of a database management system. Typically additions and amendments to files would be done as a batch, rather than one at a time, whereas in a database management system changes are made immediately. Another disadvantage of text retrieval systems is that they generally do not offer the same facility for the production of management reports as database management systems. Data manipulation is not a strong point, and managers who place a high priority on management information may prefer the flexibility of relational database management systems.

The generally poorer updating speeds of text retrieval systems, however, must be balanced against their speed of retrieval. In the case of large databases, relational database management systems compare badly with text retrieval systems in the speed at which they retrieve data. One reason is that when a relational database management system is retrieving data, it must retrieve them from wherever they are stored on the database and then assemble the relation for the user. Moreover, relational systems do not offer the same range of search facilities as text retrieval systems. Given that the user is often familiar with the retrieval power of text retrieval systems, such as the search engines available on the World Wide Web, there is pressure on the developers of commercial library management systems to provide similar retrieval capabilities.

Although some library management systems, such as those mentioned above, are designed on relational principles, and others, such as BRS/Search, InMagic and CAIRS, are built on powerful text retrieval engines, there is a clear trend for library management systems to combine the features of both types of system.

Hypertext

Hypertext has already been mentioned as a special form of text retrieval solution that makes it possible for users to navigate between sections of an electronic information resource or between separate resources, using links embedded in them. In Chapter 1 it was introduced as an important component in the World Wide Web, providing means of web publication (HyperText Markup Language or HTML) and retrieval (HyperText Transfer Protocol or HTTP). Examples of applications that may be used in the library environment include:

- electronic encyclopedias, which allow the user to follow associative trails from one chunk of text to another or to access other media (for example, graphics or sound)
- computer-assisted instruction packages, which encourage self-paced learning, again by encouraging users to follow associative links (for example, to background information)
- full-text legal resources that allow users to follow links to relevant statutes, case reports or definitions of legal terms
- library guides, giving general information, physical layout of buildings, information about collections and so on.

Some of the packages used to develop library applications use a notecard or notepad analogy to suggest what they do. From the user's point of view, the hypertext-based system presents screens of information which may recall the five-by-three index card. These cards, or pages in the case of the Web, are referred to as *nodes*. A node often represents a single concept, such as an encyclopedic entry or a legal definition. Note that, although the focus here is on hypertext, there are hypermedia applications, in which case a node might not be a chunk of text but a piece of music (for example, in an electronic encyclopedia), a graphic (for example, a floor plan in a library guide) or a video clip (for example, someone speaking).

Each node is linked to other nodes on the database and the user is encouraged to follow associative links: for example, by selecting highlighted text or by selecting a 'button', which is an icon on the screen representing a particular option or procedure. Where an author intends two nodes to be viewed sequentially, there will be a link between the two. In some applications, the network of interrelated nodes is called a stack. The stack is a matrix of nodes, through which the user can follow an associative trail.

How does the user access and browse this matrix of information? There are basically three techniques:

- follow the associative links between nodes: that is, follow the explicit links created by the author of the hypertext resource
- search across the stack for keywords, as one would search an database management system or text retrieval system
- use a browser, which represents graphically the position of a particular node in the stack.

The *browser* is an attempt to overcome one of the problems associated with use of a hypertext system, namely, that a user can become disorientated and lost ('cognitive overhead' is one expression used to describe this phenomenon). A browser is a form of mapping device, which typically presents the user with a graphical representation of where the current node is in relation to other nodes. Another tool for helping users navigate through the matrix of nodes is an audit trail, which allows them to backtrack to previous nodes of information. In large hypertext-based resources, however, audit trails may become too long to be of much help to users. In this case, they may have to rely on browsers, although it is worth pointing out the problems of representing nodes within a particularly large resource, given the size of most computer screens.

In some hypertext applications, it may be desirable for the user to be able to create new nodes and develop new links: in effect to annotate hypertext documents. This might be a useful feature in a personal information management system, although not perhaps in a library package.

Hypertext is generally associated with the so-called graphical user interface. User interfaces are discussed at the end of the next chapter, but it is worth noting, in this context, the importance of the interface, that is, the combination of computer hardware and software that allows the user to maintain a dialogue with the computer system. Features of the *graphical* user interface that are of particular relevance are:

* windows: a single screen will present the user with one node of information, but the use of windows enables the user to open more than one window on the screen, each window displaying a different node
* icons, which are graphical representations of nodes, options or commands and which present users with a choice of actions
* pointing devices, such as 'mice', that allow users to move a pointer on the computer screen and to select actions represented by icons or by highlighted text within the current node.

User interfaces are discussed in more detail in Chapter 6.

Expert or knowledge management systems

First, what is an expert system? It is a special kind of computer software, a form of artificial intelligence that can take the place of a human expert in a narrowly defined area of knowledge. A typical expert system can ask a user questions, offer advice to the user and demonstrate how it came to the conclusions that it did. Examples in the library environment include:

* intelligent front-ends, which mediate between a user and a remote database, relaying information to the user, translating the user's selections into commands for a text retrieval system and reporting results to the user

- the 'online pathfinder' expert system, mentioned in Chapter 2
- intelligent computer-assisted instruction (CAI) packages, which engage the user in a dialogue that resembles a Socratic tutor-student interchange
- cataloguing assistance
- automatic indexing, for example, Reuters' TIS (Topic Identification System)
- non-Boolean text retrieval, and
- training packages.

How does an expert system imitate a human expert? It may help to consider the basic components of an expert system:

- knowledge base, which contains information about objects (physical or conceptual), information about the relationships among them and rules for solving problems in a given knowledge domain
- inference engine, which applies the rules from the knowledge base to the information elicited from the user to produce conclusions
- user interface, which enables the system to communicate with the user, with the knowledge engineer (the person who builds the knowledge base with the help of an expert) and, in some cases, with other systems: for example, text retrieval systems.

The inference engine is somewhat different from the software used in other systems, such as database management systems. The latter use algorithms to solve problems, that is, sets of step-by-step instructions, whereas expert systems use *heuristics*, which can be compared to a rule of thumb type of reasoning. This may involve forward chaining (working forward from the information in the knowledge base), backward chaining (starting with possible solutions and searching the knowledge base for relevant facts) and a mixture of both techniques.

There are several ways of organising information in the knowledge base. The most common in library applications is a rule-based system. For example, in NZRef, which is a referral system, the system elicits a *wanted* (information required by the user) and a *given* (information the client already knows), and refers to the knowledge base for an appropriate rule, for example:

IF	wanted is meaning/definition
and	given is place
THEN	*Placenames of New Zealand*/ A.W. Reed

Figure 5.4: Sample rule-based expert system (Smith 1992, p. 40)

The main tools for development of expert systems are:

- expert system shells, which provide an inference engine, interfaces and a database on which the knowledge base is built – this is the most attractive option for those with little experience of systems development and programming
- AI (Artificial Intelligence) programming languages such as LISP and PROLOG, or non-AI languages such as C – these are more flexible tools than shells, but require a degree of programming skills that few systems librarians possess
- toolkits, which include a range of ready programmed techniques, such as reasoning mechanisms – these are easier than languages for developers, but are more flexible than shells.

One of the problems associated with expert system development is the considerable length of development time, even using a shell. Many of the working systems and prototypes are quite small and have failed to live up to the apparent potential of expert systems. Nevertheless, some useful systems have been developed, especially in the reference environment. It is also worth repeating the point made in Chapter 2 that, although rule-based expert systems (like the sample shown above) and frame-based expert systems take considerable development time, normative expert systems may be an area of development to consider.

In recent years what has been noticeable is not so much the development of ever more sophisticated knowledge-based systems for information management, but the adoption of AI concepts into 'mainstream' computing. One of the interesting areas of development has the integration of knowledge-based systems and the hypermedia features discussed earlier with more conventional computer systems, such as database management systems.

Personal bibliographic software

One of the features of online retrieval systems that was mentioned in Chapter 2 was the ability to 'tidy up' bibliographic data that have been downloaded from an online source to produce a polished bibliography. Personal bibliographic software is the software that is used to reformat references downloaded from online information sources such as Dialog. Packages such as Pro-Cite and EndNote can be used to store bibliographic citations and to output lists of references in one of several internationally-recognised bibliographic styles. This is of particular interest to those in the academic and research community who need to 'recycle' their references and have to adapt their bibliographies to publishers' preferred styles. Librarians, especially academic librarians, have an interest in bibliographic software, not least because it encourages users to download search results, rather than print them out. In some university libraries, in particular, librarians have been called on to advise individual users and even the wider academic community on the best choice of bibliographic packages.

Features of personal bibliographic software include:

- ease of use (given that packages are specialised)
- pre-defined data structures (since it can be assumed that the records being handled by the software are bibliographic)
- pre-defined output formats, using a range of standard bibliographic styles, such as the American Psychological Association (APA) style
- automatic generation of a bibliography from a manuscript, by scanning a paper and recognising embedded references
- boolean searching
- batch importing of records
- flexible sorting of selected records
- output to a printer or to a disk file for manipulation in another package (for example, a word processing package)
- detection of duplicates
- search and replace and global addition of text
- merging of databases
- production of structured bibliographies (for example, listing citations under terms taken from the descriptor field)
- access to index files as 'authority' or 'look-up' lists (Hanson 1995, pp.14-18).

Although personal bibliographic software is obviously geared primarily for the end-user, there is a variety of library applications: for example, management of special collections, indexing of local journals, production of reference databases, maintenance of current awareness services, thesaurus creation (an unusual application for software designed for the creation of bibliographies) and production of reserve reading lists in an academic library (Biggs 1995).

Spreadsheets

So far, this chapter has focused on the management of textual data, which accounts for most data management in the library environment. This last section, however, looks at the management of numerical data and specifically at the use of spreadsheets. The previous chapter referred to spreadsheet packages being used in library management for decision support: for example, in the exploration of 'what if' scenarios. An electronic spreadsheet is an applications program that allows a user to process, manipulate and display large amounts of mainly numerical data. With a good spreadsheet program, the user can perform a wide range of numerical calculations, often with the help of built-in formulae. The data are organised and displayed in a grid of rows and columns, resembling the ruled worksheets used by accountants and other financial planners.

	A	B	C	D	E	F
1			*January*	*February*	*March*	*Qly totals*
2	*Books*		962	2031	3278	6271
3	*Serials*		52	161	205	418
4	*Audiovisual*		12	58	47	117
5	*Inter-library loans*		34	187	225	446
6						
7	**Monthly totals**		1060	2437	3755	7252

Figure 5.5: Sample spreadsheet - library circulations statistics

Electronic spreadsheets were first developed by a Harvard business student, Dan Bricklin, and his friend Bob Frankston, prompted (so the story goes) by Bricklin's frustration at having to complete assignments that required the manual preparation of financial planning sheets for imaginary organisations. One of the main problems with using a paper worksheet is that a single mistake discovered halfway through a worksheet can be time-consuming to correct. The first electronic spreadsheet for microcomputer, VISICALC, was marketed by Bricklin and Frankston in 1979. It is fair to say that the popularity of spreadsheet and word processing packages in the business and financial worlds greatly encouraged the growth of the microcomputer industry in the 1980s.

The example above shows a very basic spreadsheet, used in this instance to process and display library circulation statistics. The circulations data are stored and displayed in cells. In the display the cells are the rectangular areas at the intersection of each row and column. Each datum (the singular of data) can be identified by its position in a row and in a column: for example, the cell which stores the total circulation figure is F7. Each cell can contain three data types:

- numbers (integers or decimals)
- formulae, each of which includes a function plus the coordinates of the cell or cells on which the function operates (for example, cell C7 contains a formula which could be expressed 'C2+C3+C4+C5')
- text: alphanumeric characters used merely to identify numerical data (for example, 'Books').

Should one figure be entered incorrectly, the number can be re-entered in the appropriate cell and any numerical values dependent on the value in that cell will be recalculated. In the above example, changing the figure in C4 affects values in C7, F4 and F7.

Main features of spreadsheet packages

Some of the vendors of integrated library management systems, of the kind described in the last chapter, do offer a spreadsheet facility, but these are generally of a quality inferior to that of the products in widespread use in business and financial environments, which may be stand-alone products or part of integrated packages that also include word processing and database management software. The main features of a good spreadsheet package are:

- creation of spreadsheets: for example, enter textual labels, numerical values or formulae into specified cells; construct formulae using common arithmetic operators, such as addition and multiplication, logical operators, such as AND, OR and NOT, or comparison operators such as equals or greater than; copy data that have been entered in one cell into another cell or a range of cells

- provision of built-in functions – many common operations can be performed using built-in formulae: for example, statistical, mathematical, financial and logical functions

- editing of spreadsheets: for example, inserting, amending or deleting cells; easy movement round spreadsheets; inserting or deleting rows and columns; cutting and pasting (moving) individual cells or ranges of cells

- changing formatting of cells: for example, justification of text labels within a cell, column widths or the display format for numerical values

- macro programming, which allows the user to record a series of commands and keystrokes used to perform a specific activity (for example, creation of a new spreadsheet) and to be able to repeat the activity on a future occasion by use of a single keystroke

- graphic display of data – most spreadsheet packages can display numerical data in graphic form: for example, as line graphs, bar charts and pie charts (see below)

- printing of spreadsheets: for example, users can specify what part of the spreadsheet is to be printed, whether numerical values or formulae are to be shown, and whether or not to include text labels and grids (as in other applications, users can see a screen display before printing)

- saving and filing spreadsheets, that is, save a spreadsheet or a set of interrelated spreadsheets for future retrieval, along with any associated charts.

Graphic display of data

One of the features listed above is the ability to display numerical data in graphic form. The user must be able to specify which range of values (for example, a row of totals) is to be represented and how it is to be represented (for example, type of graph, headings, axis labels). Such a facility is of use to the library manager not only for decision-making but also for the presentation of data: for example, a presentation to a funding body. Below is an example of a bar-chart representing average loans figures per hour, which may help a library manager decide how best to deploy counter staff:

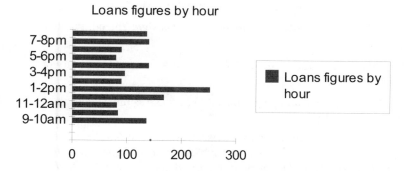

Figure 5.6: Graphic display of average loans figures per hour

Other spreadsheet facilities

It was also suggested above that sets of spreadsheets might be saved together. It is desirable to be able to link spreadsheets so that a formula in one spreadsheet may depend on the value of a cell in another spreadsheet. One reason for creating such a link might be that the dependent spreadsheet summarises data from a few different spreadsheets (for example, loans figures or expenditure data from a group of branch libraries).

As in the use of hypertext applications, it may be possible for the operator to use windows, in order to view different parts of a document on a split screen. The screen itself acts as a window on to the spreadsheet, allowing the user to view one part of the spreadsheet; but there may be instances where it would be useful to be able to view more than one part of the spreadsheet simultaneously, for example, where the user is making changes in one part of a spreadsheet and wishes to see the consequences of these changes in another part of the spreadsheet (for example, a row of totals) or even in another spreadsheet.

Spreadsheet applications

Spreadsheet projects in the library environment include:

- tracking budgets
- developing estimates
- comparison of budget plans and actual expenditure
- tracking of statistical trends: for example, collection figures or circulation statistics
- 'what if' comparisons, that is, displaying results based on changes in one or more factors, such as cutting print serials subscriptions and re-allocating resources to document delivery services.

References

Biggs, DR (ed.) 1995, *ProCite in libraries*. Learned Information, Medford, NJ.

Hansen, GW & Hansen, JV 1996, *Database management and design*. 2nd ed. Prentice-Hall, Upper Saddle River, NJ.

Hanson, T (ed.) 1995, *Bibliographic software and the electronic library*. University of Hertfordshire, Hatfield.

O'Leary, J & O'Leary, LI 2002, *Computing essentials 2002-2003*. Complete edition. McGraw-Hill/Irwin, Boston, MA.

Smith, AG 1992, 'NZRef: A rule-based reference advisory system', in *Intelligent library systems: Papers from the Intelligent Library Systems Conference organized by the Centre for Intelligent Information Management, Wagga Wagga, New South Wales, 25-27 September 1992*, J Weckert and C McDonald (eds.), Centre for Information Studies, Wagga Wagga, NSW.

Review questions

1. Explain the point of an index file, such as an inverted file index, in text retrieval.
2. Suggest one alternative to a sequential computer search through an index file.
3. Explain what a relation is in database management and suggest its equivalent in non-relational database management systems.
4. Explain how two relations are linked in a relational database management system.
5. Explain the difference between a query language and a fourth-generation language.
6. Outline the respective advantages of text retrieval software and database management systems.
7. Identify three main retrieval techniques in a hypertext package.
8. Name the main components in expert systems software.
9. List the main features of personal bibliographic software.
10. List the main features of spreadsheet software.

Further resources

Hernandez, MJ & Getz, K 2003, *Database design for mere mortals : A hands-on guide to relational database design*. 2nd ed. Addison-Wesley, Boston, MA.
There is any number of books on database design, but this is more approachable than most.

Meadow, CT, Boyce, BR & Kraft, DH 2000, *Text information retrieval systems*. 2nd ed. Academic Press, San Diego.
Some knowledge of programming (or even algebra!) would help in making the most of this book, but it is suitable for students of library and information management, and it makes few assumptions about one's knowledge of IT.

CHAPTER 6
Computer systems and technology

The focus of this book so far has been computer applications, such as text retrieval, database management systems or library management systems. This chapter examines the components of computer systems. It begins with a look at computer systems in terms of hardware, data and software. Each of these three is then discussed, starting with a detailed look at the major components of hardware. Second, it looks at how computer systems represent and transport data and the basic principles of data processing, followed by an explanation of the various categories of software. Closing the chapter is an outline of the classification of computer systems, ranging from microcomputers to mainframes, including an examination of the varying interfaces between computers and humans – the means by which humans and computer systems communicate.

Learning objectives

At the end of this chapter, you will be able to:

- list and explain the functions of the four main hardware categories of a computer system
- list and describe the most common hardware components of a computers system
- explain how data are represented and transported within a computer system
- discuss the basic principles of semiconductor technology
- list and explain the three categories of software
- outline the evolution of language translators
- list and outline the classification of computers systems, and
- discuss the three main categories of interface between humans and computer systems.

Keywords

Hardware	Clock	DVD-ROM	bus
Peripheral	ALU	drive	resolution
Data	Registers	modem	file format
Software	Buffers	binary	semiconductor
Barcode Reader	RAM	bit	logic gate
OCR	ROM	byte	compiler
Scanner	EPROM	ASCII	user interface
CPU	CD-ROM	EBCDIC	user friendly
Control Unit	CD-Recordable	Unicode	GUI

What is a computer system?

As the previous chapter suggested, a system is formed of parts where each part interacts with the other parts to achieve some common purpose. In general terms, the common purpose for a computer system is to convert data (raw facts) into information (organised and useful data) by performing operations on that data. This can be represented as follows:

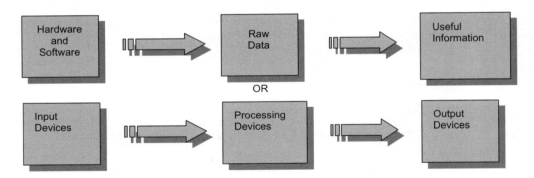

Figure 6.1: The functions of a computer system

Consequently, computer systems can be viewed as consisting of three main components:

Hardware – Hardware are the 'touchable' parts of a computer system: for example, keyboard, mouse, barcode wand, CD-ROM, printer, screen, scanner, etc.

Data – Data are the raw facts entered into a computer system, which are later processed or retrieved to produce information: for example, bibliographic data converted into a stock take report.

Software – Software is the set of instructions telling the computer what to do. They allow computer operators to use the hardware to input, process, and store and retrieve data: for example, word processors, database management applications, and operating system software.

The vast majority of this chapter is devoted to a more detailed look at each of these three components.

Hardware

As previously mentioned, hardware are the physical 'touchable' parts of a computer system. Hardware devices separate from the main computer system are referred to as peripherals. The following diagram shows the four main categories of hardware.

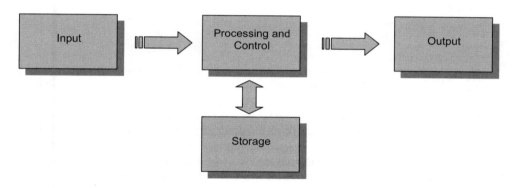

Figure 6.2: The four main categories of hardware

Input

This is how data are entered into a computer system. Input devices provide a means by which humans can interact with computers. Some common input devices are:

Keyboard

The keyboard is the main input device for a computer system. It consists of a board with numerous buttons corresponding to letters of the alphabet, digits and other special characters and keys. When a key is pressed, it is converted to a series of 0's and 1's, which uniquely represent that key. This is then passed into the computer system for processing. The most common keyboard layout is called the QWERTY (named after the first six characters on the keyboard). This keyboard layout was actually designed to slow typing down as much as possible! It was originally designed for the old mechanical typewriters that used hammers to strike paper to form letters. These hammers would jam together if typists were too fast. With modern electronic keyboards, this is not a problem, however, we are stuck with the inefficient QWERTY layout because the cost of re-training and supply of new keyboard layouts is too high. Despite this, many other keyboard layouts such as the Dvorak, Maltron or Quinkey, have been invented which vastly increase a typist's speed and accuracy.

Mouse

This is a device manipulated by the hand, which moves a cursor around on the screen. The device also has buttons which, when pressed, can be used to select options on the screen.

Barcode reader

This device is used to convert the barcode found on books and other goods into a sequence of numerals. It speeds up the data input process by replacing keyboard input of these numerals as well as reducing the chance of typing errors.

Scanner

A scanner works much like a photocopier. A page is scanned and the output is sent to the computer itself instead of being reproduced on another piece of paper. It is used to convert text or images from paper into a computer readable form. This process is often called digitising. Digitising enables images or text to be stored for later retrieval or manipulation. Most scanners come with software products enabling text to be scanned and converted to characters, as opposed to a series of dots in the shape of characters. This is called Optical Character Recognition (OCR). Some libraries are using high-tech scanners to digitise their books. This enables long term storage of the information, manipulation of the data, as well as providing access to the resources of a library through other computer systems around the world. Despite its advantages, the digitising process introduces many copyright issues.

Types of scanner include flatbed scanners, drum scanners (which are top of the range and provide high resolution images – discussed later) and scanners designed for specialised purposes such as microfilm scanners and slide scanners.

Speech recognition

Computers are designed to make life easier for us. Speech recognition is a positive step in this direction. Most devices mentioned require humans to compromise with the language that computer systems use. A speech recognition device monitors spoken words and inputs them into the computer system as we speak. Obviously, this input method is the most natural for humans. While developments in this area are slow, considerable progress has been made over the last decade. Speech recognition systems have been developed for specific languages that claim 95% accuracy. There are many variables that still need working on, not least the differences between people in terms of voice tone, talking speed, accents, genders, dialects and languages.

Processing and control

This refers to how data are processed by the computer system and how the computer system controls the many functions it performs. Both of these functions, and many more, are performed by the Central Processing Unit or CPU (often referred to as the 'brains' of a computer system). The speed of a CPU is measured in MIPS; Millions of Instructions Per Second.

The CPU can be represented diagrammatically as follows:

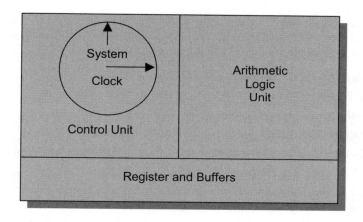

Figure 6.3: Diagrammatic representation of the CPU

Control unit (CU)

The CU directs the flow of data through the computer. Its tasks are to tell the other parts of the computer system what to do and when to do it. The CPU can perform millions of instructions per second, but only one at a time. The System Clock is used to ensure that a particular instruction doesn't use too much CPU time. The system clock works much like a metronome in music. The speed that the system clock 'ticks' is measured in megahertz. For example, a 200MHz-computer system has a clock that ticks 200 million times per second. Each instruction is allocated a certain number of 'ticks' of the system clock. This ensures that one instruction doesn't 'hog' too much CPU time at the expense of the other instructions that need completing. Although the clock speed is a major factor in determining the processing speed of a computer system, it is not the only factor. A situation may occur in which a computer system has a very fast clock but is still quite slow at processing data due to a bottleneck of speed elsewhere in the system.

Arithmetic logic unit (ALU)

The ALU performs all calculations and comparisons. It performs six functions; addition, subtraction, multiplication, division, boolean operations (that is: AND, OR and NOT) and comparisons (that is: less than, equal to, greater than). In reality however, it performs only three since, subtraction (addition of negative numbers), multiplication (repeated addition) and division (repeated subtraction) are all functions of addition.

Registers and buffers

These are temporary storage locations used by the CPU to speed up data processing. They act as halfway houses when data are being transferred between the ALU, CU, memory and the input and output devices. There are numerous registers to assist in data processing, each one only holding one piece of data. The principal registers are:

Accumulator – stores the last result processed in the ALU

Instruction register – holds an instruction in the CU prior to decoding

Address register – holds the location of the next piece of data

Storage register – holds data going to and from RAM (see below)

Program counter – holds the location of the next part of the program to be executed.

A buffer, on the other hand, is different from a register in that it can store more than one piece of data and is designed to act as a temporary storage area between the CPU and the input and output devices. It is used to free up the CPU to do other tasks. For example, if a large amount of data is to be printed, the buffer is used to store data while the printer is operating. This is because the CPU can process the data much faster than the printer can print it. Once the CPU has processed the data it stores them in the buffer, freeing the CPU up to do other tasks. This process is called spooling. A buffer may be part of the CPU or part of the input or output device.

Interface cards

The various components described above move data along a matrix of pathways called a main systems board or motherboard. It is also worth knowing – if one does not already know it – that most of the computers sold today have the option of plugging components into the motherboard in order to make the computer do something better, for instance, by adding RAM (see below), or do something not allowed for in the original design, for instance, communicate with another computer or exploit wireless technology (see next chapter). These add-on components are sometimes called plug-in boards, for obvious reasons – sometimes they are called interface boards or interface cards (see the example of a network interface card in the following chapter), expansion cards, adapter cards or controller cards.

Storage

This is a vital and essential component of a computer system. Without it we would continually need to input data into the computer system. Imagine typing in bibliographic information for a hundred books with no storage mechanism. Whenever we wanted to perform an operation on these data we would have to retype them!

Storage devices come in two main categories: Primary and secondary.

Primary storage

Primary storage, sometimes called main storage, can be random access memory, read only memory or a combination of both.

Random access memory – called RAM, this is where data and programs are transferred to (from secondary storage) when the CPU requires them. It is volatile in that the contents of RAM are only available when the computer is on. When required, the CPU transfers data or programs from secondary storage to RAM. It does this because the CPU can access data thousands of times faster from RAM than from secondary storage. An extremely fast type of RAM, called cache (pronounced kay-sh) is often found on modern computer systems. This is a section of computer memory that can be accessed at very high speeds and in which information is stored for fast retrieval. A cache size of 256Kb is common. Cache is a very expensive form of RAM, and consequently, only small amounts are used in computer systems.

Read only memory – called ROM, this contains data and instructions required by the computer that never change. Consequently, these instructions are permanently etched into the chip when manufactured and so are not lost when the computer is turned off (non-volatile). No data can be stored in ROM since it is read-only.

Combination of RAM and ROM – some ROM chips can be altered after manufacture. These are called PROMs (Programmable ROMs), EPROMs (Erasable PROMs) or EEPROMs (Electronic EPROMs). A special kind of EEPROM called Flash Memory can be erased and re-written in blocks, instead of one byte at a time (bytes are discussed later). They are used in hardware devices where change is constantly taking place. Flash memory enables the functionality of hardware to be upgraded without replacing the hardware.

Secondary storage

Secondary storage, sometimes called auxiliary storage, is non-volatile and is used to store data and programs for later retrieval. There are many kinds of secondary storage, each with advantages and disadvantages. Most storage devices use either magnetic or optical storage media.

Not lost when the computer is turned off

Magnetic storage devices use the principle that magnetically charged material has both a North and South Pole. These two poles are used to represent 0's and 1's and hence binary numbers. When data are read from magnetic media, the read/write head is used to convert the different magnetic poles into binary numbers that the CPU can process. Conversely, when writing data to magnetic media, the read/write head converts the binary signals from the CPU into magnetic charges. Care needs to be taken that magnetic radiation doesn't spoil any stored data.

Optical media devices use lasers to burn tiny craters or pits onto the surface of a plastic or metallic disk. The presence or absence of a pit on the surface of the disk is used for binary storage. Although slower than magnetic media, optical media are more robust (stored data are not affected by magnetic radiation) and have larger storage capacities for their size.

Some common examples of secondary storage devices are:

Hard disk – this form of magnetic media is used for bulk storage of data and programs. They are generally found within the case of the computer and hence are not portable. Some hard drives are removable and so provide convenient portable storage between computers. They are generally reliable and robust with fast access to stored data. They are called hard disks because the metal oxide on which the magnetic information is stored is placed on a solid, hard disk. This enables the disk to spin at much higher speeds than otherwise without distortion to the surface of the disk. RAID (Redundant Array of Independent Disks) drives are combinations of two or more drives combined in such a way as to increase the performance and fault tolerance of the drive. RAID drives come in three different levels 0, 3 or 5 for varying performance and fault tolerances. They are usually used on file servers where the hard drive is under constant interrogation and performance and fault tolerance is imperative.

Floppy disk (diskette) – Floppy disks are a magnetic medium used primarily for small data storage. As technology has developed, the storage capacity of floppy disks has increased from 120Kb to 120Mb (over 1, 000 times more storage) despite the fact that the physical size of these disks has decreased from 8" to 3.5". They are called floppy disks because the metal oxide is placed on a flexible plastic disk. Since the disk is flexible, it cannot spin as fast as a hard disk. Consequently, floppy disks have much slower access speeds than hard disks and are much less reliable. They are however, much more portable than hard disks, although even this distinction is being blurred with new technologies such as removable hard drives.

The floppy disks in current use have a capacity of 1.44 MB (megabytes – memory is discussed later in the chapter) – an insufficient capacity for many database, spreadsheet and multimedia applications. As a result, a number of floppy disk cartridges have been developed, the best-known being Zip disks, SuperDisks and HiFD disk drives. The most commonly in current use is almost certainly the Zip disk, which has a capacity of 100 and 250 MB and which requires a special drive (see below).

CD-ROM – this is an optical storage medium for bulk storage of data and programs. Unlike, hard or floppy disks, the contents of a CD-ROM cannot be changed and hence is ideally suited for static data such as bibliographic details, newspapers, journals, periodicals, directories, dictionaries and encyclopedias. They are extremely portable and offer excellent reliability for long term storage with reasonable access times. Each CD-ROM disk can hold up to 650Mb of data.

CD-R – increasing use is made of CD-R or CD-Recordable, also known as WORMs (Write Once, Read Many disks), which allow users to write to them once, using a special drive. Many CD-Rs cannot be written over or erased once they have been written to and are therefore especially useful for the archiving of data (and of course creating one's own music CDs) or any other application which requires the data, once saved, to be retained without alteration.

There are also erasable optical disks known as **CD-RW** or compact disk rewritable, which look as if they may replace floppy disks – or at any rate, the 3.5" diskettes.

DVD-ROM – DVD is a new optical storage technology for bulk storage of data and programs including audio and video. DVD stands for Digital Versatile Disk (originally called Digital VideoDisk). DVD technology hit the market in 1997 and works like a CD-ROM. Its difference is that whereas a CD-ROM uses one side of the disk to store data a DVD disk uses both sides, and each side can store data on one of two layers. The laser beam used to read the DVD operates at two intensity levels, one for each of the two layers on each side. DVD utilises the MPEG-2 file and compression standard enabling a DVD disk to hold up to 17GB of information – twenty-eight times greater than a CD-ROM (see below for an explanation of compression and multimedia files). Consequently, a single DVD can store four-and-a-half hours of a movie. It has been said that DVD technology will eventually replace our current storage methods for music, video and movie. A DVD-RAM device enables users to create their own DVD-ROM disks.

Tape – this is a magnetic storage medium mainly used for the backing up of important data to safeguard against data loss or computer malfunction (for example, loss of bibliographic, borrower and loans data). The tape itself is very similar to, and often the same as, that used in video cameras. It offers reasonable long-term security, large storage capacities, while being of small physical size. Its major disadvantage is its slow access times. Searching for data on a tape is much like searching for one's favourite song on an audiocassette tape.

Paper – although it may seem strange to include paper (sometimes called a hard copy) as a storage medium, many organisations still rely heavily on it. For many, physically seeing data printed on paper makes them easier to read and provides confidence against data loss. However, long term storage of paper is a problem due to its deterioration and its physical size. Compare, for example, the shelf space required for an entire set of printed encyclopedias with just one CD-ROM. The biggest disadvantage of paper storage is that it represents a departure from the computer system itself, thereby making the manipulation and processing of the data on the paper impossible. Of course, the majority of libraries store their books in paper format, despite the fact that there is a growing effort to digitise books for electronic storage and retrieval.

Many other storage media are available. With advances in technology, new storage methods are becoming more reliable, cheaper and faster, with larger storage capacities and smaller physical sizes.

Many software packages are available which enable data to be compressed before being written to a storage device. In many cases, data can be compressed to about half the original size thereby doubling the storage capacity of a device (more on data compression in Chapter 7).

Output

Output devices provide a means by which information (processed data) can be displayed to humans. Some common output devices used by libraries are:

Monitors

Also called Visual Display Units (VDUs), these provide a temporary display of information and options on a screen (sometimes called a soft-copy). This is the major output device of a computer system. Most monitors nowadays are color although the older monochrome (single color) monitors may still be seen. Their size, number of colors and their resolution categorise monitors.

Size – the most common size is a 14" monitor. This is a measure of the diagonal distance from one corner of the screen to the other. These are adequate for most applications but for heavy graphics use or desktop publishing a size of 15", 17", 21" or even higher may be more suitable.

Colours – the first computer monitors could display only one colour (hence the term monochrome display). Over the years we have evolved from one color to over sixty-five million colors. This improves the clarity of images on the monitor but requires high-speed hardware to support it.

Resolution – this refers to the number of dots that can fit on one screen. If one could look closely enough at a computer screen or even a television, one could see that images are created by dots. Each dot on a screen is called a Pixel (short for Picture Element). The more dots per screen, the more clarity to an image. Typical screen resolutions are 640x480, 600x800 or 1024x768. In the case of 11024x768 resolution, there are 1024 cells running horizontally across the screen and 768 vertically down the screen.

Printers

Printers are devices that produce print on paper and can be grouped into two broad categories.

Impact printers - these print by the striking of a hammer or pin on an inked ribbon, or by physical contact with the paper. Some examples of impact printers are dot-matrix printers, daisy wheel printers, line printers and plotters.

Non-impact printers – non-impact printers are all other printers and produce print without physical contact with the paper. Some examples of impact printers are laser printers, bubble-jet printers and thermal printers.

Generally speaking, impact printers are noisier, slower and of less quality than non-impact printers, while impact printers are cheaper to purchase and maintain.

Voice output

These devices scan printed text and convert it into voice output or into a document in Braille. An example of a voice output device is a Kurzweil Personal Reader.

Computer output microform

Called COM, these are used for the production of microfiche catalogues, rarely used now in libraries.

Input and output devices

Some devices are both input and output devices. Following is a list of some of the common devices, which are both input and output.

Touch screens

Touch screens can be used to display information (output) and select options (input). Options are selected by touching the relevant option on the screen. They are useful for the presentation of data that never changes and where keyboard input is not required, such as location guides in large shopping complexes, public transport timetables or introductions to collections and services for library users.

Drives

There is a variety of drives used in computer systems, but they all share the same characteristic: that they can read data from a specific type of storage device (input) and write data to the device (output). The most common are the hard disk drive and the floppy disk drive, but increasingly others are required for the input and output of data: for instance, a CD-drive (which is an internal drive for the current generation of desktop computers) and a Zip-drive, which is typically (at present) an external device that can be purchased separately and wired up to a desktop computer.

Modems

Short for MOdulator DEModulator, a modem converts the digital signals sent by a computer into an analogue signal for transmission over a telephone line (modulator), and vice-versa (demodulator). Modems will be discussed in greater detail in Chapter 7.

Maintenance of hardware

Most organisations make a considerable investment in information technology, and if they are wise they pay attention to its maintenance. As already suggested, magnetic media are especially prone to damage, and need to be kept away from strong magnetic fields, which can cause corruption of data. Moreover, while magnetic media do lose their magnetic properties over time, that loss can be slowed down by storing them in optimum conditions – in cool temperatures, for example (although not too cool). Sometimes computer equipment, such as mainframe computers (discussed later in this chapter), are stored in separate rooms, preferably under lock and key for the sake of security. This makes control of the atmosphere easier, avoiding the effects of dust and other corrosive elements (such as cigarette smoke). Other potential problems include:

- the effect of changes in temperature and humidity on magnetic tape, which can cause stress (as can improper rewinding)
- the impact of prolonged high temperatures and humidity on some optical media: for instance, humidity causing hydrolysis of the binder between recording material and the polycarbonate substrate (Hunter 2000, p. 55)
- food and drink spills
- water, either in the form of rain from a nearby window or in the form of a sprinkler system that is set off by smoke
- voltage surges, which can be largely avoided through the use of special surge protectors.

Organisations also need to have some kind of disaster plan in place. As discussed in the previous chapter, data need to be backed up in case of loss or corruption, and kept off-site or at least in a secure place such as a fireproof safe. Typically copies of some software will also be kept securely, in the event that data do need to be recovered. In the case of websites, it is quite common to maintain one's website on at least two separate servers – one a mirror site – in case of disaster striking the main server.

Data

The second component of computing systems is data. To understand something about computer processing, it is necessary to understand how data are represented within a computer.

Data representation

At the risk of stating the obvious, computers 'speak' a different language from human languages. One of the tasks of the input and output devices mentioned previously is to convert our language into computer language and vice-versa. This section is devoted to understanding the language of computers.

How are data represented in a computer system? A CPU can only recognise data if they are in the form of electrical pulses. These pulses can be in one of two states: a high-voltage state or a low-voltage state. For convenience we label these states OFF and ON, or 0 and 1 respectively. For this reason, data are represented using binary notation (base 2), a number system that uses only two digits (0 and 1). Data expressed in this computer-readable form are described as being in digital form. Contrast this with our decimal (Arabic) system (base 10) that we use every day which has ten digits (0 through to 9).

The smallest unit of data that a computer can recognise is referred to as a bit (Binary digIT). As mentioned previously, this is either 0 or 1. However, this unit is a little inconvenient for representing storage capacities. It would be much like expressing someone's height in millimetres instead of metres. Hence, to make life a little easier, the byte was created. A byte is a grouping of eight bits. Therefore the sequence 00101100 11110100 contains 16 bits or 2 bytes. As an aside, you may come across the term 'nibble'. This refers to half a byte (as you probably guessed) or 4 bits, but is rarely used.

The total number of different combinations of eight 0's and 1's is 256 (00000000, 00000001… 11111110, 11111111). This is one of the reasons we group eight bits into a byte. A byte can then be used to code any of the following familiar characters:

- Alphabetic   a, b, c, … z, A, B, C, … Z
- Numeric   0, 1, 2, … 9
- Symbols   !, #, &, $, {, ?, *, =, …
- Special Characters   control characters, space, end of line, end of file, and others characters.

How do computers know which of the 256 combinations of 8-bits belongs to which character? It just so happens that there is an approved international standard setting out the 8-bit sequence of zeroes and ones for every character in our language. In fact there are three internationally approved codes:

American Standard Code for Information Interchange (ASCII)

ASCII (pronounced ass-key) is the more common of the three codes and has been adopted by most computer manufacturers. The following table illustrates just nine of the 256 characters available in the ASCII code. Note the distinction between upper and lower case letters.

Character	ASCII
A	01000001
B	01000010
C	01000011
a	01100001
0	00110000
1	00110001
2	00110010
$	00100100
+	00101011

Figure 6.4: ASCII representation of characters

Extended Binary Coded Decimal Interchange Code (EBCDIC)

EBCDIC (pronounced ebb-see-dik) is an industry standard specifically developed for computers. Its widespread use is due to the fact that it was a standard adopted for IBM computers. EBCDIC is also an 8-bit code.

Unicode

Unicode is a much more recently developed code than the other two standards and unlike them is a 16-bit code. The reason for developing a 16-bit code is that the 8-bit codes are inadequate to cover languages such as Chinese and Japanese, which require far more than 256 combinations of bits. Development of Unicode was supported by leading companies such as Microsoft, IBM and Apple. It is 'currently the standard for Apple, HP, IBM, JustSystem, Microsoft, Oracle, SAP, Sun, Sybase, and Unisys and has been adopted by many vendors' and is required for a number of *de facto* standards, including XML (Kochtanek & Matthews 2002, p. 105). It is also perhaps worth noting that there is a representation of the Unicode characters, UTF-8, which will allow for the gradual transformation of ASCII-based applications to the full range of Unicode scripts (Arms 2000, p. 171).

Measures of storage capacity

The code that is used in a particular computer system is referred to as machine code or machine language.

To calculate the decimal value of a binary code, the first digit on the right should be multiplied by one (2^0), the second multiplied by two (2^1), the third by four (2^2), the fourth by eight (2^3), the fifth by sixteen (2^4), the sixth by thirty-two (2^5), the seventh by sixty-four (2^6) and the eighth by one-hundred and twenty-eight (2^7). The eight products are then added together. To take an example, the code for the letter 'a' has the decimal value 97 (1 + 32 + 64). In other words, as one moves from the right-hand bit leftwards, each successive column represents a higher power of two (hence base 2), whereas in a decimal number each successive column represents a higher power of ten (hence base 10).

It is worth noting that in theory ASCII codes only require seven bits (the furthest left bit is always zero). In practice however, ASCII is an 8-bit code. The eighth bit (added to the left) is called a parity bit and is used to check the validity of the byte after transmission. This is explained in Chapter 7, where the focus is on data communications.

Remembering that a byte is the equivalent of one character, it soon becomes obvious that even the byte is too small a unit to represent storage capacities. Using the byte would be like a lecturer giving a student an assignment that had to be 10,000 characters long! Hence, a kilobyte and a megabyte were created. A Kilobyte (Kb), despite popular belief, is *not* 1,000 bytes but 1,024 (2^{10}) bytes. Similarly, a Megabyte (Mb) is 1024 Kb; a Gigabyte (Gb) is 1024 Mb and a Terabyte (Tb) is 1024 Gb. Nowadays, RAM is being measured in Megabytes and hard disk capacity is being measured in Gigabytes.

Hence,	16 Mb	= 16 x 1, 024 Kb	= 16, 384 Kb
		= 16, 384 x 1, 024 bytes	= 16, 777, 216 bytes
		= 16, 777, 216 x 8 bits	= 134, 217, 728 bits

Non-textual data

As the earlier account of monitors mentioned, the images that one sees on a computer screen are created by a matrix of dots, called pixels (picture elements). The more pixels per screen, the clearer the image we see. Each colour that goes into a pixel must be coded – like all computer processed data, these codes are stored as binary code or, in other words, as a series of ones and zeros. These are stored in computer memory as a grid or map, which is the reason that we refer to them being stored as a bitmap. The quality of an image depends on two factors:

- resolution, mentioned earlier, which is measured in dots per inch or dpi (inch here refers to an inch of the item represented)
- bit-depth, which is the number of bits representing a pixel.

Ideally, we all want high-resolution images, but there are disadvantages, because high-resolution images require large files, which not only has storage implications but also means that download speeds are slow. For this reason, some of the file formats described below (for instance, types of JPEG and GIF) load a low-resolution image first and then start to build a higher resolution image, so that if someone accesses an image library on the Web the low-resolution image can be used for quick reference. Common file formats include:

- JPEG – Joint Photographic Experts Group format (.jpg), one of most common image file formats on the Web, especially for colour images
- GIF – Graphics Interchange Format (.gif), which is also commonly used for Web delivery, principally for greyscales, and allows for faster download speeds than JPEG

- TIFF – Tagged Image File Format (.tif), which offers high quality images and is therefore of considerable interest in the archiving of images

- BMP – Bitmap format (.bmp), which is used in Windows applications (discussed later)

- Photo CD (.pcd), a Kodak product used to scan slides and negatives on to CD

- PDF – Adobe's Portable Document Format (.pdf), which is used for viewing in Acrobat Reader, but has become a *de facto* standard for the distribution of electronic documents (Lee 2001, p. 48) and is also used in many institutional settings, especially court systems, for the storage of electronic documents because of its preservation of all the fonts, formatting, colours and graphics of the source document, 'regardless of the application and the platform used to create it' (Hunter 2000, p. 61).

It is worth noting the 'extensions' for these formats – the three-letter codes, with preceding full-stop, that appear above in parentheses. Extensions are commonly used in computing in the naming of files in order that computers recognise the file type. They appear at the end of a file name: for instance, the graphic for this book's cover might be stored under the name: cover.tif (or cover.jpg, if the designer wanted to send a copy to the publisher for approval).

Second, some of these formats involve compression of data (compression is still to be discussed) for fast exchange: for instance, a JPEG file has been compressed using an algorithm (set of rules) developed by the Joint Photographic Experts Group. Such formats are often described as 'lossy', which means that some data are left out, resulting in some loss of picture quality. TIFF format is generally used for archiving purposes because it is far less lossy than, for instance, JPEG and GIF, which are better adapted to web delivery. Sometimes, of course, image files will be stored in two formats: TIFF for long-term storage and one of the others for web delivery.

Images have been covered here because they are a significant component in the digital library, but there are other file formats of which one should be aware: for instance, RealAudio, which is used for audio files and Quicktime, used for moving images.

Communication channels and data transportation

Once the data have been converted into machine language, how are they moved within the CPU and the rest of the computer system?

Communication between the ALU, control unit, and registers, as well as between RAM and input and output devices takes place by the use of a bus. A bus is simply a 'highway' in which data can travel. The width of the bus, measured in bits, is called the word length of the computer and may vary from computer to computer. A typical bus width for modern computer systems is 32-bit (although some can be as high as 128-bit or more). This means that 32 bits (4 bytes) can be transported within the computer system all at once. It is much like having a 32-lane highway between cities. The more lanes, the faster the traffic can move (and a computer system always has lots of 'traffic' to move around). The word length of a computer is another major factor contributing to the overall processing speed of a computer system.

Semiconductor technology

Here, the building blocks of computer systems are explored more deeply.

Having established how data are represented in a computer system, the next question to consider is how these data are physically stored and manipulated once they enter the computer. This is made possible with the use of semiconductor technology. A semiconductor, as the name suggests, is a special material that can act as both a conductor (allowing electricity to flow) and an insulator (preventing electricity from flowing). By combining semiconductors in special ways, entire circuits can be produced to perform different functions, for example, addition, memory, comparisons, multiplication, etc.

A complete semiconductor circuit printed on a single chip is referred to as an integrated circuit (IC). The present generation of computers (from 1980 onwards) uses very-large-scale integrated circuits (VLSIC) that can have from 200,000 to 2,000,000 circuits on a single chip (according to Moore's Law, this figure doubles every 18 months). Semiconductor integrated circuits can be designed for use either as part of an Arithmetic Logic Unit (ALU) or as a memory chip (primary storage). It is possible, however, to combine the three components of the CPU (ALU, RAM and Control Unit) all on the one chip. A chip that combines the ALU and Control Unit is called a microprocessor and a computer with a microprocessor and several memory chips is called a microcomputer.

The circuitry within a computer system contains so-called logic gates, which are devices for reproducing logical operations. Surprisingly, every function performed by a computer system can be broken down into a combination of only three logical operations; AND, OR and NOT.

AND

The AND logic gate has numerous inputs but only one output. An output of 1 (or ON) is only produced if all of its inputs are 1. The symbol for the two-input AND gate is as follows.

Figure 6.5: The AND logic gate

A and B represent two inputs and Z is the output.

The behavior of logic gates is often represented using truth tables (sometimes called logic tables). A truth table displays all possible inputs along with the corresponding output. The truth table for the AND gate is as follows.

A	B	Z
0	0	0
0	1	0
1	0	0
1	1	1

Figure 6.6: The truth table for the AND logic gate

OR

The OR logic gate also has numerous inputs but only one output. An output of 1 (or ON) is produced if any of its inputs are 1. The two-input OR gate is represented by the following symbol.

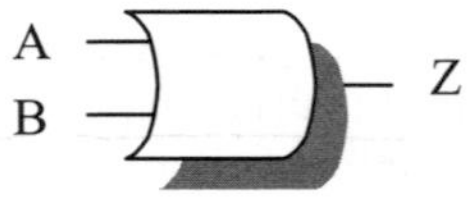

Figure 6.7: The OR logic gate

A and B represent two inputs and Z is the output. The Truth table for an OR gate is as follows.

A	B	Z
0	0	0
0	1	1
1	0	1
1	1	1

Figure 6.8: The truth table for the OR logic gate

NOT

This logic gate has one input and one output. An output of 1 (or ON) is only produced if the input is 0 and vice-versa. A NOT gate is represented by the following symbol.

A ▷o● Z

Figure 6.9: The NOT logic gate

A represents the input and Z the output. The Truth table for a NOT gate is as follows.

A	Z
0	1
1	0

Figure 6.10: The truth table for the NOT logic gate

As previously mentioned, various permutations of the AND, OR and NOT gates are used to perform tasks such as memory, addition, subtraction, and comparisons.

Software

The third and final component of computer systems, is software. Without computer software, a computer system is useless. Software is the set of instructions that tell the computer what to do. A computer system with no software would be like having a motor car without a driver. Software can be grouped into three categories, operating system (OS) software, utility software and application software.

Operating system software

This is the most important kind of software for a computer system. Without this, no other software will work. In fact without operating system software, the hardware of the computer system would not work. System software is the link between the hardware and other software packages. It is the key to unlocking the computer systems resources. Operating system software can be split into four basic sub-systems:

Kernel

This is the heart of the Operating System. It coordinates the activities of other software and manages the use of RAM. It works much like traffic police at an intersection. The kernel tells each activity when and for how long it can use the CPU and how much main memory it can use. The kernel is loaded into RAM automatically whenever the computer is turned on. Some operating systems use secondary storage as a replacement for RAM when the entire RAM is being used. This is called virtual memory.

Device manager

This coordinates the transferring of all data to and from input and output devices. It monitors each device on the computer system (printer, keyboard, mouse and so on) ensuring that they all 'talk' the same language. Each device attached to the computer system will have a device driver: a small program enabling it to communicate with the rest of the computer system.

File manager

This keeps track of every file in the computer system and maintains a record of exactly where each file is. It enables files to be deleted, moved, renamed, copied and saved.

Shell

Sometimes called the command processor, the shell enables communication between the user and the rest of the operating system.

Types of operating system

Operating system software can be a mixture of single or multi-user, single or multi-tasking with single or multi-processor capabilities.

Single or multi-user

Single user operating systems allow only one person to access the computer system at any one time whereas multi-user operating systems can have many users sharing the computer system resources.

Single or multi-tasking

A single tasking operating system can perform only one task at a time. When that task is finished it then starts the next. Multi-tasking operating systems on the other hand, give the appearance of doing more than one task at once by giving each concurrent task a slice of CPU time until all tasks have been completed.

Single or multi-processor

A single processor operating system can only handle a computer system with one CPU. Some computer systems however have more than one CPU. In these cases, a multi-processor operating system is required to ensure that all CPUs are utilised.

Examples of operating systems

Some examples of operating system software are:

Microsoft – Disk Operating System (MS-DOS)

This operating system, the most common in its time around the 1980s, is a single user, single tasking, single processor operating system. It is a command driven operating system, that is, commands are issued from the keyboard to perform functions. For example, if time were to be entered via the keyboard the computer system would display the current time on the monitor. The system relied heavily on the user remembering the hundred or so commands that could be typed.

Its major disadvantages were that it was limited to using only 640Kb of RAM and that file names were restricted to what is called an 8.3 format, that is, eight letters could be used to describe the contents of a file, followed by a stop and then an optional three letters – the extension mentioned earlier. On top of this restriction, certain letters were not allowed to be used in file names, such as ?, >, *, < and the space. An example of a valid filename would be *library.doc*. However, *My Budget, documents.txt*, and *holidays.file* would not be allowed since the first contains a space and is greater than eight characters in length and the second has an extension that is greater than three letters. Updated versions of MS-DOS improved the memory restrictions, but not the 8.3 file naming restriction.

Macintosh operating system

This is a single user, multi-tasking operating system, developed in the 1980s and based around a graphical user interface or GUI (see below). It was the first of a new generation of microcomputers that displayed information on the screen for users to choose from and represented entities (such as files or actions) by using icons. It incorporated a mouse for selecting items on the screen and ushered in the term 'user-friendly' computing.

Microsoft Windows 95

Windows 95 was a single user, multitasking, single processor operating system developed in 1995, which offered a graphical user interface and provided users with Plug-n-Play™. Plug-n-Play™ operating systems automatically detect new hardware devices and install the appropriate software drivers to give users access to the new hardware.

Microsoft Windows NT

Windows NT is a multi-user, multi-tasking, multi-processor operating system developed by Microsoft. It offers a graphical user interface (GUI) identical to Windows 95 but offers advanced security and networking capabilities for corporate use.

Windows has been further updated by Windows Millenium Edition, specifically designed for home-users, and more recently by Windows XP – Microsoft's most powerful desktop operating system at the time of writing and, like NT, suitable for use as a network operating system.

UNIX

This is a multi-user, multi-tasking, and multi-processor operating system developed by Bell Laboratories. It is considered a portable operating system because it can be used on many different kinds of computer systems (machine independent). Unlike DOS, the primary and secondary storage capacities are not limited. UNIX can share the CPU among different applications (multi-tasking) as well as amongst several users (multi-user). Unfortunately there is no UNIX standard and so there are several versions of UNIX on the market. One version to receive a lot of attention in the literature in recent years is Linux, which was developed by Linus Torwalds while a graduate student at University of Helsinki. At present it is one of those products that is freely available for development. UNIX is ideal for large-scale applications, and a wide range of library management and records management systems run on it.

PICK — LIBRARIES

Originally developed by Dick Pick and Don Nelson in 1965, PICK is a multi-user, multi-tasking, multi-processor operating system commercially available since 1974. PICK is tailored for database management applications and hence is an ideal operating system for libraries and other institutions that rely heavily on data management. It automates most of the data processing within a computer system with the aim of freeing up the user to concentrate on the data themselves. PICK contains a powerful, near English, database management language called ACCESS and a Terminal Control Language (TCL) that can be used to execute over 200 system utility programs. At the heart of PICK is a database system that handles variable-length fields and a highly efficient virtual memory management system. PICK has a user-friendly interface, is machine independent, like UNIX, and can be implemented on computers ranging from microcomputers to large mainframes.

All these aspects have helped PICK to sustain a share of the computer operating system market for over thirty years. Leading library management systems like Dynix, URICA 2000 and Geac ADVANCE run on a PICK operating system. The fact that UNIX has very much become an industry standard (or set of standards) led to the development of software that would allow a PICK-based system to run on a UNIX platform.

Although there has been some compromise, the wide use of different operating systems with different file formats combined with the wars for market share have made 'cross-platform delivery' difficult. While some operating systems, such as UNIX, are becoming standards, others have simply disappeared (Lee 2001, p. 45).

Utility software

Utility software are programs designed to maintain and diagnose a computer system. In most cases they come with the operating system but are not essential for the successful operation of the computer system. Utility software perform tasks such as the:

- backing up and retrieval of data
- retrieval of accidentally deleted files
- diagnosis of hardware faults
- repair of file storage errors
- detection and removal of viruses
- reorganising of files on a storage device.

Many third party software vendors sell utility software for various operating systems.

Application software

The operating system and utility software provide access to the resources of the computer system. Application software is the kind of software that performs the tasks that we want the computer system to do: for example word processing, database management, games, searching and sorting.

Application software can be either:

Commercial

Commercial software is written by software vendors for various markets. Commercial software can usually be customised for an individual or an organisation but are written with a view to meeting the needs of the marketplace. Word processing applications, games, database applications and library management systems are examples of commercial software.

Custom

Custom software is specifically written for a person or organisation. The advantage of custom written software is that it is tailored specifically for a particular use; however, custom software is very expensive and may require regular maintenance. Take, for example, software written specifically for an insurance company. It is unlikely that a software vendor will have a product specifically written for its use. In this case it would need to employ a software writing company to create a custom software package. However, because laws and regulations regarding insurance are constantly changing, this piece of custom software would require regular maintenance. (Chapter 8 looks further at advantages and disadvantages of commercial and custom software, in the context of library management systems.)

Language translators

A subset of the commercially available software that deserves special attention is language translators. These software applications allow users to write and develop custom software.

Language translators allow computer programmers to write sets of instructions in specific programming languages. These instructions are converted by the language translator into machine code. The computer system then reads these machine code instructions and executes them. Hence, a language translator is a program that translates from one computer language to another. Why should this be necessary?

It was mentioned earlier in this chapter that CPUs could only understand machine code or machine language (expressed in binary code). Machine code is hardware-specific, and hence there are as many machine codes as there are hardware designs. Although machine code makes complete sense for computers, it is a very difficult and tedious language in which to write programs. Hence programmers developed other less difficult languages in which to write programs. Over the years, these programming languages are moving closer and closer to human language. Consequently there are several generations of computer programming languages.

First generation languages (1GLs). 1GLs constitute the actual code that computers understand; that is machine code. In the early days of computing, programmers needed to learn the specific pattern of 1's and 0's of all computing instructions in order to tell the computer what to do. For example, a machine code instruction to load a value of 1 may be `10101001 00000001`.

Second generation languages (2GLs). 2GLs are called assembly languages. Each machine code instruction is given a mnemonic, making it easier to remember specific codes. The above example in assembly language would be `LDA #$01`, where LDA stands for LoaD the following value into a memory Address.

Third generation languages (3GLs). 3GLs are called procedural languages or high level languages. They are easier to understand because they resemble our own English language more than 1GLs and 2GLs. However, specific training is still required to program in these languages. Some examples of 3GLs are BASIC, COBOL, Pascal, Fortran, C, C++, Perl and Ada. One of the latest languages to hit the market is called JAVA. Developed by Sun Microsystems, this language allows programmers to write applications that can be used on any operating system (platform-independent). Its main use is in web pages where JAVA is used to write applets (short applications) to enhance the look and feel of a web page.

Fourth generation languages (4GLs). 4GLs are sometimes called problem-oriented languages or non-procedural languages, and require less training than 3GLs. In these languages one tells the computer what to do, not how to do it. Programmers and end-users use 4GLs to develop software applications. Some examples are SQL, ACCESS, Informix and FOCUS.

Fifth generation languages (5GLs). Called natural languages, 5GLs translate human instructions, including spelling mistakes and bad grammar, into machine code. They are designed to give people a more natural connection with computers. These languages are the objects of considerable research. It is hoped that they would be able to remember as people do, and then improve upon it.

With the exception of first generation languages, all computing languages need to be converted to machine code to enable the computer system to execute the instructions. Two kinds of language translators are used to achieve this.

Compilers. Compilers translate an entire computer program into machine language *before* execution.

Interpreters. Interpreters, on the other hand, translate programs one line at a time *during* execution. Compiled programs execute faster than translated ones since the conversion process takes place before execution.

Classification of computer systems

The previous sections provided a fairly detailed look at the three major components of computer systems: hardware, data and software. This section takes a step back to look at the ways in which computer systems are classified. There is a wide variety of computer types. Most literature, however, distinguishes four main kinds: supercomputers, mainframes, minicomputers and microcomputers. The criteria used to categorise computer systems include:

- computer system architecture (design of internal circuitry)
- processing speed (measured in millions of instructions per second or MIPS)
- amount of main memory
- speed of output devices
- number of users
- cost.

Supercomputers

These are exceptionally powerful computers designed to run at the fastest possible speeds. They are particularly useful for large-scale number crunching such as weather predictions, weapons research and oil exploration. They cost tens of millions of dollars and are generally owned by government agencies. The Cray series of computer systems is an example of supercomputers. Their processing speed is measured in thousands of MIPS.

Mainframe computers

Most large organisations rely heavily on at least one mainframe. Their processing speed is measured in tens of MIPS and they cost several hundred thousand to a couple of million dollars. They generally take up the size of a room and can handle hundreds of users accessing it at any one time. Insurance companies, banks, airline reservations systems and large library management systems use mainframes.

Minicomputers

Occupying less physical space and offering less processing speed, these offer a cheaper alternative to mainframe computers, costing from several thousand to half a million dollars. The distinction between minicomputers and mainframes is quite blurred due to constant advances in technology. Many stand-alone library management systems (that is, systems that have a computer dedicated to them and to no other significant functions) run on minicomputers.

Microcomputers

These are smaller and somewhat slower that all the previous systems but are a lot cheaper and smaller. They include desktop and laptop computers. They cost between a couple of hundred to several thousand dollars and are the most common of all computer systems.

Technological advancements have significantly blurred the distinction between computer types. Microcomputers are being developed today that are significantly faster than the mainframes of yesteryear.

Using a computer system: the user interface

This section explores how the user communicates with the computer system. The medium through which communication takes place is called the user interface. The user interface refers to the software and hardware that allow the user to maintain a dialogue with the computer system. A typical user interface includes a keyboard and a monitor. Until recent years, this dialogue was text-based, but since the development of the Macintosh in the 1980s, a graphical user interface (GUI) has added a new dimension to communicating with computer systems.

There are three broad categories of user interfaces; command-line, menu-driven and graphical user interfaces.

Command-line user interfaces

Command-line user interfaces are focused around the two hardware components of a keyboard and monitor. Instructions are given to the computer through a series of commands typed in on the keyboard. It has the disadvantage that commands must be remembered and hence is the least user-friendly of all the interfaces. A blank screen with a blinking cursor waiting for a command can be quite intimidating for a novice computer user. However, it does offer some great advantages. Command-line user interfaces require very little main memory, offer greater flexibility and in some situations can be a lot faster at executing instructions. Because of this, modern user interfaces offer command-line execution as an alternative to the common GUI. Some examples of command-line user interfaces are MS-DOS, earlier versions of UNIX, and TCL (Terminal Control Language). Some of the older online information systems used by libraries, for instance (at the time of writing!), Dialog, offer command-line user interfaces, and there are information librarians who like them because of the speed factor.

Menu-driven user interfaces

Menu-driven user interfaces are also focused around the hardware components of a keyboard and a monitor (although sometimes a mouse is incorporated). In a menu-driven user interface, users are presented with a menu of options from which to select. Clearly this is a more user-friendly approach since commands need not be remembered, just selected.

Some users find this approach slower and more cumbersome, however. As a result, most menu driver user interfaces also permit users to enter instructions using a command-line user interface. An example of a menu driven interface is the one offering a user the menu options of author, title, subject or keyword search on an online catalogue. A user might have the option of using the menu system or typing in AU to begin an author search (an increasingly uncommon option, it must be said).

Graphical user interfaces (GUI)

GUIs are interfaces that utilise a pointing device along with the common keyboard and monitor. Using a mouse or other pointing device, the user can select actions, commands or options that are displayed on the screen as graphical representations, called icons. GUIs present users with all the possible choices and allow them to decide which action to take based on the presented information. Compare this with command-line interfaces where users are presented with a blank screen and must remember commands to type in. A typical user action in a GUI might be to use a mouse to click on an icon of a filing cabinet to display the contents of a secondary storage device. The alternative in a command-line user interface may be to enter the command DIR. OS/2, Macintosh Operating System and Microsoft Windows 95 are all examples of GUIs. GUIs can also be referred to as a WIMP environment because they make extensive use of the following items:

Windows

Windows are rectangular display areas on a computer screen. Usually there are many windows on a screen, one for each running application. Each window can be selected to give it the focus of any keyboard entry that may be needed.

Icons

Icons are graphical representations of various options. These icons can be selected to perform the option it represents: for example, an icon is used to represent a word processing application which, when selected, will execute that application.

Mouse

A mouse is a cursor positioning device, manipulated by the hand, which moves the screen cursor in the same direction as the movement created when the mouse is rolled over a flat surface. (A cursor is a special character: for example, in this instance it might be an arrow that can be positioned over an icon.) Mice also have buttons on them which, when clicked, select various items that the cursor is resting over. The buttons can also be held down at the same time the mouse is moved to select more than one object or to move an object from one location on the screen to another (called drag and drop).

Pull-down menus

Pull-down menus are categories, usually listed across the top of a window, which when selected with a mouse (or equivalent keyboard combination) reveal a list of menu options relating to that category. Each of these menu options can then be selected using the mouse or the keyboard.

The following diagram may help to illustrate three of these four components of GUIs.

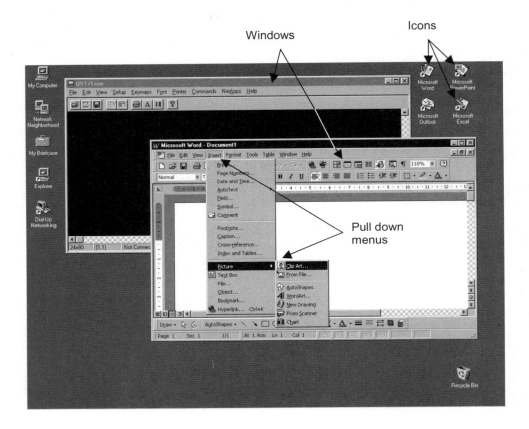

Figure 6.11: A graphical user interface (GUI)

References

Arms, WY 2000, *Digital libraries*. MIT Press, Cambridge, MA.

Hunter, GS 2000, *Preserving digital information: A how-to-do-it manual*. Neal-Schuman, New York.

Kochtanek, TR & Matthews, JR 2002, *Library information systems: From library automation to distributed information access solutions*. Libraries Unlimited, Westport, CT.

Lee, SD 2001, *Digital imaging: A practical handbook*. Library Association Publishing, London.

Review questions

1. What are the four main categories of hardware?
2. What is the task of the control unit?
3. Explain the two types of computer storage.
4. How are characters represented within a computer system?
5. List and explain the three types of software.
6. What are a bit, a byte and a Megabyte?
7. What are the three building blocks of all functions within a computer system?
8. What is a GUI?
9. Why is digital storage better than paper storage?
10. What does user-friendly mean and why is the user interface to a computer system so important?

Further resources

American National Standards Institute, < http://web.ansi.org/>.

Luber, AD 2002, *PC fear factor: The ultimate PC disaster prevention guide*. Que, Indianapolis, IN.
  Aimed at non-technical computer users, this book tells users how to prevent computer disasters where possible and, when disaster does strike, how to recover systems.

Maran, R & Whitehead, P 2000, *Computers simplified: Simply the easiest way to learn*. 5th ed. IDG Books, Foster City, CA.
  Suitable for school students, this is a very readable introduction to personal computer technology, from the hardware to the Web.

O'Leary, J & O'Leary, LI 2002, *Computing essentials 2002-2003*. Complete edition. McGraw-Hill/Irwin, Boston.
There is no end of print books on computing, but this one is especially broad in its coverage and it is regularly updated. It also contains a substantial glossary for those who find the technical language hard-going at times.

The PC guide, <http://www.pcguide.com/>.
The goal of The PC Guide is to provide the best useful information on PCs, to help PC users get the most from their machines--and their money. Areas covered include: step-by-step summary guide to buying a PC, requirements analysis, designing and specifying PC systems and components, understanding PC sources, vendors and prices, purchasing PCs and components, and 'after the purchase'.

White, R 2002, *How computers work*. 6th ed. Que, Indianapolis, IN.
Everything you ever wanted to know about computers? Unlikely, in one book, but there is considerable breadth and depth in its treatment of the topic. Especially strong on hardware components.

CHAPTER 7
Communications and networking

The ability to transfer files and information from one computer system to another has dramatically changed our perception and use of computer systems. Data communications between computer systems has enabled the sharing of computing resources, data and information. This chapter is devoted to discussing how computer systems communicate through the use of computer networks.

Learning objectives

At the end of this chapter, you will be able to:

- list the benefits of networking computers
- explain the difference between a LAN and a WAN
- list and explain the various communications media and their advantages and disadvantages
- explain the common transmission methods used between computer systems
- list and explain the advantages and disadvantages of some common error detection and correction methods
- define the term protocol and explain its importance in data communications
- define the seven layers of the OSI Reference Model and list common protocols used in each layer, and
- list and define common networking hardware.

Keywords

LAN	Noise	RS232	Token ring
WAN	Parallel	Parity	ISDN
Topology	Serial	Analogue	Z39.50
Bus	Synchronous	Digital	Gateway
Ring	Asynchronous	CRC	Router
Star	Simplex	Protocol	Hub
Microwave	Half-duplex	OSI	Repeater
Satellite	Full duplex	TCP/IP	Modem
Bandwidth	Flow control	Ethernet	Proxy server

Communications and networking is a broad topic within the computing industry. To assist the learning process, this chapter is divided into the following six topics:

1. Why network computer systems? – an introduction as to why we need to implement communications between computer systems.

2. Network models – a look at the difference between a local area network (LAN) and a wide area network (WAN).

3. Network media – the various media used in the transmission of data.

4. Data transmission methods – the varying methods of transmitting data between computer systems including data detection and correction methods.

5. Protocols – an introductory discussion of the rules or protocols used in the transmission of data.

6. Communication hardware – where a brief explanation of some of the hardware used in data communications is provided.

Why network computer systems?

It is impossible for one library to hold all of the world's library resources. However, it is possible for one library to have *access* to all of the library resources in the world through computer networks. Many of the most exciting developments in library services are due to improvements in the area of data communications. These are laying the foundations of the electronic library predicted in the literature. A day may arrive when a person walks into a library, sits down at a computer and has the ability to access any book, journal, newspaper, periodical, video and so forth from anywhere around the world. Computer networks are advantageous for two reasons:

*   the sharing of computing resources
*   the sharing of data and information.

Sharing of computing resources

A major benefit of networking computer systems is the ability to share computer system resources. Expensive items such as printers, hard disk drives, modems and scanners can all be shared, saving money and hardware maintenance costs. As an example, one printer can be shared by many people and a hard disk can be used to provide users with a common place for their personal information as well as a common place to share public information.

There is currently a trend to save on the costs of desktop computers by using something called thin client. Many organisations, instead of putting the latest and most powerful microcomputer on everyone's desk, will buy their employees thin client or network computers. These do not store the software or data required by the employees, but act as intelligent terminals, networking to a server that does store the organisation's software and data files.

Sharing of data and information

Probably the dominant reason why computers are networked is to share data and information among users. Users can share ideas and opinions by sharing information on a common networked hard drive, for example. Software products or common data such as bibliographic records can be shared over a network. Common storage areas ensure that there are not multiple versions of the same information. Networks provide the ability to share ideas and information and collaborate on projects, despite the physical distance of project members.

Consider the following data communications applications (based on applications discussed earlier):

- linking of local library management systems into bibliographic networks, with a view to resource sharing (for example, increased inter-library loans or reciprocal borrowing agreements)
- linking of a library management system with the computer resources of a parent body in a local area network (for example, a local council's mainframe-based system or a university's campus-wide network)
- use of a non-library terminal (typically a microcomputer) to access a local library system or a remote system or other electronic resources via the Internet
- use of an electronic mail facility to send a request to another library's electronic mail account
- transfer of bibliographic records from a cataloguing cooperative such as Kinetica
- linking of local library systems with vendors' systems for the purpose of online ordering and claiming of library materials
- use of electronic networks for online invoicing and payment: for example, library materials or inter-library loans
- transfer of user data from a non-library system (for example, a college mainframe or minicomputer) to avoid re-keying data already in machine-readable form
- use of the Internet to transfer documents in machine-readable format.

Network models

Networked computer systems can be in one of two broad categories: Local Area Networks (LANs) or Wide Area Networks (WANs). The distinction between the two is purely geographical, although with advances in technology the boundaries between the two are blurred.

Local area networks

LANs are generally restricted to linking computer systems within or between offices, usually within the same building. They incorporate the sharing of printers and hard drives as well as providing electronic mail facilities to aid communication between LAN users. LANs come in one of three topologies: bus, ring or star.

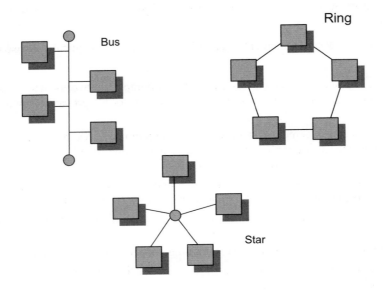

Figure 7.1: The bus, ring and star local area network topologies

Bus

In a bus topology, all devices are connected to a central cable, called the bus or backbone, which is terminated at each end. Bus networks are relatively inexpensive and easy to install and are used by Ethernet networks (discussed later). Their disadvantage is that if one connection fails, the network becomes unusable.

Ring

All devices in a ring topology are connected to one another in the shape of a closed loop, so that each device is connected directly to two other devices, one on either side. Messages travel around the ring, with each node keeping only those messages addressed to it. They can span larger distances than a bus network because each node regenerates the messages passing through it. Ring topologies are relatively expensive, more difficult to install and, as with bus topologies, if one connection fails, the network is inoperative. For this reason, most ring topologies use multi-access units (MAUs) which bypass faulty connections, keeping the ring structure intact.

Star

With a star topology, all devices are connected to a central hub. Star networks are relatively easy to install and manage, but bottlenecks can occur because all data must pass through the hub. The main disadvantage of star networks is that they require more cabling than other topologies, such as a bus or ring networks. In addition, if the central hub fails, the entire network becomes unusable.

Wide area networks

WANs involve communication between computer systems over a wide area. Generally speaking WANs are for communicating between cities and countries and in most cases a WAN is a collection of LANs. The most common WAN to librarians is the bibliographic network. Most of the applications listed previously involve the transfer of data (for example, bibliographic records, inter-library loan requests or book orders) over a substantial distance.

Network media

Three elements must be present for the transmission of data to take place:

- Sender
- Medium (a channel along which data are transferred)
- Receiver.

The media used to link two computer systems together can be either direct or indirect. Direct uses a physical connection between the two systems using cables, whereas indirect uses the air as a carrier for a transmitted signal. For each of these methods, a number of different media are used to achieve data communication.

Direct media

Direct connections involve physically connecting one computer system to another using cables. Three common cable media are described here.

Twisted pair

Twisted pair cabling consists of two insulated copper wires twisted around each another (thus the term twisted pair). The relative potential difference between the two wires is the signal. The twisting in the wires reduces line noise since any electromagnetic interference is induced into both wires, thereby canceling each other out. Twisted pair cabling can reach distances of up to a hundred metres. Further distance can be achieved by shielding the twisted pairs with wire braid or using repeaters, which regenerate a signal before re-transmitting it. (Repeaters are discussed later.)

Coaxial cable

Coaxial cable consists of a centre wire surrounded by insulation, which in turn, is surrounded by a grounded shield of braided wire and plastic insulation. This shield is used to reduce electromagnetic interference. Coaxial cabling is the primary type of cabling used by the cable television industry and is also widely used for computer networks. Although more expensive than twisted pair, it is much less susceptible to interference and can transmit data more quickly than standard twisted pair. Networking coaxial cable generally comes in two forms, 10base2 and 10base5. These can reach distances of up to 200m and 500m respectively before the signal requires amplification.

Optical fibre

Fibre-optic cabling transmits data as pulses of light instead of electrical impulses. It has 26,000 times the transmission capacity of twisted-pair cabling despite the fact that it is around one twentieth of the size. Fibre-optic cable is slowly replacing the old twisted-pair telephone lines. Optical fibre cables can carry very high volumes of data at high speeds (the speed of light) and offer the major advantage of not being susceptible to electrical interference. They are lighter, smaller and less expensive than coaxial cable. Another advantage of fibre optic cable is that it cannot be tapped, and since data are transmitted as pulses of light, breaking the cable disrupts the flow of data, preventing it from being 'read'. Optical fibre can reach distances of a few kilometres before requiring amplification.

The following diagram compares the physical sizes and transmission capabilities of these three forms of cabling.

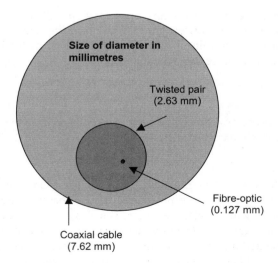

Figure 7.2: Comparing physical sizes of twisted pair, coaxial and fibre-optic cabling

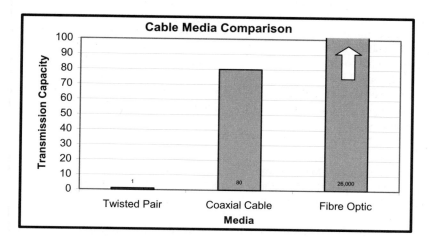

Figure 7.3: Comparing transmission capacities of twisted pair, coaxial and fibre-optic cabling

Indirect media

The technology developed for mobile or wireless telephones is now widely used for computer communication: for instance, RF or radio frequency technology supports wireless LANs (WLANs), in which data are transferred over the air, with little need for direct connection.

The following are the three most common media for transmitting data using air as a carrier.

Infrared (IR)

Some computing devices and peripherals achieve data transfer by using infrared signals (the same signals used by a TV remote control). Transmitted infrared signals are quite weak and can only be received within a radius of around ten metres and must be in the line of sight of the transmitter, hence this medium is only used within a room to provide a cable free data transmission environment. Some laptops come equipped with IR transmitters and receivers. These can be used to transmit data between two laptops or for using a wireless keyboard or mouse.

Microwave

Microwave is a form of high frequency radio signal (operating at thousands of MHz) in which the signal is not broadcast but is transmitted in a straight line through the air. Due to the curvature of the earth and the fact that microwave signals cannot bend, microwave links are only useful for distances of around 100 km or so. This makes it ideal to transmit data between buildings in a city or a large University campus. Some libraries have used microwave technology to transmit data between a city library and the city's mobile libraries. Even with its distance limitations, many organisations still choose microwave for long distance communication. In these instances microwave dishes are placed around 100 km apart depending on the terrain. Microwave dishes receive signals from one dish and re-transmit the signal to the next. Hence, during transmission, data hop from one microwave dish to another until the destination is reached. It is imperative that each dish is in the line-of-sight of the other and so dishes are often placed on top of hills, mountains and buildings to enable a longer distance between hops and to prevent trees and the like from obstructing the transmitted signals.

Satellite

Satellites work similarly to microwave but are used for transmission over longer distances. A communication satellite orbits about 35,000 km above the earth's surface and rotates at an exact position and speed giving the impression that it remains over a fixed point on the earth's surface. The satellite receives signals from stations on the earth's surface. The signals are then amplified before being re-transmitted to the next earth station in direct line-of-sight. Satellites are used to overcome the problem that microwave dishes have with the curvature of the earth as the following diagram illustrates.

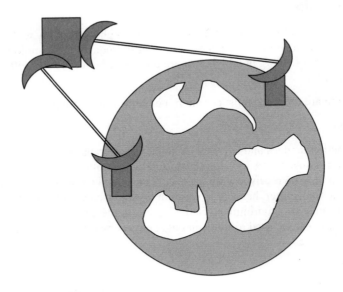

Figure 7.4: Satellite transmission

Selecting a communications medium

Three things must be considered when selecting which media type to use for transmitting data.

Distance

A signal transmitted along any medium will diminish as the signal moves away from its source. If the distance between sender and receiver is too long, the signal may require boosting to ensure that the transmitted data are still interpretable at the receiver's end. This is done with repeaters or amplifiers similar to those used in television broadcasting.

Bandwidth

The bandwidth refers to the capacity of a channel and is measured by the number of bits per second that can be transmitted along a medium. The transmission of video and audio generally requires a constant bandwidth to ensure satisfactory image and sound. However, the cost of the transmission increases in proportion to the bandwidth required.

Noise

Signal noise or distortion is caused by electromagnetic interference, and results in the corruption of data. Care needs to be taken to ensure that electromagnetic interference does not 'pollute' the transmission path. Moreover, increases in data transmission rates result in increases in the likelihood of data corruption.

Data transmission methods

This section will cover the following topics dealing with the varying methods used to transmit data, including some of the methods used to detect and correct transmission errors:

- data representation and data storage (review of last chapter's discussion)
- parallel and serial transmission
- synchronous and asynchronous transmission
- simplex, half-duplex and full duplex transmission mode
- analogue and digital signals, and
- error detection and correction methods.

This may look a little daunting, but each concept is easy to understand. Nevertheless, before considering these different methods of transmitting data, it is worth reviewing some relevant points about data representation and storage, as discussed in Chapter 6.

Data representation and data storage (review)

The last chapter identified the basic unit of data in a computer as a bit (Binary digIT). A group of eight bits is called a byte and is the unit used to represent characters in machine-readable form. The two most commonly used codes for character representation over the years have been ASCII and EBCDIC, but there is now considerable interest in Unicode. ASCII, to take an example of an industry standard, was developed specifically for data communications. Characters are identified in ASCII by only seven bits. The eighth (leftmost) bit was referred to as a parity bit and this is used for detecting errors during transmission. Error detection and correction will be covered in more detail at the end of this section.

Parallel and serial transmission

Data communication is essentially the transmission of binary digits (bits) from a sender to a receiver. There are two standard methods for doing this: parallel and serial transmission.

Parallel transmission

Parallel transmission involves sending the bits that make up a byte side by side so that the bits that belong together arrive at the receiving device simultaneously. This method of transmission requires a cable with at least eight wires (one for each bit in the byte). Consider the following diagram indicating the parallel transmission of the letter 'a' (ASCII=01000001).

Figure 7.5: Parallel transmission

Parallel transmission becomes impracticable if data are to be transmitted over distances longer than about five metres. This is due to the fact that the longer the data have to travel the greater the chance that electrical interference among the eight wires will occur, resulting in the transmitted bits arriving at different times and causing nonsense data. Consequently, parallel transmission is generally used for transmission of data within the computer system and between the hardware components of the computer system, such as connecting a printer to a computer.

Serial transmission

Serial transmission involves sending the bits that make up a byte one after each other. Illustrated below is the transmission of the same letter 'a'.

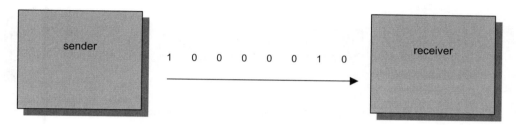

Figure 7.6: Serial transmission

In theory, parallel transmission is around eight times faster than serial transmission (since parallel can transmit eight bits at a time instead of one). Nonetheless, serial transmission can still reach extremely high transmission speeds. The extra control offered by serial transmission also results in a more reliable form of transmission and so is used for long distance communication (as opposed to parallel transmission that has a maximum distance of around five metres).

Consequently, the remainder of this section is devoted to the different forms of serial transmission. As mentioned previously, parallel communication is utilised within the computer system itself through the bus (see Chapter 6 for a discussion on buses). Therefore, whenever data are transmitted serially, they first need to be converted from the computer system's parallel form into a serial form. Each computer has a port called an *RS232 serial port* whose job is to convert parallel to serial (when sending serial data) and serial to parallel (when receiving serial data).

Synchronous and asynchronous transmission

The relationship between the sender and the receiver is quite intimate in computer systems. Both must know exactly what the other is going to do and when. As with people, if the receiver of information is not listening, the sender's message is not understood. In serial transmission, there are two transfer methods that can be used; synchronous and asynchronous.

Synchronous

This is the faster and more expensive of the two methods. Synchronous transmission sends all data at once in what is known as a data stream. Both the sender's and receiver's system clocks must be synchronised to ensure that the receiver knows when data transmission will start and finish, including the precise time that the next bit of information will arrive. Consequently, the system clock in synchronous transmission is vital to maintain control during transmission.

Figure 7.7: Synchronous data transmission

Asynchronous

This method has *no* timing mechanism. Data are transmitted one byte at a time, with each byte starting and/or ending with start and stop bits respectively. In this way the receiver can identify each byte received. The advantage of asynchronous transmission, apart from its cheaper cost, is that data can be transmitted whenever convenient for the sender (unlike synchronous where all data are sent in one continuous stream). Consequently, the majority of serial transmissions are performed asynchronously.

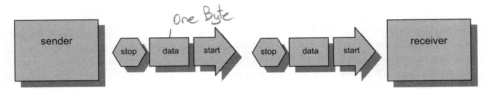

Figure 7.8: Asynchronous data transmission

Asynchronous flow control. The start and stop bits allow the receiving device to determine the start and end of each transmitted byte. In asynchronous transmission, there may be varying time intervals between each transmitted byte (unlike synchronous transmission). As a result, how does the receiving device know when the next byte is coming, and how does the sender know if the receiver is ready for the next byte of data? There are two methods for controlling the flow of asynchronous data.

1. *Software flow control (XOF/XON)* – the receiver informs the sender when it is ready to receive data. It does this by transmitting special bytes called XOFF and XON. An XOFF (transmit off) signal is transmitted to the sender when the receiver wants to temporarily halt the flow of data, and the XON (transmit on) signal is transmitted to the sender when the receiver wants to resume the flow of data.

2. *Hardware flow control (RTS/CTS)* – the cable connecting the two devices has an extra wire in it, dedicated to controlling the flow of bytes. The sending device asks the receiver if it is ready to receive data using an RTS (Request To Send) signal. The sender then waits until the receiver responds with a CTS (Clear To Send) signal. When the CTS signal is received, data transmission occurs. For hardware flow control to operate successfully the cable must have the extra wire and both sender and receiver must be configured for hardware flow control communication.

The exchange of XON/XOFF and RTS/CTS signals between serial devices is called *handshaking* and occurs numerous times during data transmission.

Simplex, half-duplex and full duplex transmission mode

In addition to the method of data transfer (parallel or serial), and the type of transmission (synchronous or asynchronous), there are three modes of transmission: simplex, half-duplex and full duplex.

Simplex

Simplex refers to data transfer that occurs in one direction only. It is not frequently used in communications systems but can be used where data are broadcast only. Simplex behaves the same as traffic moving down a one-way street or the broadcast of radio or television signals.

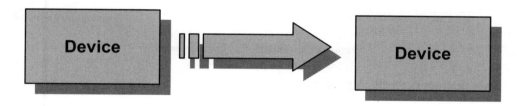

Figure 7.9: Simplex transmission mode

Half-duplex

Half-duplex refers to data transfer that occurs in both directions but only one at a time. Each communications device takes it in turn to send data while the other receives, and vice-versa. Half-duplex behaves the same as traffic on a one-lane bridge or two people using a walkie-talkie or CB radio.

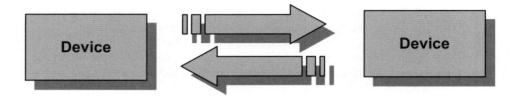

Figure 7.10: Half-duplex transmission mode

Full duplex

Full duplex refers to data transfer that occurs in both directions simultaneously. Each device can send and receive data at the same time, saving on transmission time. Full duplex behaves the same as traffic on a two-way street or two people talking on a telephone, since it is possible for both people to talk at the same time. Full duplex is the most common form of data transfer and is the fastest of the three but requires more expensive equipment.

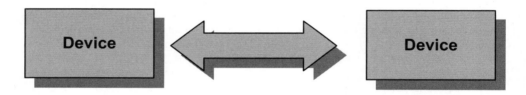

Figure 7.11: Full-duplex transmission mode

Analogue and digital signals

Data can be transmitted in one of two forms, analogue or digital form.

Analogue

Analogue signals are transmitted using a continuously changing quantity as a reference. Data transmission consists of sending signals as continuous waves. An example of an analogue signal is the transmission of radio waves, television waves or sound waves. Analogue signals are of particular interest to computer systems since the majority of the world's telephone systems transmit analogue signals and it is these telephone systems that are often used as the medium for data communications. The telephone system, which is designed primarily to transmit the human voice, translates sound waves into analogue signals for transmission, which are reconverted into sound waves at the receiving handset. An analogue signal may look something like the following:

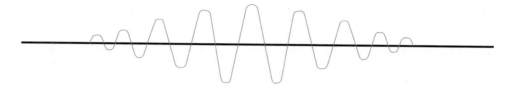

Figure 7.12: Analogue signals

Digital

Digital data transmission consists of sending signals in the form of discrete on (high) and off (low) states. The following diagram illustrates the digital representation of 11010010. A high-voltage state represents the binary digit 1 and a low-voltage state represents the binary digit 0.

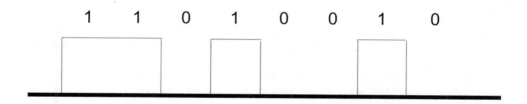

Figure 7.13: Digital signals

Digital is by far the more versatile, efficient and fast method of transmission over both short and long distances. However, as previously mentioned, most of the established communication channels (such as the telephone network and radio and television broadcasts) use analogue because it was the only method around when they were invented.

This poses a problem for data communication since the two systems, digital and analogue, are incompatible. There are two strategies to overcome this problem:

- convert the digital signals from the computer into analogue signals for transmission over the existing telephone network
- change the world's telephone network system to a digital system.

As silly as the second option might sound, the major players in the telecommunications industry do offer digital networks such as ISDN (see below) or fibre optic thus making it possible to link digital devices without the need to convert digital signals into analogue. Also, a significant proportion of the old twisted pair cabling has been replaced with the newer fibre-optic cabling paving the way for a digital future. With respect to television signals, pay TV companies bring digital signals directly into the home and some countries have already introduced digital TV.

Not surprisingly, converting digital signals into analogue is the more frequently used strategy. Devices called modems are used to convert digital signals into analogue and vice-versa. Modems are discussed later in this section.

Error detection and correction methods

It was mentioned previously that transmitted data can lose some of their integrity during transit, due to either hardware faults or noise (such as electromagnetic interference). How can we be sure that the data received are the same data that were sent? As one can imagine, undetected transmission errors could be devastating. (It is worth noting here that an error in binary is where a bit that should be a 1 is a 0 and vice-versa.) Fortunately there are a number of methods that can be used to detect and correct transmission errors. Following are four of the most common error detection and correction methods.

Parity checking

Chapter 6 discussed how characters are represented using ASCII and how only seven out of the eight bits are required to represent a character. During data transmission, the eighth bit can be used as a parity bit. This parity bit is used to detect errors. This eighth bit is calculated and appended to the seven bits just prior to transmission. There are two kinds of parity: odd and even. When two computer systems transmit data using parity checking they must ensure that they are both using the same kind of parity. In odd parity, the number of 1's is added up and the eighth bit is made to be a 0 or a 1 to ensure that the total number of 1's in the byte is an *odd* number. For even parity the same occurs except that the eighth bit is made to be a 0 or a 1 to ensure that the total number of 1's in the byte is an *even* number. For example, the letter 'P' in 7-bit ASCII is 1010000. If this was transmitted using odd parity, a one would be added to become **1**1010000 (number of 1's = 3) and similarly for even parity a zero would be added to become **0**1010000 (total number of 1's = 2).

When the data are received at the other end, the computer system counts the number of 1's to ensure that there is an odd (or even) number. If a discrepancy is found, the sending device is notified and the character is re-transmitted.

This is the simplest form of error detection and works for the majority of cases. It does not detect all errors however, as the following example demonstrates. Say that odd parity is used on the same letter 'P'. The sending device transmits 01010000. Imagine that bits 4 and 5 have errors so that the receiving device receives 01001000 (notice that bits 4 and 5 have changed from a 0 to 1 and 1 to 0). This byte still has an even number of 1's and so an error is *not* detected. As can be imagined, parity checking is not for everyone. Imagine a bank using this method to transfer money between accounts!

Check sum

This method treats each byte that is sent as a binary number, and each of these bytes is added together. To complete the transmission of the data, the sum of the bytes is sent. At the other end, the receiving device has been busily adding up all the bytes so that when the check sum is received at the end of the transmission, it is compared with its own value. If the check sum differs, then the data are re-transmitted. For large files, check sums are calculated based on small portions of the file so that if an error is detected only a portion of the file needs to be re-sent.

Cyclic redundancy check (CRC)

CRC treats the transmitted data as one long binary number. This long number is divided by an agreed constant (CRC-16 uses 16 as the divisor) and the remainder is sent to the receiving computer after all data have been sent. This remainder is then compared with the remainder that was calculated by the receiving computer and, if they differ, the offending data block is re-transmitted.

Hamming code

So far the parity checking, check sum and CRC methods are all used to detect errors only. To correct the error, the data block must be re-sent. The hamming code is a method used not only to detect a transmission error but also to locate the faulty bit and consequently correct it without having to converse with the sending device.

For a 7-bit ASCII code, an extra four bits are added (unlike parity checking where only 1 extra bit is added) making a total of eleven bits. Each of the four bits is assigned as a parity bit for only some of the eleven bits, such that each bit is checked by exactly two other bits. When an error occurs in transmission, a process of elimination can determine the offending bit, and consequently, the bit can be toggled from a 0 to a 1 or vice-versa.

This begs the question, why doesn't everybody use the hamming code? The reason is that an extra 57% of data is transmitted (an extra four bits out of seven) to achieve this result, when in reality, errors in transmission occur less than 1% of the time. For most, a 57% increase in transmission time is not a fair trade-off for the advantages. Despite this, the hamming code has applications where data security and integrity are crucial, such as the defence forces and government agencies.

Protocols

So far, this chapter has discussed a number of varying methods for transferring data and connecting computer systems together. It is imperative for two computer systems to agree on a method of data transfer *before* data are transmitted. Imagine the results if the sender and receiver were using different parity checking. The only data that would be accepted would be the ones that had errors in them!

The set of conventions or rules governing the transfer of data between computer systems is called a protocol. Despite the fact that there is a variety of computer systems in existence, they can all communicate with each other if they use identical protocols. The protocol determines things such as: the type of error checking to use, the type of data compression, how the receiving device indicates that the message has been received, and many more. Already a number of these protocols have been discussed, such as parity checking, serial, asynchronous and full duplex.

The Open Systems Interconnection (OSI)

To simplify the transfer of data, the International Standards Organisation (ISO) has defined a layered system of communication protocols called the Open Systems Interconnection (OSI). This consists of a 7-layered *OSI Reference Model* for defining specific aspects of transmission control, as well as *OSI Protocols* for each of these seven layers.

Although the OSI is an international standard, the OSI protocols contained within its seven layers have not been universally accepted. A major reason for this is that there are numerous other suites of protocols that were already well established in the market place when the OSI Protocols were released. Some of these are:

- TCP/IP (Transmission Control Protocol/Internet Protocol) – a suite of protocols used on the Internet, which has become a standard for many academic and government environments
- SNA (Systems Network Architecture) – a layered protocol like OSI developed by IBM
- AppleTalk – a suite of protocols developed by Apple to network Apple Macintosh computers together
- DECnet – a set of protocols developed by Digital Equipment Corporation
- Novell Netware – developed by Novell for their network operating systems.

Despite the fact that the OSI protocols have not been accepted, the OSI Reference Model has. It is used by many organisations to *develop* new protocols and to explain the functions of protocols already in existence. As a consequence, the OSI Reference Model will be used here to assist in explaining the many popular protocols in the market place today.

As previously mentioned, the OSI organises the communications hierarchy into seven layers where each layer addresses specific aspects of transmission control. The data to be transmitted are encapsulated down through the seven layers before being physically transmitted across the network media. The receiver then 'unwraps' each of the seven layers, in turn, to get to the transmitted data. This process is akin to a person wrapping up a gift in seven different colors of paper before giving it to somebody. The person receiving the gift then unwraps each layer, one at a time, to find the gift in the middle. The following diagram may help to illustrate the process.

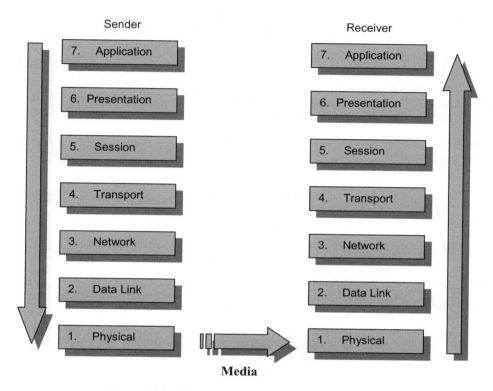

Figure 7.14: The seven layers of the OSI reference model

It is beyond the scope of this text to describe every communications protocol that exists for each of the seven layers. There are literally thousands of protocols in use around the world. It will, however, briefly explain each layer as well as the most commonly used protocols in each layer.

1. Physical layer

This layer manages the putting of data on to the network media and off again. The three most common physical layer protocols are:

Ethernet. This protocol, developed by Xerox Corporation for LANs, utilises either CSMA/CD or CSMA/CA technology. Carrier Sense Multiple Access (CSMA) with Collision Detection (CD) is the standard for Ethernet networks where each network device constantly monitors network traffic. Devices wishing to transmit onto the network wait for 'silence' before attempting to transmit data. If two devices attempt to transmit at exactly the same time, a collision is detected and both devices wait a randomly assigned time interval before attempting to re-transmit the data. With Collision Avoidance (CA), rules are set up between devices to avoid collisions in the first place. Ethernet can be used on bus and star topologies.

Token ring. IBM developed token ring for implementation on a LAN ring topology. A token (a special pattern of bits) circulates the ring passing through each device on the network in turn. Devices must have possession of the token before transmitting onto the network. In this way collisions are avoided.

To explain the protocol, consider the following example:

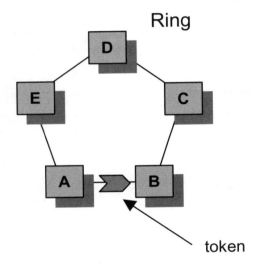

Figure 7.15: A token-ring local area network

Device A wants to transmit a message to device D and so waits for a free token to arrive. When it arrives (from E) it attaches the data to be transmitted to the token along with the transmitter's (A) and receiver's (D) address. Before passing the token on to B, however, A changes the free-token pattern to a busy-token, thereby informing other devices that the token is in use. Device B receives the busy-token, realises that the token is being used and that the data are not intended for it, and passes the token to the next device (C) in the ring. Likewise C passes it to D. Device D realises that the data have reached their destination and strips off the data for processing.

It then attaches a new message to the busy-token (indicating that the data were received successfully) along with the transmitter's (D) and receiver's (A) address. The token passes through E to A, where A receives the message. To complete the data transmission process, device A transmits a new free-token and the token circulates the ring again until a device wishes to transmit data.

ISDN. Short for Integrated Services Digital Network, ISDN is an international standard for sending voice, data and video over digital telephone lines. ISDN supports data transfer rates from 64 Kbps (Kb per second) to 2 Mbps (Mb per second). ISDN is for Wide Area Networks (WANs) and is usually implemented over fibre-optic cables.

Recent years have seen the wide development of digital subscriber line (DSL) services, using existing telephone lines to provide high-speed connections and good bandwidth.

2.   Data link layer

This layer is responsible for passing data from one device to another. The most common data link protocols are a set called 802 developed by the Institute of Electrical and Electronic Engineers (IEEE). Two of these 802 protocols are:

> **IEEE 802.3** – defines the MAC layer for bus networks that use CSMA/CD, the basis of the Ethernet standard.
>
> **IEEE 802.5** – defines the MAC layer for token-ring networks.

Other common protocols in the data link layer are:

Frame relay. A packet switching protocol for use in WANs, by which data are divided up and sent in packets instead of one continuous stream of data (circuit switching). The packets are sent separately and can even follow different paths to their destination. When all packets have arrived at the destination they are sorted to form the complete message.

ATM. Short for Asynchronous Transfer Mode, ATM is a WAN protocol that transmits data in cells or packets. Older technologies use large data cell sizes, however, ATM uses cell sizes of only fifty-three bytes in size with very basic routing information. This ensures that no one data type (video, audio or data) can 'hog' the transmission line. Transfer speeds can range from 25-622 Mbps. ATM is a cross between packet switching (where there is no dedicated transmission route) and circuit switching (where a dedicated transmission route is established). ATM creates a fixed route between the sender and receiver whenever data are transferred. Some believe that ATM will revolutionise the Internet bandwidth problem.

3.   Network layer

This layer is responsible for routing data from one network node to another. Some of the common network layer protocols are:

IP. Short for Internet Protocol, IP is usually linked with TCP (discussed in the next layer). However, IP by itself works much like a postage service. Messages are addressed and dropped off at the destination, but no direct connection exists between the sender and the recipient. Each host computer on the Internet has an IP address consisting of four numbers separated by periods; for example, 137.166.16.198. This IP number uniquely identifies the host computer throughout the world. As mentioned in Chapter 1, these numbers are also associated with a fully qualified host name since names are easier to remember than numbers. Hence `137.166.16.198` has a fully qualified host name of `www.csu.edu.au`. Either its IP address or fully qualified host name can be used to address a host computer, however, it is always safer to use the fully qualified host name since its IP address may change from time to time.

IPX. Short for Internetwork Packet Exchange, this protocol is used by Novell Netware operating systems. It is similar to IP in that it is usually linked with a higher level protocol (in this case SPX) and by itself delivers messages based on connectionless communications.

SLIP. Short for Serial Line Internet Protocol, this is one of two methods of connecting to the Internet via a modem. SLIP is the older but simpler of the two methods and is used to carry TCP/IP traffic only.

PPP. Point to Point Protocol, PPP is the second of the two protocols used to connect to the Internet via a serial port. PPP is the newer of the two protocols and offers some advanced features. Unlike SLIP, PPP is a multi-protocol transport mechanism. Not only can PPP be used to carry TCP/IP traffic but IPX, AppleTalk, NetBIOS and many others, all at the same time.

Frame relay. Some protocols span across two or more OSI layers. Frame relay is an example of this, spanning both the data link and network layers. It is a packet-switching protocol for connecting devices on a WAN and supports transfer speeds from 1.544 – 45 Mbps.

X25PLP. The X.25 packet level protocol forms part of the X.25 standard developed in 1976 covering the first three OSI protocol layers.

4.   Transport layer

This layer is responsible for the integrity of the transmitted data, from sender to receiver, using error detection and correction methods. There are two common protocols in this layer.

TCP. Standing for Transmission Control Protocol, TCP is usually combined with IP to form TCP/IP networks. Whereas IP is concerned with the packets reaching a destination, TCP establishes a connection between the two hosts, thereby guaranteeing delivery of data. TCP is also responsible for ordering the packets when they arrive at the destination, since some packets may arrive out of order. TCP/IP is a routable protocol and hence is a popular one, since network traffic can be controlled and minimised. As far as library-related systems are concerned, TCP/IP is *the* network protocol.

UDP. User Datagram Protocol is a connectionless protocol that, like TCP, runs on top of IP networks. UDP offers very few error correction services but instead offers a more direct way of transmitting data. UDP's main application is in the broadcasting of messages over an IP network. Network diagnostics programs such as Ping, NSLookUp and TraceRoute use UDP.

SPX. Short for Sequenced Packet Exchange, this protocol sits on top of the IPX network layer protocol. Generally referred to as IPX/SPX, SPX provides the connection services that IPX lacks. SPX and IPX have the same joint functions that TCP and IP have respectively and like TCP/IP, IPX/SPX is routable.

5.   Session layer

The fifth layer of the OSI model, the session layer, is responsible for establishing and maintaining the communications channels. In reality this layer is often combined with the Transport Layer. However there are three common protocols associated with this layer.

NetBIOS. Short for Network Basic Input Output System, NetBIOS is an extension of DOS BIOS adding special functions for LANs.

NetBEUI. NetBEUI is an extension of NetBIOS. Short for NetBIOS Enhanced User Interface, it is primarily used by network operating systems such as Windows 95, Windows NT, Windows for Workgroups, LAN Manager and LAN Server. It was originally designed by IBM but later extended by Microsoft and Novell.

SAP. Service Advertising Protocol is a Netware protocol used to inform other devices of services and addresses of servers on a network.

6.   Presentation layer

This layer is responsible for presenting the data in a form acceptable to the application. For example, this layer would convert character codes into either ASCII or EBCDIC and vice-versa, depending on the application. Once again, this layer is often combined with the Transport Layer and hence there are few protocols associated with it. One, however, is:

RPC. Remote Procedure Call is a protocol allowing a program on one computer to execute a program stored on a server.

7.   Application layer

This layer meets the needs of specific applications and handles all inter-application communication. There are many protocols in this layer. However, the protocols based on the TCP/IP and OSI suite of protocols are the focus here.

Common TCP/IP protocols

Telnet. This is a terminal emulation protocol used to connect to a server on the Internet. From here, commands can be typed in as if the user were sitting in front of the server.

FTP. This protocol is used on the Internet to send (upload) and receive (download) files from remote servers.

X Windows. A windowing and graphics system developed by the Massachusetts Institute of Technology. Almost all UNIX graphical interfaces are based around X Windows.

SMTP. Simple Mail Transport Protocol is used to send email messages between client and server and between servers. It is used for sending email only.

POP. Post Office Protocol is a protocol used by clients to retrieve email messages from a mail server.

IMAP. Like POP, the Internet Message Access Protocol is used to retrieve messages from a server. It offers some advanced features that POP3 doesn't offer: for example, searching of email messages while they still reside on the server. Stanford University developed IMAP in 1986.

SMB. Server Message Block is a message format for sharing files and directories and devices. NetBIOS, previously mentioned, is based on the SMB format. A product called Samba is based on SMB, which allows UNIX and Windows machines to share files and directories using TCP/IP.

DNS. As mentioned previously, all computers connected to the Internet have an IP address that uniquely identifies it, and each IP address has a fully qualified host name associated with it, such as www.csu.edu.au. Domain Name Service is a protocol used to convert fully qualified host names into IP addresses and vice-versa. Hence, when someone tries to connect to www.csu.edu.au, DNS is used to convert it into its IP address 137.166.16.198.

DHCP. Dynamic Host Configuration Protocol is used to assign IP addresses to devices attached to the Internet. This means that a device may have a different IP address each time it is turned on.

HTTP. Hypertext Transfer Protocol is a protocol used on the World Wide Web and defines how Web pages are requested, formatted and transmitted.

Ping. Ping, a UDP/IP protocol, is used to check whether a device is turned on and is part of the Internet (alive) or not.

Common ISO protocols

Although the OSI protocols have not been accepted readily, ISO have numerous protocols that are gaining in support every year. Major software vendors are beginning to ensure that their products support these ISO protocols. Some of these protocols follow:

X.400. This is an ISO standard for addressing and delivering email messages. Although included in the OSI model it supports Ethernet, X.25, TCP/IP and dial-up connections.

X.500. X.500 is an ISO standard defining a hierarchical structure for storing, retrieving and accessing directory information such as a person's email address, company, state or country and so on. X.500 is slowly being accepted by software vendors and many companies are ensuring that their inhouse protocols and applications are X.500 compliant. Novell's NDS (Network Directory Services) is X.500 compliant, for example.

LDAP. Lightweight Directory Access Protocol (sometimes called X.500-Lite) is a cut-down, simpler version of X.500, which supports TCP/IP (unlike X.500). Due to its TCP/IP compatibility, LDAP makes it possible for almost any application on any machine to access directory information such as email addresses.

There is constant pressure on standards organisations to approve and internationally standardise new and revised protocols. One such protocol is Z39.50 (referred to in earlier chapters), which has already had a significant impact on the library community.

Z39.50. Formally called 'Information Retrieval Service Definition and Protocol Specifications for Library Applications', Z39.50 is a standard approved in 1988 by the National Information Standards Organisation (NISO) in America. Revised in 1992, this Applications Layer protocol provides a uniform method for users to access information resources such as online library catalogues. (The ISO equivalent is ISO23950:1998, 'Information and documentation — Information retrieval (Z39.50)'.) Consider the significance of this protocol for the library environment. From the perspective of the library user, any Z39.50-compliant information resource – library catalogue or database, especially – can be accessed using the same user interface. What the protocol does is not only to allow the applications to communicate but also to allow the user to access the information resource using the familiar user interface of the client system. In other words, the user does not need to worry about the differing interfaces of library catalogues and proprietorial database platforms (such as ProQuest and Ovid).

Many organisations are attempting to develop client and server support of Z39.50. It is easy to imagine the benefits obtained if all libraries around the world implemented Z39.50. This would pave the way for information sharing between any two libraries across the world and vastly increase each library's resources. Most library management systems (discussed in Chapter 4) include a Z39.50 client module that should provide access to any Z39.50-compliant database. It should be noted, however, that vendors and/or libraries need to ensure that their software is upgraded so that it is compliant with the most recent version of Z39.50.

Z39.50 has its critics: for instance, those who see 'scalability' problems in the fact that 'multithreading' several institutions (libraries are not the only users of this protocol) at the same time can create a communications overload between client and server and consequently a bottleneck. It is also attacked for being too complex or not very 'web-like', and there are newer standards such as XML that seem likely to replace it; however, Z39.50 does have the merit of permitting simultaneous enquiry on heterogeneous databases and currently there is research into linking it to standards such as XML and RDF. Continued development takes place within an informal group of implementers and developers known as the Z39.50 Implementers Group, or ZIG.

Other important protocols

Simple Object Access Protocol (SOAP). This is an XML-based protocol designed to provide an open, extensible way for applications to communicate over the Internet and pass data and instructions to each other, regardless of which operating system or language the applications may use. SOAP facilitates communication by defining a simple, extensible message format in standard XML and providing a way to send such XML messages using HTTP.

Wireless Application Protocol (WAP). This is a set of communication protocols designed to enable mobile users with wireless devices to access and interact with Internet applications such as email and the Web. It is intended that it will work with most wireless networks and can be built on any operating system. It should therefore provide service interoperability, even between different families of device.

Communication hardware

The last section of this chapter is devoted to listing and describing some common networking devices. With all the previous discussions on protocols it might be refreshing to read about things physical instead of abstract. Before departing from protocols altogether, however, it would be a good opportunity to introduce first a piece of networking hardware called a gateway.

Gateways

As discussed, there are numerous suites of protocols such as OSI, TCP/IP, Netware and AppleTalk to name a few. To make it possible to connect these somewhat incompatible systems, gateways are used. Gateways are a combination of hardware and software and are used to route data packets and convert from one protocol to another. They are generally used to connect WANs together or LANs to WANs.

Hubs

A method of connecting sections of a LAN, a hub contains multiple ports to which to connect devices. Messages arriving to the hub are copied to each port (broadcast). Hence all sections of a LAN can see all packets. This broadcasting aspect of hubs is undesirable since it dramatically increases network traffic.

Bridges

Bridges are used to connect two LANs together regardless of whether the LANs are alike or not. Bridges aren't too fussed about protocols but simply forward packets without performing any processing on them. A special kind of bridge, called a switching hub, is available. A switching hub is really a multi-port bridge which remembers the addresses of the devices attached to each port. Consequently, messages arriving at the switching hub can be routed directly to the correct port instead of being copied to each port on the hub.

Routers

A router is similar to a bridge except that it has the ability to filter out messages and re-route messages based on certain criteria. For example, messages falling into an IP address range of 137.166.80.xxx may be routed down one path (administration building, for example), while all others may be routed down another (library).

Repeaters

A repeater is used to regenerate an analogue or digital signal. A signal passed along a cable will eventually deteriorate. Repeaters can be used to amplify the signal and then re-transmit it to reach a longer distance than that which a cable is normally capable of reaching. For analogue signals, a repeater can only amplify the signal received, whereas a digital signal can be reconstructed before being re-transmitted. Some network devices have in-built repeater characteristics to ensure the integrity of the data signal.

Modems

A modem is short for MOdulator DEModulator and its function is to modulate signals from the computer to the telephone line and vice-versa. In other words, when a computing system is transmitting data, a modem converts the digital signals from a computer into an analogue signal that can be transmitted over a telephone line. Conversely, when a computing system is receiving data, it converts from an analogue signal to a digital signal.

The following diagram may help to illustrate:

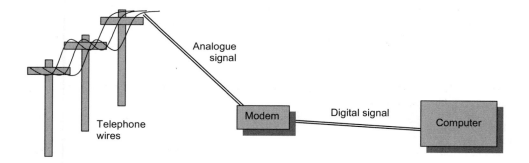

Figure 7.16: The function of a modem

A modem provides computer users with a method of transferring data when they are in a location with no network connection. The modem is a key hardware device in data transmission and mobile computing, since the telephone system is probably the largest cabling infrastructure throughout the world. Modems can be either internal, in other words, the modem is inserted into a spare expansion slot inside the computer, or external, in which case the modem is attached to one of the spare serial ports of a computer. Fortunately the RS-232 serial port is a standard interface for connecting any modem to a computer. Most modern computers have at least one RS-232 serial port. With the growing use of wireless technology, it is also worth knowing that there are wireless modems, which connect to the serial port and transfer data through the air.

Although there is a standard interface for attaching modems to computers, numerous protocols for data transmission exist that a modem may or may not support. Some of these protocols are international standards such as CCITT V.32 bis, while others, such as US Robotics HST, have been developed privately.

There are many characteristics that separate one modem from another. Following is a short list of some of these:

Bits per second (bps)

BPS is a measure of the transmission and reception speed of a modem. Some common speeds are 28,800 bps, 36,600 bps and 56,600 bps. However, the slowest device in the overall connection between sender and receiver determines the transmission speed. Unfortunately, there are few telephone lines that will transmit at speeds greater than 28,800 bps.

Voice/data/fax

Some modems support the transmission of voice (just like a normal telephone), data and facsimile. In some cases the voice and data may be transmitted simultaneously. Modems supporting voice usually have a built-in speaker and microphone. With a fax modem, facsimiles can be sent from a word processing application or received into a graphics application for reading or manipulating.

Auto answer

Some modems have the ability to answer incoming calls automatically (much like an answering machine does).

Flash memory

Modems that have flash memory instead of ROM can be updated regularly without having to purchase a new modem.

Data compression

One way modems can reduce transmission time and increase transmission speed is to use data compression techniques. Data are compressed just before transmission, enabling faster throughput of data. Various methodologies exist for compressing data and so it is essential that the data compression method is agreed on when two modems initiate communication. One such method, or protocol, is called V4.2bis which can achieve compression ratios of 4:1 while another called MNP Class 5 can achieve 2:1.

Modems will not be with us forever. This is because a lot of the world's telephone systems are being converted from analogue to digital through the use of fibre optic cabling, thus making the modem redundant.

Network interface card (NIC)

The network interface card is inserted into a spare expansion slot within a computer (see the reference in Chapter 6 to plugging cards into the motherboard). NICs are usually designed for specific network media and network protocols: for example, one NIC may support twisted cabling for an Ethernet network, while another may support a token-ring network. Every network card has a unique address called a MAC (Media Access Control) address or Ethernet address. This is used to identify uniquely each machine on a network.

Multi-access unit (MAU)

A MAU is a special kind of hub that is used to overcome the vulnerability of a ring topology. Without a MAU, a ring network would fail if one node on the network were faulty. With a MAU, each node on the ring connects to the MAU. If a node fails, the MAU detects this and shorts out the non-operating node to maintain the ring structure.

Terminators

Terminators are used on bus networks to terminate each end of the bus. Their function is to absorb signals to prevent them from being 'reflected' back down the cable.

Proxy servers

Although not a special data communications device like those just discussed, a proxy server is a computer server that is put to special use in data communications, because it is the hardware device through which communications between an organisation's internal network and the outside world typically must pass. Combined with appropriate security software, the proxy server forms a *firewall*, the purpose of which is to help protect an intranet from external threat. The software examines the content and source of each message and blocks those that fail to meet the organisation's security parameters. Like most web browsers, proxy servers also make use of cache memory (see Chapter 6), which means that web pages that have previously been downloaded by members of the organisation are stored, so that if they are requested again they can be accessed from the proxy server's memory, saving the time that might be spent retrieving them again from the Web.

Review questions

1.   What are the advantages of networking computer systems?
2.   What is the difference between a LAN and a WAN?
3.   List and briefly explain some common communications media.
4.   What is the difference between serial and parallel, synchronous and asynchronous?
5.   List and briefly explain three common error detection and correction methods.
6.   What does the word protocol mean and why are protocols necessary?
7.   What is the OSI Reference Model?
8.   What is TCP/IP?
9.   What is the difference between a gateway and a bridge?
10.   Why is a modem necessary? Why won't they be around forever?

Further resources

ACM Transactions on Internet Technology
Published quarterly by the Association for Computing Machinery, which aims to advance the skills of information technology professionals and students worldwide.

American National Standards Institute, < http://web.ansi.org/>.

Griffiths, P 2000, *Managing your internet and intranet services: The information and library professional's guide to strategy*. Library Association, London
This work covers topics such as organisation of a Web site, service provision, registration of domain names, the authoring and design of a website, accessibility and ongoing management of the content.

International Federation of Library Associations, *Internet and networking: Technology standards and organizations*, < http://www.ifla.org/II/standard.htm>.
A valuable resource for the library and information management community, IFLA provides links to such organisations and resources as international and national standards organisations, Internet organisations, metadata resources for digital libraries and inter-library loan protocol resources.

Lawrence, E *et al*. 2002, *Technology of Internet business*. Wiley, Milton, Qld.
This book is aimed at a general readership, as distinct from an IT expert, and is highly readable

White, CM 2002, *Data communications and computer networks: A business user's approach*. 2nd ed. Thomson/Course Technology, n.p., Australia.
As for the Lawrence text, this is a readable approach to networking. It contains a very impressive glossary.

CHAPTER 8
Library systems development

This chapter examines the development of computerised library systems. It builds on previous chapters, which dealt first with computer applications in libraries and then with the supporting technology. The chapter opens with an outline of the main options for systems development facing library managers. Where practicable, the emphasis is on a top-down approach, which takes as its starting point the data-processing and information needs of the library and not simply the availability of the technology. The chapter introduces the traditional systems analysis and design approach, before focusing on the way in which libraries generally go about acquiring new systems, which is to purchase prewritten software packages. Specific aspects of the systems development are examined, including project management, writing specifications, selecting systems, implementing systems and the final systems evaluation.

Learning objectives

At the end of this chapter, you will be able to:

- identify the main stages in the systems life-cycle
- discuss key management issues in the development of library systems
- contribute to a library automation project.

Keywords

Inhouse development
Turnkey system
Consortium
Systems life cycle
Systems analysis

Feasibility study
Functional requirements
Request for proposals
Ergonomics
Smart barcodes

Options for systems development

Systems development may take one of three forms:

- replacement of a manual system with a computerised system
- upgrading and addition to an existing computerised system
- replacement of an existing computerised system with another.

Much of the literature on library automation focuses on the first of these, because replacement of a manual system was the most common reason for undertaking systems analysis and design. A growing proportion of libraries, however, already have computerised systems, and replacement or modification of these systems may be a requirement. The options for systems development may include:

- development of an inhouse system
- purchase of a turnkey system (hardware and software supplied by the one vendor)
- purchase of prewritten library-specific software
- purchase of a general purpose software package, such as those discussed in Chapter 5
- contracting with an existing bibliographic network
- forming a consortium for the purposes of automation
- making use of the existing computer system and staff of a parent organisation.

Development of an inhouse system

Before the market in prewritten library-specific software became established, the most common means of developing computerised library systems was inhouse development. Advantages of inhouse development centre on the fact that inhouse systems are custom-designed. Provided the process of systems analysis and design is done properly, the product should be a system that reflects the specific needs of the library better than any prewritten software. The main disadvantages of inhouse development are the time and cost of software development, and the reliance either on staff with considerable expertise or external consultants (see below). Given the huge amounts of programming code required for a library system and the increased functionality expected from most systems, inhouse development is a highly unlikely course of action, except for relatively simple systems.

Turnkey systems

A turnkey system is a system that comprises both hardware and prewritten software. It is so called because of the comparative ease of implementation: the vendor will generally install the system, leaving the librarian to switch on and get started (hence 'turn-key'). Typically, the vendor will also provide some training: for example, training key staff in the case of a large library, and a maintenance contract that may include supply of new software versions and amendments as they are developed. Turnkey systems are also generally integrated systems that provide library management functions such as cataloguing, acquisitions, circulations and serials control. Main advantages to note are speed of implementation, low costs compared to inhouse development, stability of costs, proven performance (provided the vendor already has customers) and, generally, good maintenance contracts.

Prewritten library-specific software

A library might decide to purchase prewritten library-specific software without being tied to purchasing hardware from the same vendor. This may be because the library already has access to hardware (its own or that of a parent organisation) or can obtain the hardware more cheaply than it can from a turnkey vendor. It is perhaps worth pointing out that libraries do have much more ability to 'mix and match' than they did in the 1980s because of the demand that hardware and software conform to open standards and the increased use of a client-server architecture.

Purchase of pre-written software has many of the advantages of a turnkey system, but the question of maintenance is not so clear-cut. Where a library relies on different suppliers for hardware and software, there may be a problem in making suppliers accept responsibility for problems.

Many of the system vendors design different versions of their systems so that they can be used with more than one automation platform. (Automation platform refers to the operating system and hardware on which the applications software runs.) This might be regarded as a desirable feature if the library plans to move at a later date to a new platform. Prewritten library systems are predominantly integrated systems, but there are also many stand-alone packages for specific functions, such as serials control and media management.

Prewritten generic software

Some libraries opt to use general purpose software, such as database management systems or text retrieval packages, and adapt these to library needs. This may be because the library already has access to such a package (for example, a system used by a parent organisation) or because the library is especially small and its parent organisation cannot afford to purchase library-specific software. Advantages include the fact that many of these packages have been developed for use in the business and financial sector and are already well tested and well documented. Another advantage is that because general purpose software has a much larger market than library-specific software, it is generally less expensive than the latter, a factor which may influence selection in a small library. Because of their general nature, however, these packages are less likely to be appropriate to library data processing and information needs than either custom-designed or library-specific software. They can be adapted for library use, but this requires more expertise than use of prewritten library-specific software or turnkey systems.

Bibliographic networks

The principal motives behind the development of bibliographic networks have been the perceived benefits of shared cataloguing and the growing need to share resources through enhanced inter-library loans and reciprocal borrowing (see Chapters 2 and 3). Other facilities are now offered, such as acquisitions and circulations functions. As well as sharing data and resources, libraries may be able to share other costs, such as hardware and software development and systems administration.

Networking is not an option that all libraries can consider. A suitable network may not exist, and even if one does exist, the costs of membership may be prohibitive. There is little evidence so far that library networks have benefited their member libraries financially. Library managers are generally motivated by the desire to improve service provision to users and not by the belief that they can cut costs. Methods for evaluating the benefits of library networks include:

- measuring avoidance costs (for example, savings from avoiding original cataloguing or from borrowing material instead of purchasing it)
- measuring direct costs
- studying collection overlap (a low level of overlap being regarded as most beneficial)
- identifying and assessing success factors, such as fill rates of inter-library loans and response times (Woodsworth 1991, pp. 66-67).

Consortia

Some libraries opt to form a consortium instead of joining an existing network. The difference between a network and a consortium is that whereas a library network 'assumes a formal organization, composed of member libraries that have some shared goal or goals, and that realize the goal(s) in part through reliance on computing and telecommunications technologies,' a library consortium is a group of libraries 'that work together on a number of projects that may or may not be technologically grounded' (Woodsworth 1991, p. 2)

Forming a consortium to develop an automated system may suit a group of small libraries that sees benefits in sharing hardware, software and maintenance costs. They are generally organised on a local basis. The main benefit, apart from the sharing of development and maintenance costs, is resource sharing on a local level. The shared bibliographic file is a source of information for inter-library lending and for collection development (some duplication of stock among member libraries can be avoided), a common circulations function makes the placing of reservation holds quicker, and member libraries can use an electronic mail facility to communicate requests. The quality of service can be demonstrably improved, but again there is no evidence that such consortia produce cost benefits to member libraries.

Computer systems of parent organisations

In terms of cost alone, use of the existing computer facilities and staff of a parent organisation offers immediate benefits. The ability to use an existing automation platform cuts out a considerable factor in development costs. Strategies for system development include:

- use of existing software (for example, a generic DBMS)
- development of new software by computer staff and/or by an external consultant
- purchase of prewritten library-specific software compatible with the operating system in use.

One of the added advantages that some library managers see in using the facilities of a parent organisation is that the library can use the expertise of existing computing staff. All the system maintenance work can be done by computing staff, whereas the purchase or development of a stand-alone library management system requires a member or members of library staff to take responsibility for system maintenance.

There are disadvantages, of course, such as the fact that computing personnel who have had no previous contact with librarians may find the special needs of libraries mysterious. The history of computerised library systems development is full of stories about the inability of librarians and computer department personnel to communicate with each other. Where the central computer is in a different building from the library, there may be specific personnel problems: for example, public libraries requiring file-saves or back-ups to be done in the evening when the staff of the computer department are no longer on duty.

The systems approach

Much of the literature on systems development refers to the fact that systems have a life cycle. This may seem a pessimistic viewpoint for a library that has just invested heavily in a computerised library system. The system life cycle can be represented like this:

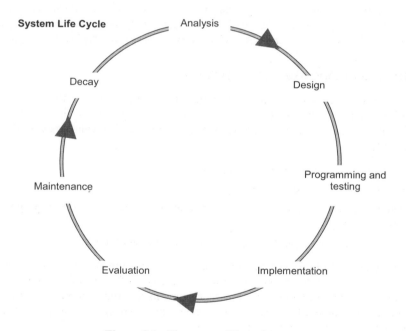

Figure 8.1: The system life cycle

Systems development should be a top-down process, beginning with an analysis of management needs. Traditional (inhouse) systems development consists of the following steps:

- analysis, which includes analysis of organisational needs and objectives, analysis of the means of meeting organisational objectives, a feasibility study and an analysis of the functional requirements of the proposed system
- design stage, in which the functional requirements are transformed into a detailed set of physical requirements: for example, output, input, user interface, database design, processing and security requirements
- programming and testing phase, when the detailed system specifications are translated into program code and the programs are tested: for example, using test data
- implementation, which is the process of installation, converting from the old system to the new one and testing how the system works as a whole (for instance, checking performance times and capacity for handling peak loads).

These phases include not only the birth stages of the system life cycle, but also its running life through to its eventual decay and replacement. This involves not only system maintenance but also a post-implementation evaluation. Given the investment in time and money involved in systems development and the *apparently* new-found interest in accountability, it is important for a library to check whether or not the system is performing according to the objectives laid down in the systems analysis. In the course of time, this evaluation will also become the basis for the development of a replacement system.

Limitations of inhouse development

The strategy outlined above, sometimes called structured systems analysis and design, is the traditional approach to systems development. In very general terms, it is the strategy for developing a custom-designed inhouse system. There are disadvantages with this approach: for example,

- time taken to develop and test the software
- errors found in the system after implementation
- dependence on skilled staff or consultants, who may leave without writing proper documentation
- costs escalating over the development and implementation period.

In the early days of library system development, it may have been necessary for a library to undertake this kind of development, because of the lack of appropriate library-specific software. With few exceptions, current developments and redevelopments, however, follow the alternative strategy of purchasing prewritten library-specific software or else a turnkey system. This offers the following advantages:

- speed of implementation (the software is already developed)
- fixed costs, in general (the software is already developed)
- lower costs, in general, than for inhouse development (the substantial costs of design and programming are in effect shared by the libraries that buy the product)

- lower risk than for inhouse development (the software has already been tested, unless it is an entirely new product)
- a maintenance contract, which can include software redevelopments and enhancements (avoiding reliance on local expertise, which may not always be available).

There are disadvantages to the purchase of prewritten systems. One is that they are written for the average library, and will not reflect management needs as closely as a custom-designed system. This should not be exaggerated, however, because of the degree of parameterisation offered by many prewritten systems (see Chapter 4). Second, just as inhouse development entails reliance on local expertise for maintenance and redevelopment of systems, so purchasing a prewritten system entails reliance on a vendor. There are cases in which programmers have left a company without leaving proper documentation. Moreover, some companies go bankrupt or are taken over by other companies. It is a very volatile industry.

There are documented cases in which library directors opt for inhouse development. The motivation is generally frustration with existing commercial systems: for example, search facilities that are considered unacceptably slow or inadequate, circulation systems that are not designed for fast throughput, crude or inconvenient management information systems or badly designed screen processes.

Any inhouse development these days, however, involves adapting a software package, such as a database management system, rather than writing a new system from scratch in programming code. This offers more customisation than purchasing a prewritten system, but it requires more time and expertise than the latter.

Purchase of prewritten library systems

This section discusses the purchase of prewritten systems, either complete turnkey systems or the software component. The structured approach to systems analysis and design outlined above can be adapted to the purchase of prewritten systems. The main difference is that the lengthy design and programming phases are replaced with the writing of a detailed set of specifications and the selection of a turnkey or software package that best meets the specifications. The structured stages to purchase a system are:

- systems analysis
- writing of specifications and selection of system
- implementation
- maintenance and evaluation.

The remainder of this chapter looks at each of these phases in turn.

Systems analysis phase

As for inhouse development, the systems analysis stage should include:

- an analysis of organisational needs
- an evaluation of alternative means of meeting organisational objectives
- a feasibility study
- an analysis of functional requirements.

Why a new computerised system?

The first stage in the analysis process is to determine the library's needs. A library manager will generally only undertake computerised systems development if it can be demonstrated that computerisation or an upgrade in computerised systems will provide demonstrable benefits to the library and/or its parent organisation. The decision to investigate the possible development may be prompted by a problem in existing systems, such as the inability of an existing circulation system to cope with the demands of a busy loans department, or by a perceived opportunity: for example, an improvement in the quantity, quality or timeliness of information supplied to users/organisations. Benefits may be tangible, that is, benefits that can be quantified and evaluated in dollar terms, or intangible, that is, benefits that cannot be expressed in dollar terms.

In the library environment, the benefits claimed for computerisation are generally of the intangible variety and relate to improved service to users, such as:

- enhanced information service through access to online databases or to web resources
- improved access to the library's information resources through enhanced catalogue access
- improved dissemination of information about the library's information resources (for example, listings of video material for teachers)
- faster data processing (for example, shorter queues at circulations counters)
- improved circulation control, resulting in greater availability of library material
- improved accuracy, resulting in better public relations
- enhanced inter-library cooperation, resulting in access to wider collections
- increased productivity, releasing staff from clerical duties to assist users more directly.

Tangible benefits are rather more difficult to demonstrate. These may include:

- reduction in repetitious clerical routines, leading to decreased staff establishment (or, less commonly, immediate redundancies)
- improved financial management (for example, in acquisitions function)
- improved management control (for example, monitoring of staff and vendor performance)

- enhanced inter-library cooperation may lead to rationalisation of collection development on a regional or national level.

Research into library systems development suggests that library managers are more interested in potential improvements in user services than in the reduction of operating costs.

Evaluation of alternatives

Once organisational needs and objectives have been identified, the next step is to define in general terms the kind of systems development required. Although the library manager may be influenced by existing knowledge and experience of computerisation, including experience of specific systems and configurations, the emphasis at this stage is on functional needs.

At this stage, the library manager should try to gather information on the alternative means of achieving organisational needs. The solution may be an integrated automation package that computerises all the library's basic functions, but there may be other alternatives. A library manager concerned about the inadequacy of an existing manual circulation control system may opt to computerise only that function (although the introduction of such stand-alone systems is a decreasingly popular option). The library manager may already have a preconceived notion of what system to purchase. It is important, however, to explore the various options so that the library gets the system best suited to its needs. Means of identifying available systems and technology are to:

(1) Discuss with other users in similar organisations
(2) Carry out relevant reading (books, journals, trade literature)
(3) Visit suppliers and dealers
(4) Go to exhibitions and demonstrations
(5) Attend short courses and seminars ...
(6) Consult:
  - professional associations
  - special interest groups
  - training organisations
  - specialist centres
  - relevant academic departments
  - database producers and hosts
  - information consultants   (Webb 1996, p. 41.)

To these sources of information one could add Internet resources, such as discussion or mailing lists, newsgroups and websites. There are also user groups, which are groups of organisations that use the same system and exchange information and experiences, sometimes, but not necessarily, over the Internet. Note too that library directories can give pointers to the systems in use in libraries comparable to your own.

Logically, if a top-down approach is taken, the analysis of organisational needs and functional requirements should form the basis of software evaluation, since the library manager is looking for the prewritten system that most closely meets requirements, and this depends largely on the software features. The choice of software will then determine the choice of automation platform used. In practice, the hardware may be selected first (for example, where a parent organisation already has appropriate hardware or where it can secure discounts for the purchase of certain hardware). In this case, the alternatives to be considered are restricted.

Feasibility study

Once there is a clear idea of the kind of system envisaged, the next step is to explore the feasibility of the proposed course of action. The main areas to be considered are:

- technical feasibility: whether the proposed course of action can be implemented with the existing hardware, software and technical expertise
- economic feasibility: whether the benefits outweigh the costs.

In the business and financial sectors, the economic feasibility study may involve a formal cost-benefit analysis, to discover whether or not the benefits outweigh the costs of the proposed project. In the library environment, the former will generally include intangible benefits that cannot be expressed in dollar terms. This does not mean that a cost-benefit analysis should not be attempted. The exercise puts a value on the proposed benefits and may be required by funding bodies.

Costs include both the initial costs of development and recurring costs. Initial costs may include:

- purchase of hardware and/or software
- purchase of manuals from vendor
- training (conducted initially by the vendor)
- file conversion
- site preparation.

Recurrent costs include:

- purchase of consumables (for example, magnetic tape, computer printout paper)
- maintenance costs or contract
- enhancements of the software as it is developed
- extra staff salaries (for example, Systems Librarian).

Working parties

Once the decision has been made to go ahead with the proposed development, it is common practice to form a working party (or project management group or steering party committee). In a large library, this might involve the heads of department led by a project manager. The working party, on occasion, may include a trade union representative. It should be added, however, that the degree of staff involvement, and of course trade union involvement, does depend largely on organisational culture, which in turn depends on the type of organisation concerned (for example, public or private) and on societal values: for example, many Asian cultures are not, if the literature is to be believed, as conducive towards participative management as most westernised cultures (although it is too easy to exaggerate cultural differences).

Proponents of participative management argue that staff should be involved from an early stage. There are two main reasons. One is that staff have a good working knowledge of existing systems, data processing, and information needs and problems, and will have much to contribute to the project. Second, if staff have some input, they are much more likely to regard the project as theirs than to regard it as something imposed from above. They become *stakeholders*.

There have been references for years to the stress that development of computerised systems inflicts on staff: for example, fear of unemployment, underemployment, deskilling or occupational health and safety problems (OH&S). Staff involvement brings these issues into the open from an early stage and encourages them to be addressed. It is argued, therefore, that non-professional staff should be involved in project development, and not merely a small automation working party made up of library and IT professionals. A minimal strategy is to use a regular newsletter to report on the progress of the project and on the decisions made by the library manager or working party.

Analysis of functional requirements

Part of the analysis process is to draw up a set of functional requirements. The questions asked at this stage include:

- Which operations is the system to cover?
- Which databases need to be created?
- How are these databases to be created?
- What kind of records are to be in the database?
- What information will be sought from the database?
- How will the information sought from the database be presented?
- Which are the vital features and which are merely desirable additions?
- Who will use the system regularly?
- What level of experience can be expected of users?

(Rowley 1996, p. 193)

At this stage, the library may send out a Request for Information (RFI) to vendors, giving a brief overview of requirements and asking vendors if they could satisfy them (not to be confused with a Request for Proposals; discussed below).

System selection

The outcome of the analysis should be a set of functional specifications, which becomes the basis for the following stages of systems development:

- production of a detailed set of specifications

- identification of appropriate systems and invitation of tenders from vendors
- selection of the system that most closely meets the library's functional, technical, financial and other requirements.

A detailed set of specifications is required if the library is to send out requests for proposals, because vendors must have information on which to base their proposals. A set of specifications also provides project teams with criteria on which to evaluate proposed systems and compare them.

Request for proposals (RFP)

The traditional way of eliciting the required information from vendors is to send a Request for Proposals. The most common strategy is to approach a short-list of vendors, whose suitability has been established in the earlier information-gathering stage. This is generally a formal document. It should:

- identify areas which should be addressed in each vendor's proposal, such as references to users of the system, details of training programs and documentation, technical specifications (for example, model and memory capacity of CPU), costs of loading data files and maintenance details
- give the vendors sufficient information on which to base their proposals: or example, background information on the library, an outline of the selection process, a contact name, mandatory and desired functional requirements and performance specifications, and terms and conditions that must be included in the contract.

It is also common to include forms, in order to make it easier to compare proposals: or example, a price quotation.

It is often suggested that a RFP is a waste of time for systems selection. RFPs were designed as a way to ensure that the claims of a vendor were backed up in writing, especially in the case of products that needed extensive development or customisation. The argument against RFPs is that such a process is not appropriate for makers of standard, off-the-shelf products and that the licence agreement should protect libraries by stating that the software performs as documented. The main argument for using a RFP is that it facilitates the next step: system selection.

Selection process

The next step is to evaluate the proposals submitted by vendors. Provided there is a sufficiently manageable short-list of proposals, it will assist the decision-making process if the library manager or working party can visit libraries already using the proposed systems and discover first-hand from colleagues whether or not they are happy with the product and the company. It may also be advisable to arrange demonstrations of the most suitable systems, although demonstrations that use small test databases tell very little about processing or retrieval times.

The information on which the selection decision is made is very complex, and much of the literature recommends the use of decision matrixes to assist the process. One strategy is to begin by listing detailed functions (more detailed, for example, than the features listed in Chapter 4) and to use these as the basis for decision matrixes, in which competing systems are given scores. In order to calculate a score, one might:

- allocate each function a raw score on a scale of 0 (not available) to 10 (meets all criteria);
- allocate weights on a scale based on the relative importance of each function, where the scale may be 1 to 10, 1 to 100, or any other limits which meet your needs, for example, 'Accept *MARC* records' - 100, 'Accept diacritics' - 15;
- multiply raw scores by weights to obtain a weighted score;
- add weighted scores for comparison.

(Fraser & Goodacre 1993, p. 4.)

It is also advisable to indicate whether any of the features listed are *mandatory*. Clearly, if any system fails to provide a mandatory feature then it should be eliminated straight away. This does mean that special care should be taken when indicating those features which are mandatory, since it is undesirable to eliminate an otherwise excellent system on the basis of a feature that the library *could* manage without.

The remaining step in this phase of development is to negotiate a contract with the successful vendor and to inform the other vendors who sent proposals of the decision.

System implementation

Implementation comprises five main steps:

- site preparation
- installation of software and (if appropriate) hardware
- staff training and preparation of documentation
- creation or conversion of databases, such as bibliographic and borrower files
- running the system.

Some of these activities will be the responsibility of the vendor, particularly the installation of the software and (in the case of turnkey systems) the installation of the hardware. The contract may also cover vendor responsibility for staff training, documentation, and the creation or conversion of databases.

Site preparation

Much of the work of implementation can be done prior to installation. Preparatory work includes:

- preparation of hardware requirements: for example, installing extra power points, organising telecommunications links, preparing conduits for cables, arranging accommodation for CPU (if special conditions such as controlled humidity are required), organising storage for back-ups (such as a fireproof safe or separate location) and rearranging lighting

- purchase of material not supplied by the vendor, such as extra equipment (for example, modems, power conditioning systems such as uninterruptible power supplies), consumables (for example, magnetic tape for back-ups, paper for printers) and new stationery (for example, new borrower cards, purchase order forms).

The list of new equipment should also include health and safety features, such as ergonomic furniture. The term ergonomics refers to design of technological systems that takes into account studies of human physique and behaviour. In addition to ergonomically designed furniture, libraries may need to acquire filter panels or screen coatings to reduce the glare of computer screens, document holders to attach to monitors in order to avoid frequent eye and head movements, acoustic hoods and sound-absorbent barriers to reduce noise, such as the noise of impact printers, and air conditioning systems.

Installation of hardware and software

Normally the hardware will be installed by the hardware vendor or the turnkey vendor, although the library will want to test the equipment to see if it operates according to specifications. The organisation to which the library belongs may also have statutory safety checks to perform on new equipment. Once the hardware has been checked, the software can be installed. The vendor may set up a test account. The term account refers here to a database supplied by the vendor. The main account is the one on which the library's data files will be stored and processed. A test account can be used to:

- train staff (for example, the key staff trained by the vendor)
- set up parameters, which can be copied to the main account once the library is ready to run the system
- test a representative set of records.

Staff training and documentation

Interestingly, libraries that have never conducted formal training programs previously feel the need to conduct training programs for new computerised systems. As a minimum requirement, staff should receive an effective demonstration of the new system prior to the system running. Ideally, however, they should also have hands-on experience. Where a test account has been established, it can be used to give this experience. Training sessions should preferably:

- keep the number of participants small
- find a balance between hands-on experience, on the one hand, and presentation and discussion, on the other
- be brief, where possible, with follow-ups, rather than attempting to provide all the required training in one session.

Vendor-supplied documentation varies enormously in quality. Some of it has a deservedly bad reputation. User documentation includes documentation in the form of screen layouts (such as menus and help screens) and printed documentation. The latter includes:

- policy manuals
- procedures manual, used in staff training
- manuals geared towards particular groups of staff: for example, circulations counter staff, supervisory staff and systems staff.

The procedures manuals produced by the vendor may be too complicated for quick reference (for example, at a busy service point), and some libraries may produce their own task-orientated manuals (ideally word processed for easy amendment). Increasingly, such manuals are made available by library management in online form, most often on an intranet, but this does ignore the fact that print manuals are often more convenient and faster to consult (information management issues again!).

The library manager should also consider the needs of the library user. Once the system is running, user education programs (assuming they already exist) will have to include education in the use of the system. This may take the form of spoken instruction, written handouts and/or web-based instruction. The library manager who is sensitive to the feelings of the library community will also keep users informed of systems developments and of any changes to procedures and services.

Creation of databases

Creation of databases refers to the input of data such as:

- bibliographic data
- borrower data
- supplier data (for acquisitions)
- holdings (copy or item) data.

Some data, such as supplier data, can be keyed into the system with no trouble. Bibliographic and borrower files, however, will be very time-consuming to create if they have to be manually input. Conversion of files takes two forms: conversion of manual files into machine-readable files and conversion of existing machine-readable files into a format that the new system can handle.

In the case of borrower data, it may be possible to load data held elsewhere by the parent organisation. For instance, an academic library may be able to obtain data from the administration division of the academic institution: for example, by downloading the data in ASCII format and uploading the data into the library system. The ability to do this may have been specified by the library to prospective vendors. When borrower data are in manual format, however, there is rarely any alternative to keying in the data. Where libraries are unsure what proportion of their registered borrowers are active borrowers (for example, in the public library service), they may start a re-registration program prior to running the system.

When the library is converting from manual bibliographic files, however, it faces the following choices:

- use existing staff to key data into the new system (expensive, but there is quality control) or hire temporary staff
- pay an agency to handle the conversion: for example, some bibliographic networks will conduct retrospective conversions
- use an optical character recognition (OCR) reader to convert existing manual records into machine-readable form
- download bibliographic data using a communications link with a bibliographic network or order records on a magnetic medium using identifiers such as ISBNs
- purchase a bibliographic database from an external agency: for example, a library that has bought the same system, and transfer records as required from that database to the main bibliographic file (this assumes a lack of copyright problems, acceptable bibliographic standards and an acceptable level of stock overlap)
- convert 'on the fly', which refers to the creation of brief bibliographic records at the point of issue, prior to lending material or after discharge of material (on the principle that this material is in most demand).

It is worth adding that when it comes to system migration, the version of MARC used may become a factor, and it will be necessary to test bibliographic and authority records that are transferred from the old system. It is also necessary to check how the copy or item specific information is linked to the bibliographic records during the migration process.

If an external agency such as a bibliographic network is used as a source of bibliographic records, the holdings data, which are unique to the library, will need to be input locally. The barcode number (see Chapter 4) is generally the link between the physical item and the bibliographic record. It should match a number in the holdings (item) file on the database. There are two main strategies for barcoding material:

- use of *smart barcodes*: these are generated at the time the bibliographic record is created, so that the link between barcode number and record is already made (in other words, when the barcode is generated it already refers to a specific work, and a short description appears on the barcode label) – typically systems generate sheets of smart barcodes, leaving library staff to identify the correct items and attach the barcodes (using the brief bibliographic data printed on the labels to assist matching)
- use of *dumb or generic barcodes*: barcode labels are attached to library material *before* retrospective conversion or cataloguing, so that the barcode does not yet refer to a specific work (hence it is 'generic') – when the bibliographic record is created or loaded from another database, the barcode number must then be read into the appropriate holdings record (for instance, using a light-pen and barcode reader), thus creating the required link between the number and the record.

Where libraries decide to convert on the fly, it may be too difficult for staff to find barcodes on sheets, particularly while users are waiting, in which case generic labels (dumb) barcodes may be preferred.

Running the system

There are four basic strategies for the process of converting from the old system to the new:

- *direct conversion*, in which the new system *in toto* replaces the old system – the most inexpensive option, provided nothing goes wrong
- *parallel conversion*, in which old and new systems run in parallel: for example, using the new acquisitions subsystem to create brief bibliographic records and generate orders, but retaining the old manual system for final financial control until the new system has proved itself – an expensive option in terms of staff time but some consider it safer than direct conversion
- *phased conversion*, in which the system is introduced gradually: for example, a particular function such as circulations (libraries may be under pressure to phase in circulations quickly, because it has a high public profile, and to let the people who are paying for the system see it in operation) – in the case of library management systems, phased conversion may be facilitated by the modular nature of some packages
- pilot conversion, in which the system is introduced in a particular location first: for example, a branch library or a consortium member.

Systems evaluation

Systems development does not end with implementation. The system should be evaluated. The process is both retrospective and forward-looking in that its purpose is to:

- check performance of the system against the system specifications, identifying whether or not the project goals have been met and whether or not there are problems that need addressing
- improve the performance of the system – evaluation forms the basis of future systems development, whether future systems development comprises modifying or and extending the system or replacing it with a completely new system.

Studies in a number of countries suggest that library managers pay insufficient attention to post-implementation evaluation, which is surprising, given the current interest in accountability.

Once the system is running, staff will notice areas in which the system could be improved to good advantage. Library users may also provide useful feedback for those managers who conduct surveys or, like certain business managers, get out front with the end-users. Library managers may also benefit from user groups, which provide a forum for libraries to share information on common experiences and problems and provide a useful channel of feedback from libraries to vendors. Given the growing level of web access, there is plenty of opportunity to develop proactive user groups.

ICT support

In larger libraries, system development of the kind outlined here is typically led by a systems librarian, someone who may have had an amateur interest in computers, in the early days of library system development, but today is likely to be someone with dual librarianship and IT qualifications. In smaller libraries, of course, it may not be possible to create such a position, and the role may become part of another designated staff member's job description or even that of the library director – part of the multiskilling expected in the current library and information management environment. There are a number of ICT specialists, however, who may be an invaluable part of the development project. These might include:

- system analysts, whose specialism is the analysis of information needs within an organisation and the design and implementation of systems that meet those needs
- programmers, who write the enormous amounts of computer code required for a library information system (or the less enormous amounts required to adapt an existing system)
- webmasters, whose area of expertise is the design, operation and evaluation of websites.

Other ICT specialists with whom librarians are likely to work include:

- information systems managers, who have overall responsibility for the information systems in an organisation and are typically 'hybrid' managers with a knowledge of both ICTs and the business environment
- network managers, who are responsible for the running and upgrading of communication systems and for areas such as network security
- database administrators, who are responsible for the design, maintenance and exploitation of organisational databases (to coin a phrase adapted from the IT literature, they could be called data miners)
- computer technicians, who are generally the people who install hardware and software and act as 'troubleshooters' for end-users in the organisation (including librarians)
- help-desk personnel, who provide telephone support for end-users in areas such as use of software and organisational networks
- computer trainers, who provide classes on use of software and organisational information systems, and who may (resources permitting, of course!) train end-users at their desktops.

Conclusion

The emphasis in this chapter has been on the purchase of prewritten software packages and turnkey systems, which is the strategy adopted by most libraries. Nonetheless, it is not the only method of system development. Others have been outlined. The important point, however, is that systems development is seen as a top-down process that starts from an analysis of organisational and/or library needs. Choices may be limited, for example, through the availability of existing hardware, but this should not preclude systems analysis. The examination of systems development attempts to outline the main management issues, and is not intended as a checklist for project management. A couple of the resources listed below will provide more practical guidance.

References

Fraser, D & Goodacre, C 1993, *Selecting library management software*. Centre for Information Studies, Wagga Wagga, NSW.

Rowley, JE 1996, *The basics of information systems*. Library Association, London.

Webb, SP 1996, *Creating an information service*. 3rd ed. Aslib, London.

Woodsworth, A 1991, *Library cooperation and networks: A basic reader*. Neal-Schuman, New York.

Review questions

1. Outline the main options for systems development in libraries.
2. Identify advantages (if any) of using general purpose software (for example, a DBMS) to develop a library management system.
3. Suggest what benefits membership of a bibliographic network can confer in terms of system development.
4. List the disadvantages associated with 'traditional' structured systems analysis and design.
5. Outline the main costs associated with systems development.
6. Suggest the first step to make in the selection of one system from a short-list of systems.
7. Name five main steps in the process of implementation.
8. Define ergonomics.
9. Suggest the difference between a smart barcode and a dumb barcode (and the answer is not 'intelligence'!).
10. Identify four strategies for converting from an old to a new system.

Further resources

American Library Association, *Library Technology Reports*.
Reports in 2003 cover areas such as 'Integrated Library System Software for Smaller Libraries', 'Model RFP for Integrated Library System Products' and 'Radio Frequency Identifiers (RFID)'. See summaries at http://www.techsource.ala.org/ltr.

Bilal, D 2002, *Automating media centers and small libraries: A microcomputer-based approach*. Libraries Unlimited, Greenwood Village, CO.
While obviously geared to small libraries, this contains practical advice on the automation process, including a very helpful 42-page sample request for proposal.

Cohn, JM, Kelsey, AL & Fiels, KM 2002, *Planning for integrated systems and technologies: A how-to-do-it manual for librarians*. Facet Publishing, London.
A practical guide to the automation process, which takes into account the changing electronic information environment.

Hanson, A & Levin, BL (eds.) 2002, *Building a virtual library*. Information Science Publishing, Hershey, PA.
The focus in this chapter has been the processes associated with the development of library systems, but this book deals specifically with the development of digital collections.

Morris, A & Dyer, H 1998, *Human aspects of library automation*. 2nd ed. Gower, Aldershot, Hants.
In much of the literature on library automation, the human perspectives are forgotten. This was admirably remedied in the two editions of this text.

Osborne, LN & Nakamura, M 2000, *Systems analysis for librarians and information professionals*. 2nd ed. Libraries Unlimited, Englewood, CO.
A reasonably practical approach to what could be a theoretical subject. The authors follow the structured analysis and design model that has dominated since the 1970s, but there are also chapters that address the practical concerns of library and information managers (and even a chapter on object-oriented analysis and design).

APPENDIX 1
Case studies

The following case studies have been provided in order to put the theory and principles discussed in this book into some form of context. It is hoped that by reading some concrete examples of system development, readers will make more sense out of the preceding chapters, which at times have been an abstract and generalised gallop through the electronic library, the supporting systems, technology and networks, and the processes of systems development. These are obviously 'snapshots' of particular stages in organisations' systems development, taken not long before the publication of this book.

The first case study is very much an overview of systems development in an educational institution, beginning with automation of library processes in the mid-1980s, through the replacement of that library management system in the late 1990s and ending with library management's current efforts to introduce digitisation and to exploit newer technologies such as RFID. It closes with the Director's vision of the ongoing nature of the endeavour to improve customer service: *'The end of the journey is by no means in sight and the Library must continue to make significant strides to exploit new technologies in order to remain relevant to its users.'*

The second case study focuses on part of that ongoing effort, namely, the continual system upgrades required. In this case, the library is a public library service in a capital city, and responsibility for upgrades is shared by library management, the system vendor and Council's IT managers. What is especially valuable about this case study is the focus on the actual processes put in place to ensure fast and smooth upgrades, good communication and minimum disruption to public service.

The next two case studies focus specifically on the provision of access to information resources – the subject of Chapter 3. The first of these discusses how one academic library has enhanced its bibliographic records by using URLs to link bibliographic records to the value added information provided by online bookstores such as Amazon.com, a project that is still in the process of development. The second provides further information on Kinetica, one of the bibliographic networks discussed in Chapter 3. Note especially the ongoing evaluation of systems and Kinetica's priorities for future development.

The fifth case study discusses an academic library's efforts to create and deliver digital multimedia collections for teaching and research. It is especially worth noting the fact that the technologies used to digitise and deliver existing analogue material, such as video and audio presentations, are also seen as a means of developing the library's own user education programs. Another interesting point to note is that, although the focus here is one library's experience, collaboration with other libraries in the area is now being explored.

The next case study provides a stark contrast with much of the high technology endeavour described so far. The author was seconded to the National University of East Timor Library Project for a short period and experienced first-hand the impact of unstable electricity supply and the related problem of maintaining hardware in adverse climatic conditions. Clearly, disaster planning can only achieve so much. Note, too, the comment about the way in which the English language dominates the online environment and the implications for library staff in a non-English speaking society.

The final case study documents a digital library project in a European city. Note especially the critical importance of providing access to resources, as discussed in Chapter 3, and the need for robust standards in order to ensure the level of resource discovery required for the wide community at which the service is targeted.

Journey towards a digital library

Fang Sin Guek,[1] Singapore Polytechnic

This paper traces the computerisation journey at an educational institute library in Singapore. It discusses how over the years the Library was able to harness new information technology and communication capabilities in meeting the expectations of library users and in providing an effective service.

First computerisation project

The computerisation journey began in the mid 1980s. Library management took the decision to implement a turnkey online integrated automated system to meet the increased demands on library services that resulted from increased student enrolment, teaching staff and a substantial increase in funds for collection management.

At that point in time, the Library served 12,000 members, comprising mainly teaching staff and students. There was a collection of about 125,000 volumes of books, 900 audio-visual titles and subscription of over 1,400 periodical and serial titles. Materials were catalogued using AACR2 standard and a card catalogue with author/title and classified number sequences was provided. The Library's loans totalled 150,000 yearly.

The objective was to provide a totally integrated computing facility for applications such as cataloguing, acquisitions, serials, circulation and information enquiry. It also included the capabilities to manage the budget and management reporting. The system was required to have the hardware and software capabilities to meet the Library's growing requirements for offering fast and efficient services to its users.

Project evaluation

Five tender quotations were received, each with a different library application package. Proposals came from IBM for Centennial Dobis, IDAPS for Technocrat, HP for VTLS, GEAC, and AWA for Urica. The project was evaluated in three stages. In the first stage, systems which did not meet the minimum requirements were eliminated. The second stage was a detailed evaluation of the hardware and software features of the entire system. A set of criteria was used and a rating system adopted to provide quantitative comparative evaluation of the systems. For the final stage of evaluation, testing and appraisal of the applications and system management were conducted. Amongst the other deciding factors were the cost, system support for hardware

---

[1] Fang Sin Guek is Director, Singapore Polytechnic Library.

and software application, company viability, training, expandability of hardware and proven reliability.

System selection

An integrated library package which met our criteria and offered the best solution to the Library's computerisation needs was selected. It provided the following advantages over other systems:

- *flexibility* – its extensive use of parameters provided flexibility in the applications of our library policies. The vendor agreed to customise the system for our needs. In addition source code and object code were also provided.
- *support* – the hardware support was provided by a reputable computer company in the country. The operating system was easy to be mastered by someone who has some basic training in system operation and programming knowledge. The software application package was supported from another site in a neighbouring country by a dial-up phone line.
- *cost effectiveness* – the total cost of the hardware, software, installation and training was the lowest of the quotes received.
- *reliability* – the system had been tried and tested in another academic institution with a large collection of books and large student and academic staff population. The system was also selected for use by nearly forty libraries worldwide. Additionally, the system was developed by professionals in both computer science and library science, and the system was continually being enhanced.

Changing needs and new technologies

The library management system was successfully implemented in 1985 and it served the Library's needs rather well as the functions of acquisitions, serials, cataloguing and circulation were largely automated and well integrated. The main benefits of computerisation at that stage were the automation of many manual processes of record keeping for loans, purchasing of materials, fund allocation and management, and cataloguing.

Users of the Library were offered a faster and more effective way of searching using the online public access catalogue, or OPAC, which was mainly a text-based system. Long queues at loan counters were eliminated as items checked out were swiftly scanned into the library system using barcode technology. That era was characterised by reference librarians searching remote online searches using computers, dedicated phone lines and modem linkups. Management reporting for library functions was improved as statistical data were provided for analysis.

With rapid growth in the information technology and telecommunication sectors, in particular the prevalent use of the Internet in the mid 90s and higher ownership of home PCs, the library was challenged to review its offerings of services for users. At the same time, the Institute had established a fairly sophisticated computing infrastructure, and many IT services and applications were widely available campus wide. There were growing demands and expectations from users to provide multimedia resources, a web-based catalogue, and the capability for the online catalogue to be accessible on the Internet by off-campus students.

Library staff increasingly recognised that the existing system was quickly becoming inadequate in meeting the many new sophisticated needs. A major setback of the software application was its proprietary design and its problem of working well with only compatible platforms. There was also a concern that the system was not Y2K compliant.

Replacement of the library management system

In 1998, Library management decided that the existing system could not keep up with growing needs and new technologies, and that it should be replaced. The main objective for a new system was the capability to link electronically with a multitude of electronic resources to deliver value-added services to support the library's key processes. At that time, the Institute had established a fairly sophisticated computing infrastructure and many IT services and applications were web-based and widely available campus wide.

Key requirements

The main requirements identified for an integrated library and information services system were to:

- provide for features, functions and new information services necessary for library automation in a distributed, multimedia operating environment
- expand PC services to include access to multimedia applications, digital collections, online catalogue, campus-wide services, and CD-ROM and online databases in a networked environment
- provide for a high level integration in network architecture and systems that would allow connectivity to the institution's main computing infrastructure
- ensure successful migration of library data to the new library system
- ensure that the system would be able to work with hardware from different suppliers – it must be compliant with international standards such as Z39.50, allow portability of software and data, and be easy to connect and integrate
- provide third-generation library application software that would be window-based and which would offer the functionalities of a fully integrated library management and information system – these functionalities included cataloguing of library materials, online public access catalogue, authority control, acquisitions and funds allocation, loans of library materials, serials/periodicals control and a management reporting system.

Systems and network requirements

- hardware and software components with capacity for expansion to meet growth in library services for five years
- a UNIX server to host the library application server, Windows NT servers for the other applications and a UNIX or Windows NT server for its WEB server
- desktop control for one-stop service to all library services from workstations in the Library.
- a high bandwidth network enabled by ATM, Fast Ethernet, structured cabling.

Launch of a new library management system

In 1999, a new library management system was implemented to meet those new requirements and needs. The system selected was a turnkey solution which successfully migrated data from the previous library system. It was Windows-based, providing the functionalities of an integrated library management system.

The web-based catalogue had a powerful search engine and it made extensive use of hyperlinks to access additional sources of information. A graphical front-end user interface was designed by the system integrator using a proprietary software to provide a single point of service for the different library services and resources. These included the web catalogue, with patron empowerment for renewals, reservations, checking personal loan records, access to a wide variety of electronic resources available on the Internet, searching online international databases through IP authentication, and accessing library information and forms for services. Statistical data may be output in text file and exported into databases for further analysis using third party software. The Z39.50 protocol allowed the system to perform searches on one or more OPACs simultaneously.

The system fully met the Library's requirements and needs for about three years. In fact, users found the library system very user-friendly and consistently gave it a satisfactory rating in customer satisfaction surveys. However, with the passage of time, limitations in the new system started to surface. The front-end interface which was designed by the system integrator using a proprietary software was found to be restrictive, as the Library could not make changes to the graphical interface unless a fee was paid to the system integrator. Furthermore, as the user interface was designed using the Win NT4 operating system, it was becoming obsolete as Microsoft had announced that support for this product would soon be phased out. As a result, all Win NT4 applications in the institution were gradually being upgraded to Win 2000 platform.

Towards a digital library

In early 2003, Library management decided to take a significant leap forward in upgrading its Library to provide a more comprehensive electronic and digital library service. This would also enable the Library to play a key role in implementing the campus strategy for e-learning in the institution by offering a much wider range of digitised materials to support online teaching and learning. Digitised materials include past examination papers, course readings, images, sound, e-books and journals, and other important resources available within the institution.

The upgraded system will provide a powerful tool for searching library resources and the growing multitude of databases at one go. It will have capabilities for virtual reference services, an online forum for interactive discussions and personalisation services for both access and delivery of services based on the user's personal needs. A gateway will be developed to bring all these services and resources together under a single point for access.

The Library is also embarking on a project to employ Radio Frequency Identification (RFID) Technology for the management and circulation of its collection. All items in its physical collection will be converted from barcode technology to RFID system. This involves programming each RFID tag with unique information about the item to enable identification at the point of loan, return or during an inventory check. The RFID system will be integrated with the library management system for all these transactions. Users will be able to check out items through self-service machines. Returned items will be checked in through an automatic book drop and items will be sorted automatically by the system.

A continuing journey

The journey ahead promises to be a challenging and exciting one as emerging technologies such as wireless technology, 3G mobiles, wireless PDAs and PDA/Mobile hybrids become more affordable and readily available, and users become more technologically aware. Such technologies promise to bring the resources of the digital library to its users anywhere, any time and at an affordable cost. Mobile phones and Personal Digital Assistants (PDAs) will enable users in the future to search the online catalogue, check their personal borrower status, renew and reserve books, read an e-book and receive their reminders through SMS when travelling on buses, trains at any time – indeed, anywhere in the world as long as they have access to telecommunication services.

These developments are part of the Library's ongoing journey to exploit new technologies and needs to deliver an effective and innovative library. The end of the journey is by no means in sight and the Library must continue to make significant strides to exploit new technologies in order to remain relevant to its users.

Upgrading the library management system

Kelly Brennan, Brisbane City Council Library Service

Background

Brisbane City Council Library Service migrated to a new library management system in June 2000, however, system implementation doesn't end with the new library management system. Approximately once a year a system upgrade needs to take place, which involves upgrading the application, working closely with the system vendor during all stages. It is important to note that at each stage, upgrades are risk managed with risk being shared among the vendor, library staff and IT support (Unix, Desktop, Database and Network). Decision points are shared by library management, vendor management and IT management.

Key personnel

- Senior Co-ordinator, Systems, Archives and Finance
- Systems Librarian
- Manager – Library Service
- Library Management System Vendor
- Key staff in Information Technology Support (I-Division)

Why regular upgrades?

Brisbane City Council Library Service upgrades its application for several reasons, and always on the advice of the system vendor. We have a close working relationship with the vendor, who is familiar with the day to day projects which we undertake. Reasons for an upgrade of the application include the installation of patches and fixes (in other words, fixing a known issue with a module such as circulation or cataloguing), performance factors (being a large public library service, transaction loads are continually increasing, both within the library and remotely through our online library catalogue: eLibCat-www.brisbane.qld.gov.au/elibcat/) or a new version of the application becoming available. Further, if a system is not upgraded in a timely manner, and becomes two or more versions out of date, the vendor may cease support.

When a new version of the software is released, it is tested thoroughly by the vendor, but we may experience small problems due to the transaction load, the platform on which the software is running or specialist reports that we require. In these cases, patches sometimes are made available after the initial upgrade, which also require in-depth testing before being installed.

Process

The Senior Co-ordinator, Systems, Archives and Finance, in conjunction with the Systems Librarian, the LMS vendor and key personnel in the Information Technology Support (I-Division) section of Brisbane City Council (such as Unix support staff) coordinates a date for the upgrade to occur on the production hardware. We are fortunate to have both a test system and a production system, which allows all stress testing and functionality testing to occur before any changes are made to the production system. The vendor upgrades the test system, and then Brisbane City Council Library Service undertakes a month of in-depth testing before the upgrade occurs on production. During the installation, the system is unavailable. Thus, any upgrades to the production system are usually scheduled for a long weekend such as Australia Day, to minimise the disruption to the public.

A two day period is required for a full backup of the system to occur (a necessity in case rollback is required – see below), the vendor to install the new version and the Systems Librarian to install the new version of the client on several staff machines. The Systems Librarian then undertakes functionality testing to ensure that the upgrade to the production hardware was successful. Any problems that are discovered are relayed back to the vendor immediately, and they are resolved that day if possible. At any time, if the Senior Co-ordinator, Systems, Archives and Finance, Systems Librarian or the vendor feels that any major problem cannot be solved before the system is made available to the public, then the decision is made to rollback.

If key staff are satisfied that the upgrade was successful, the next day involves branch staff 'pulling back' the upgraded client from the server. When staff first access the client in the morning, they are prompted to upgrade to the new version. As there are approximately 277 staff machines that need to be upgraded, across thirty-five sites, a schedule is prepared to minimise the stress on the server, which in turn ensures that each branch has enough circulation machines upgraded when they open the doors, so that customer service is not compromised.

Testing procedure

Testing – both stress and functionality testing – is a structured process in which the System Librarian thoroughly tests all applicable modules of the new version, as well as any new functions that are made available. The release notes to the new version are available online, and these are used to identify new functionality, as well as any known issues (small issues that the vendor has been made aware of after the release). The Systems Librarian is responsible for a small group of branch staff who have been identified as having excellent problem identification skills – known as 'Superusers', they are involved in the stress and functionality testing phase. Over a period of a week these staff use training machines which have the new version of the client installed, and replicate as many transactions, both simple and difficult, as possible to try to identify any problems.

One difficulty which we encounter is in stress testing, as it is impossible to replicate the large amount of transactions that occur daily on the production system. While there is software available which can undertake proper stress testing, this would not be useful in our environment as it would not be an 'apple to apple' comparison, as the production and development hardware have different specifications.

The Superusers work off a checklist created by the Systems Librarian, which lists the minimum transactions that must be replicated. For each situation, at least ten transactions must be replicated, for example:

Circulation

- test basic checkouts
- place holds while user has bills on his or her record
- cancel holds which are 'in-transit' to pickup library
- create new user
- try to remove user who has holds on his or her record.

Any problems that are identified during this stage are tested again by the Systems Librarian, and then passed on to the vendor to be solved before the upgrade occurs on production.

Rollback procedure

A rollback procedure is documented by the Senior Co-ordinator, Systems, Archives and Finance. This procedure involves rolling back to the backup copy of the database, as well as the vendor's reinstallation of the previous version of the application on to the server. Rollback will occur if key personnel decide that there are major problems that cannot be fixed prior to staff pulling back the client in the branches.

Communication

Because branch staff are responsible for pulling the client back on the machines in their library, it is important that the System Librarian provide a simple yet detailed set of instructions for staff to follow. Further, a list of 'new or different' features is provided, before the changes are made on production, to alert staff to developments. Brisbane City Council operates a central helpdesk for staff to contact for desktop support, so it is important that the helpdesk is aware of upgrades, although all questions/issues will be relayed back to the Systems Librarian. Moreover, as the library catalogue is unavailable while the upgrade is occurring, it is important that staff relay this information to customers.

It is the intention to make each upgrade as smooth as possible, with minimum negative impact on customer service. Good documentation and communication is vital, as well as working closely with the vendor to ensure that all problems are solved before the upgrade occurs on the production hardware. Brisbane City Council Library Service has an excellent relationship with its LMS vendor, and this has resulted in each upgrade going smoothly, and the rollback procedure never having to be implemented.

Enhancing the library online catalogue with value-added information from online bookstores

Tommy Yeung[2] and Owen Tam,[3] Lingnan University Libary, Hong Kong

Throughout the years, libraries have been exploring various ways to enhance bibliographic records in their online catalogues with the aim of providing more useful information to users. In late 2002, Lingnan University Library began to insert hyperlinks (URLs) in bibliographic records linking to value added information provided by online bookstores such as Amazon.com. As of April 2003, more than 76,000 English-language monograph titles published from 1993 to 2002 (60% of the Library's English collection) have been matched against the holdings of Amazon.com, with a matching rate of 85%. More than 64,500 bibliographic records of these titles in the library's online catalogue are now enhanced with URLs to Amazon.com.

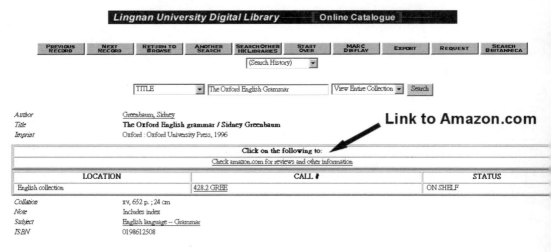

Figure 9.1: Example of enhanced online catalogue record

The project has significantly enhanced the library's online catalogue by allowing users to retrieve all sorts of value-added information not included originally in the bibliographic

[2] Tommy Yeung is Associate Librarian, Lingnan University, Hong Kong (email: tyeung@ln.edu.hk).
[3] Owen Tam is Acting Associate Librarian, Lingnan University, Hong Kong (email: owent@ln.edu.hk).

records. These include book reviews, table of contents (TOCs), book jackets and even selected chapters of a book.

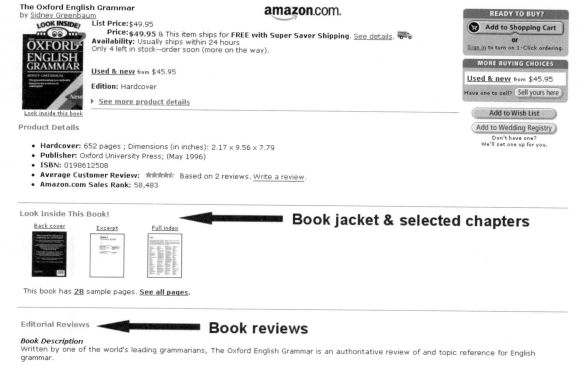

Figure 9.2: Example of value-added elements

As illustrated in the flowchart below (Figure 9.4), the whole process of record matching and linking was done by computer. In-house developed software is used to perform mechanical matching of the Library's bibliographic records (exported in MARC format from the online catalogue) against the Amazon.com online database. MARC tag 020, the ISBN number, is used as matching point. After matched titles are identified, the software generates unique and structural URLs and inserts them into MARC field 856 of the relevant bibliographic records.

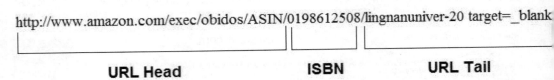

URL Head   **ISBN**   **URL Tail**

Figure 9.3: Sample URL for enhanced bibliographic record

The enhanced records are then loaded back to the library catalogue via a customised MARC load table.

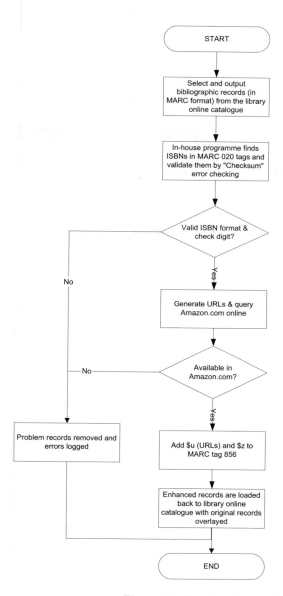

Figure 9.4: Flowchart for development of enhanced records

An underlying benefit of this project is that it has saved the Library tremendously from investing time and human resources in manually adding and maintaining the value-added information. Moreover, access statistics of the URLs and information on subsequent online purchases are important indicators for collection development.

For the second phase of the project, Lingnan has begun to link their Chinese bibliographic records to online Chinese bookstores (for instance, Books.com.tw).

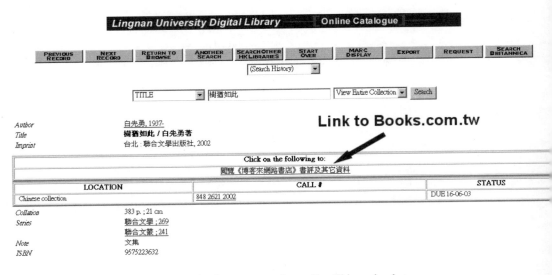

Figure 9.5: Record enhancement using online Chinese bookstores

Kinetica

Roxanne Missingham,[4] National Library of Australia

Kinetica is an example of a national bibliographic network in which the leadership of the National Library has been a critical factor. Kinetica provides Australian libraries with access to the National Bibliographic Network which contains over 33.5 million holdings and 13.5 million bibliographic records reflecting the holdings of the majority of Australian libraries. It also provides access to major international databases including Te Puna (the national bibliographic database of New Zealand), RLIN (the catalogue of the US Research Libraries Group), CURL (union catalogue of the Consortium of United Kingdom and Ireland University libraries) and OCLC's WorldCat. The extent of use of the Kinetica service reflects its importance to Australian libraries – its more than 1,100 customers undertake an average of six million searches each year.

The Kinetica service is a charged-for service supported by the National Library of Australia to assist resource sharing and library operations. The broader goal of the National Library is to assist Australians to find and access the resources held by Australian libraries. In achieving this goal the cooperation of the Australian library network is essential, as is the utilisation of new developments in technology.

Kinetica development

The National Bibliographic Database celebrated its twenty-first year in 2002. Kinetica has been in existence since 1999 and its predecessor, the Australian Bibliographic Network, commenced in 1981 with six participants – the National Library, Canberra Public Library Service, the University of Adelaide, the University of New South Wales, the State Library of South Australia and the Commonwealth Attorney-General's Department. The development of an online service supplying Australian libraries with cataloguing records and facilitating resource sharing has a long history. Printed products listing Australian publications, including subject analysis and classification data, were first produced by the National Library in 1937 in the form of the *Australian National Bibliography* (titled the *Annual catalogue of Australian publications* from 1937-1961). Union catalogues of serials were produced in print – *Serials in Australian libraries: Social Sciences and Humanities* by the National Library from 1963 to 1983 (from 1975 in microform) and *Scientific Serials in Australian libraries* by CSIRO from 1959 to 1984 (1979 to 1984 in microform).

---

[4] Roxanne Missingham is Assistant Director General, Resource Sharing, at the National Library of Australia (email: rmissingham@nla.gov.au).

Computerised production of card for Australian libraries commenced in 1967, computerised production of the Australian National Bibliography commenced in 1972 and the automated Cataloguing in Publication Program dates from 1974. Between printed bibliographies and online databases Australian libraries relied on microform services including the *National Union Catalogue of Monographs* which was produced in microform from 1983 to 1995.

Considerable investigation was undertaken by National Library staff in the late 1970s into library automation options. Discussions were also held with the Australian library community to review the need for and scope of a national automated union catalogue. In 1980 the Library selected the software developed by the Washington Library Network (WLN) which was piloted and put into full production on 2 November 1981. The database was composed then, as it is now, on two record sources. The first is records from national agencies, such as the Library of Congress, British Library and National Library of Canada. These files provide a record of much of the world's publishing output, particularly English language materials, enabling Australian libraries to acquire records in a very timely fashion for the majority of the material they acquire. The second source of records is Australian libraries, which contribute in a variety of ways. Initially all Australian libraries contributed their records online through a somewhat complex text-based system. A major enhancement, provided later, was the ability to clone (or copy) a record. Further developments included a document delivery module enabling libraries to request material from each other and for a payment, service providing consolidated billing for materials received and supplied.

As the library community approached the mid 1990s it became clear that a new system was required. The adoption of local library management systems, the wide acceptance of the Internet as a communication network and the approach of the year 2000 signalled a need to change. Again, the library investigated both technical options and the new needs of customers. After an ambitious joint project with the National Library of New Zealand, World1, was explored and abandoned, the Library tendered for a new system.

Acknowledging that resource sharing depended on a strong national database and that libraries required services based on downloading records, a new system was selected and was launched in March 1999. The software acquired for cataloguing and database services had been previously developed for the National Library of Canada. Cataloguing and web searching software used in the service is supported by a Belgian company, with the contract and all support supplied on an outsourced basis. The service is based on international standards including MARC, Z39.50 and Internet protocols. Approximately one Terabyte of memory is used for the service.

Interlending or document supply software was acquired through a tender process. The Virtual Document eXchange (VDX) of Fretwell Downing was selected and then implemented in September 1999, and has been upgraded regularly since then to enable customers to manage inter library lending. The implementation of VDX version 2.2.7 in December 2002 has enabled the service to reach a new level of performance for Australian libraries, as this version includes the ISO Interlibrary Protocol. The adoption of the protocol enables libraries using local library systems that have implemented the protocol to use their local system to request and supply material. Further they can utilise the resources of other Australian libraries through Kinetica Document Delivery (KDD) and also use the Kinetica Document Delivery Payment Service to achieve single two monthly payments to cover the difference between materials supplied and obtained from other libraries. The ISO protocol has also enabled Australian libraries to use KDD to request material from suppliers such as the Canadian Institute of Scientific Information (CISTI) and international libraries through networks such as Te Puna.

A major report into Australian Interlibrary Loan and Document Supply services (http://www.nla.gov.au/initiatives/nrswg/illdd_rpt_sum.html), benchmarking the performance of over ninety-five libraries found that there were five key factors for efficient library operations. One of these factors was the use of a union catalogue, most frequently the National Bibliographic database. The second factor was the use of an automated interlibrary loan system such as the Kinetica Document Delivery Service. These findings have encouraged more Australian libraries to utilise Kinetica and in particular the Kinetica Document delivery Service.

Kinetica services

Kinetica users are both Australian libraries and individuals. Libraries that use Kinetica can contribute to the National Bibliographic Database, obtaining a discounted rate based upon their method and timeliness of contribution (see http://www.nla.gov.au/kinetica/) or can be 'search only' customers, searching without obtaining a discount. The discounts provide an incentive to libraries to participate fully in resource sharing through enabling other libraries to access their resources. Individuals can join Kinetica and prepurchase blocks of searches. In addition to these types of membership, groups of libraries that can be billed as a single customer can obtain a consortium subscription and large users are offered 'site licences', where a subscription for a period is agreed, based on previous use of Kinetica.

The Kinetica service comprises four major components:

- Cataloguing – libraries can contribute holdings and bibliographic records online using the Kinetica Cataloguing Client (a windows based application based on Amicus software), a Web Input Form (enabling records with a medium level of complexity to be added) and through batchloading of files (a fully automated process using software developed for Kinetica)

- Web searching – the search interface, which uses the LibriVision software, offers simple, advanced and search builder style options, and can be used to support any of the databases available through Kinetica: currently the National Bibliographic Database (NBD), Kinetica Authorities, Kinetica Chinese, Japanese and Korean Service, Research Libraries Group Union Catalogue, Research Libraries Group Authorities, Te Puna Database (New Zealand union catalogue), OCLC WorldCat Database, CURL (Consortium of University Research Libraries in the United Kingdom) Database

- Document supply/interlending services – libraries can request and supply materials and utilise the payment service for consolidated billing using the VDX software
- National Bibliographic Database, the cornerstone of resource sharing in Australia, utilising the Amicus database software.

The effectiveness of the Kinetica service was demonstrated in a study in 2002 which found that records for 80% of the new material added to the collections of Australian libraries was sourced from the National Bibliographic Database, and a further 5% of records were sourced from other databases offered by Kinetica. The coverage of Australian library collections has improved the effectiveness of the National Bibliographic Database. While State and university libraries were early and significant contributors, nearly all Australian public libraries are now members through site licences.

In 1996 a new service was added to Kinetica – the Australian National Chinese, Japanese and Korean Database. This service uses the Innopac software and enables libraries to enter, search and receive records in script for these and other languages. Records are contributed by state, university and public libraries. The Innopac Millennium software was implemented in 2002, providing a greater level of functionality for users.

Continuing evaluation

The National Library continues to evaluate changes in technology and actively review the needs of Australian libraries. In 2002 a progress report confirmed the need for a centralised database at the heart of the service. In 2002 an Expert Advisory Committee on Kinetica Enhancements collected information from Australian libraries in all states and territories and presented a consolidated list of developments for consideration.

In November 2002 the company that developed the software used for Kinetica Web searching and cataloguing was declared bankrupt. A new company was formed in early 2003 that acquired the rights to develop and support the software. For Kinetica customers full business continuity occurred through this period. The National Library continued to review, with advice from the Kinetica Advisory Committee, technology options for the future of the service.

Key areas for development are improving the coverage of Australian publications particularly online resources and online government publications; increasing the connectivity between Australian libraries and resources held in libraries around the world; utilising new technology to enable libraries to become more efficient; and, most important, increasing the access for Australians to the resources held in Australian libraries and online Australian resources.

Developing online multimedia library collections and services

Tommy Yeung[5] and Owen Tam,[6] Lingnan University Libary, Hong Kong

Introduction

Multimedia materials are important and often primary sources of information for scholarly needs. As library users increasingly expect to access multimedia resources over the Web, developing online multimedia collections and finding effective ways to deliver them over the Internet have become the top priority for libraries.

This case study demonstrates how Lingnan University Library developed its web-based multimedia collections and pioneered the use of Multimedia On Demand in Hong Kong to deliver library services over the Internet.

Developing multimedia collections through digitization

Traditional multimedia materials are analogue based (audio cassettes and video tapes) and have many weaknesses such as deteriorating picture quality with use, being time consuming to produce, lack of access over the Internet or inability to be used concurrently. To overcome these weaknesses, Lingnan University Library has been digitizing selected multimedia materials in its collections and making them available for Internet access via the library's homepage.

Digitized multimedia materials include local TV documentaries, video recordings of university assemblies and public lectures by prominent speakers, and audio recording of student projects.

---

[5] Tommy Yeung is Associate Librarian, Lingnan University, Hong Kong (email: tyeung@ln.edu.hk).
[6] Owen Tam is Acting Associate Librarian, Lingnan University, Hong Kong (email: owent@ln.edu.hk).

Figure 9.6: Local TV documentaries

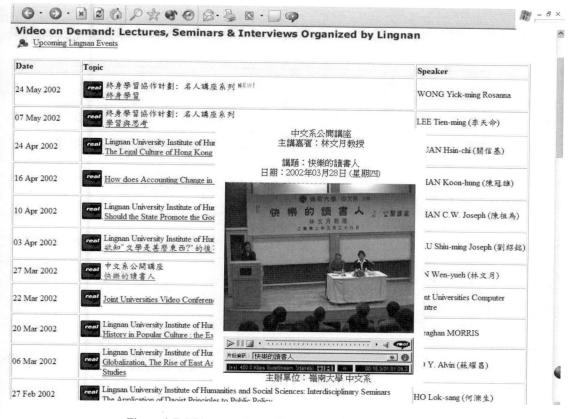

Figure 9.7: Video recording of important public lectures

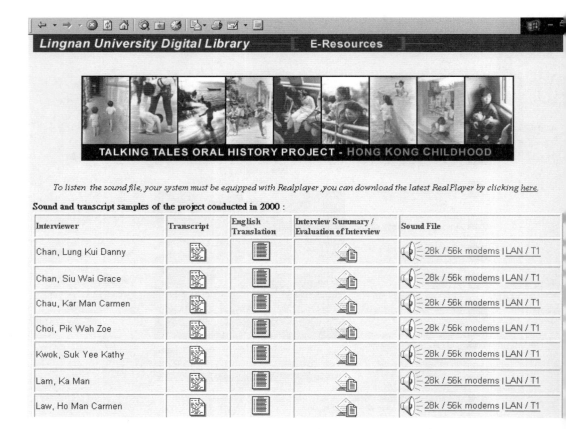

Figure 9.8: Audio recording of student projects

Multimedia On Demand - delivering multimedia resources to users seamlessly over the Internet

Once audio and video materials are digitised, they can be put on a server for users to access from the Internet. Typically, when one clicks on a hyperlink of an audio or video file on the server, the file downloads and then plays. However, because file sizes of audio and video materials can be very large, users may experience long delays between clicking and playing.

Lingnan used *streaming technology* to solve this problem. Streamed media begin to play when a link is clicked without waiting for the entire file to download. The three commonly used streaming media standards are, Apple Computer's QuickTime format, Real Network's Real format and Microsoft's Windows Media format. Each of these formats has advantages and disadvantages as well as requirements for special server and viewing software. Lingnan has chosen the Real format as it has a high data compression ratio and supports the broadest range of client operating systems.

As illustrated in Appendix 1, developing Multimedia On Demand involves many steps:

- program selection and recording
- copyright clearance
- digitisation and editing
- publishing the multimedia resources on the library homepage
- cataloguing the resources in the library catalogue with direct hyperlinks for online viewing.

Due to licensing restrictions, access to some programs is restricted to the campus network only. Such restriction is controlled by the Library's web server and streaming media server.

As of April 2003, there are nearly 1,000 hours of streaming multimedia materials available from the Library's Multimedia On Demand service.

In addition to offering on-demand access to multimedia resources, the Library also has been using streaming technology to broadcast live (webcast) important events held in the University. Such service allows remote users to participate in the events without coming to the campus.

Conclusion

The creation and delivery of digital multimedia collections for teaching and research has proved to be an exceptional resource, one that libraries are only now beginning to exploit. Besides collection development, multimedia technologies have also opened up new opportunities for provision of library services: for example, library user education activities can be recorded and streamed, or even webcast over the Internet.

Using Multimedia On Demand, Lingnan University Library has been successful in its initial effort to meet uses' needs of access to audio and video resources over the Internet. To cope with their increasing expectations of accessing online multimedia resources, collaboration with other libraries is necessary. Libraries in Hong Kong are now exploring resource sharing opportunities in this area.

Appendix: Implementation of Multimedia On Demand

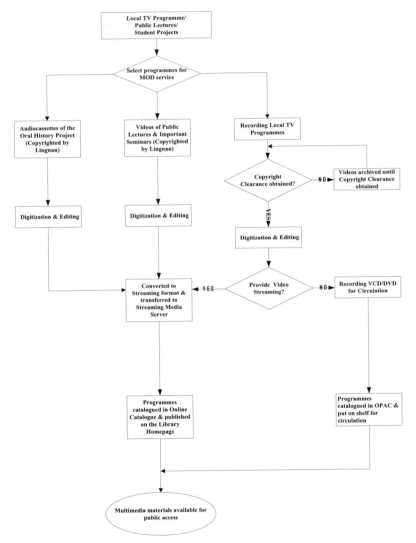

Figure 9.9: Flowchart for development of Multimedia On Demand

Reconstructing a university library: Universidade Nasional Timor Lorosae

Karen Myers,[7] National University of East Timor Library Project

Following the vote for independence in 1999, the education infrastructure of East Timor was completely destroyed in the ensuing violence. Previous libraries that existed, both public and educational, had their collections looted and their buildings, furnishings and equipment destroyed. The rebuilding of the new university, Universidade Nasional Timor Lorosae (UNTL) and its Library is one of the most important steps being taken in the reconstruction of East Timor – a huge undertaking that is vital to the progress of the new country. In November 2000, when the University opened its doors for the first time, the Library was placed temporarily in a couple of rooms in the main University building while its future home, a former gymnasium, was rebuilt. There was no library service for students in the first year of classes. A team of four library staff provided basic access to the few available resources for the benefit of teachers only. After a year in the classrooms, the library moved into its new building and opened for student access for the first time in January 2002.

The library building consists of:

- a large open space area housing the library collection, student seating and security counter, approximately the size of two basketball courts
- two rooms that will house a multimedia centre and multimedia/audiovisual classroom
- a Reserve Collection room
- two administration offices, a cataloguing room and a small storage room.

There have been numerous problems with the building, including a leaking roof that required further repair work. Alterations have also been necessary to improve library operations, climate control (especially heat and dust) and security. The library was closed in mid-2002 for this work to be done, and opened again in January 2003

Prior to 1999, Indonesians held most positions of middle and senior authority in all areas of employment. This left a huge hole in the skilled staff available to fill the gaps after they left. The four UNTL Librarians have many years of experience amongst them at previous University and Polytechnic Libraries, however, only one has had any tertiary education and formal library training. As well as the four Librarians, there are currently four assistants and one security officer on staff to manage the daunting task of establishing a full library service from scratch,

---

[7] Email: karenmyers1@hotmail.com

with very few resources at their disposal. (The annual budget for the entire education sector in East Timor is less than that of a major University Library in Australia.)

The development of the library collection and resources is largely dependent on donations. There is no Internet at the University, no campus-wide IT network and only a small telephone network. Much of the Library's IT equipment, including PCs, servers, hubs and printers, has been donated by various bodies in Australia. The donation of Athena library management software meant that two librarians could be trained to catalogue library books using the donated computers. These librarians could then teach other library staff how to use the computerised cataloguing system. A small computer network was established to provide cataloguing and circulation activities as well as student access to the catalogue.

Unfortunately, the unstable electricity supply has played havoc with the equipment, causing frequent hard drive failures. It is also impossible to keep equipment at reasonable temperatures without access to a consistent power supply, making the network susceptible to damage, as occurred in 2002 when 5000 cataloguing records were lost! Much is dependent on getting stable power and IT infrastructure in place. For example, The National Library of Australia has offered free access to Kinetica to download catalogue records, but the offer is not feasible until Internet access is available to the Library. The lack of IT support is one of the biggest problems facing the Library and East Timor as a whole. Staff additionally face the task of learning English to cope with the predominantly English nature of online services.

As well as working to establish online catalogues, computer networks and collections of resources, there is also the ongoing issue of language. Indonesian, English and Portuguese texts are currently being collected to support the various languages used in the fledgling nation. The local language, Tetum, is a spoken language with very few written resources. Indonesian texts are vital as most East Timorese of University age speak and read Bahasa. Many generous donations of books have been made including over 7,500 Indonesian books from the Asia Foundation. However, many of these are in reserve collections because of the lack of resources and the fear they will be stolen. Many English and Portuguese books remain in storage until they can be catalogued, making storage space tight.

With the assistance of the project's sponsoring body, Apheda-Union Aid Abroad, volunteers, primarily from Australia, have played a major role in helping to establish the Library service. As well as this support and training, it is proposed that relationships be developed with appropriate Australian libraries, in order to provide UNTL Library staff with advice and guidance when needed.

Development issues for the Glasgow Digital Library

Alan Dawson,[8] Centre for Digital Library Research,
University of Strathclyde

Background

The Glasgow Digital Library (GDL)[9] is intended to be a regional, collaborative, distributed digital library, based in Glasgow, the largest city in Scotland. It aims to combine theory and practice to create a digital library that can support teaching, learning, research and public information. The GDL was initially funded as a two-year research project to investigate and report on planning, implementing, operating and evaluating the library. This meant that a digital library service had to be created in order to research its management and operation, although funding was provided only to carry out the research, not create a user service. The paradox was partially resolved by obtaining additional funding for specific digitisation projects, which allowed the library to create its own content. By early 2003 the GDL incorporated six main digital collections, with a total of around 5,000 items.

This paper summarises the main issues encountered in developing the Glasgow Digital Library. A more detailed account is given by the author in the book *Digital libraries: Policy, planning and practice* (Andrews & Law 2003).

Library purpose and philosophy

The principles of operation underpinning the GDL helped determine its collection development policy and priorities for implementation. As a regional initiative based in a university, the GDL is a hybrid between public library and higher education library, so its content is not geared to particular courses nor limited to a specific target audience. It has a philosophy of thinking globally before acting locally, aiming to balance the needs of local users with a worldwide and long-term perspective on digital resources, and is therefore committed to using international standards.

---

[8] Alan Dawson is Senior Researcher/Programmer at the Centre for Digital Library Research, University of Strathclyde, Glasgow G4 0NS, Scotland (email:alan.dawson@strath.ac.uk).
[9] The Glasgow Digital Library is available at http://gdl.cdlr.strath.ac.uk/

Collection development policy

Initially there were three main priorities:

- to make use of physical collections held by project partners, for political as well as practical purposes
- to demonstrate the benefits of collaboration by pooling resources that might otherwise result in duplication of effort
- to create and co-ordinate content that was not just *about* Glasgow, but also *for* Glasgow.

These priorities were incorporated into a brief but important collection development policy agreed by all project partners.

Standards

Choice of standards for the GDL was determined by its international outlook and concern for long-term interoperability. Key standards are Dublin Core and MARC 21 for metadata, LCSH for subject vocabulary, AACR2 for resource descriptions, XHTML and W3C web accessibility guidelines for web pages, TIFF and JPEG for image format, and Z39.50 for cross-searching with other catalogues. These standards are supplemented by editorial guidelines and authority files for place names and resource types. Although local in scope, these are equally important for providing consistency of resource description and assisting information retrieval.

Compliance with these standards was rarely technically difficult but required clear policies, guidelines and disciplined work practices. Adherence to standards was regarded as an inherent part of digital library development rather than a burden to be imposed after content creation. The process was assisted by a coherent information environment and guidelines for content contributors, though central validation and editing was also carried out.

Content creation

Objects do not select themselves for digitisation. Research has to be carried out, items selected for value and relevance, captions written and edited, titles applied or invented. Even with a basic formula of text, images and web pages, decisions have to be made about image resolution, file size and format, characters sets and workflow processes.

The GDL carried out some digitisation internally on a simple desktop scanner, some was handled by project partners and some by a specialist service (including large images and glass slides). Research and content selection was also distributed amongst project staff, partners and external contractors with specialist knowledge. Images were captured and archived at high resolution (300dpi TIFF) then copied to lower-quality higher-speed JPEG files for web usage. Optical character reading was carried out where feasible and was carefully checked before publication. Digitisation itself was quick – images can be captured in seconds – but the prerequisite selection and the subsequent manipulation and management processes were far more time-consuming.

The aim of digitisation was to create an accurate copy of the source material, but in practice images were routinely manipulated after creation; they were often resized and cropped, sometimes lightened and sharpened, and thumbnail images sometimes created. This is common practice and does not usually affect authenticity of the material, yet the ease of digital manipulation and enhancement illustrates that the issues of preservation and authenticity are less clear-cut than might be imagined.

Metadata

Inevitably, metadata creation and management was a big issue. The emphasis throughout was on ensuring accuracy, consistency and completeness in key high-value fields, especially title, description, date and subject terms. One major question was whether to catalogue the original item or the digital copy: for example, was the creator of a booklet the person who wrote it or the organisation responsible for digitising it? However, the biggest issue of all was how to handle the whole metadata creation and management process. Flexibility was achieved by using a database structure that was not tied to any particular metadata scheme. Content extraction programs were written (using Visual Basic) to generate material in different formats for different purposes: for instance, separate forename and surname fields in one collection were combined to produce standard name format for web display but surname-first format for use in Dublin Core metadata and MARC records.

Classification

Maintaining Dewey Decimal Classification as well as a controlled subject vocabulary was considered but judged unsustainable for the GDL. Library of Congress Subject Headings (LCSH) were therefore used as the primary means of linking diverse collections into a coherent information structure. To overcome the LCSH problem of cultural bias toward North America, it was supplemented by controlled local subject terms where this was considered essential. The GDL subject terms were used in the web interface, with LCSH terms included in metadata where international compatibility was required.[10] Controlled authority files for place names and people names were also used to provide library-wide consistency and an alternative to the collection-centred view. These classifications helped illustrate the scope and scale of collections and influenced topic chunking, as well as making searching more reliable.

---

[10] The CDLR subscribes to the OCLC Connexion service and is evaluating its use for collaborative cataloguing and other purposes (http://www.oclc.org/connexion/).

Development methodology

A robust system for organising diverse collections of digital objects is essential for any heterogeneous digital library, with mechanisms for handling multiple contributors, collections, file formats and access methods, as well as controlling updating procedures. The initial solution adopted for the GDL was technically straightforward but enabled rapid development. Microsoft Access databases were required as a condition of funding for four of the first six collections, so Access was chosen as the primary content and metadata repository for all six collections. Library content and metadata were then generated from Access in different formats for different purposes, for instance, web pages, Dublin Core metadata and MARC 21 records.[11] This was achieved by adding HTML markup and MARC tags to the database and using Visual Basic programs to automate the integration and export of content, markup and metadata.

In effect this methodology created a modular, flexible, inexpensive content management system using common desktop software. The modular approach enabled content creation to be readily distributed amongst contributors, facilitated re-use of metadata, and allowed additional collections to be plugged in to the library relatively quickly. This approach was effective but required a consistent item naming scheme for all objects in the library and a disciplined approach from those involved.

Interface design

There were five main requirements for the GDL web interface: consistency, flexibility, scalability, accessibility and feasibility. *Consistency* meant devising a design template that could provide visual coherence across all collections without imposing blanket uniformity. *Flexibility* meant enabling users to access library content in different ways – across as well as within collections. *Scalability* meant creating an interface that would work with only three or four collections yet be able to cope with dozens or hundreds. *Accessibility* meant meeting requirements of funding bodies and standard web accessibility guidelines (World Wide Web Consortium 2003). *Feasibility* meant creating something quickly and inexpensively.

The solution was to make a virtue out of necessity and go for simplicity. Content of the library was judged inherently interesting, with plenty of striking images, so all that was needed was a clear set of labels and some example images to illustrate each collection, together with options for navigating the library as a whole – by place or subject – as an alternative to the collection-centred view. Cascading stylesheets were used throughout to provide flexibility and design consistency. The result was minimalist but acceptable and practicable.

---

[11] MARC records were created in text format and converted to machine-readable MARC format using MarcEdit software (http://www.onid.orst.edu/~reeset/marcedit/).

Searching and browsing

The GDL aims to offer several search options – across the entire library, within a single collection, or within a single field – as well as options to cross-search the GDL with other digital libraries and library catalogues. However, web users have become used to the simplest possible search interface, and there are real difficulties in offering complex search options and summarising the meaning of these options via a simple user interface.

In the short term, priority was given to creating a browseable interface to each collection, offering flexible access to content. Search options are being added one collection at a time, using different software solutions for different collections.[12] This is not ideal for a user service, but from a research perspective it is useful to investigate and understand different search mechanisms. The longer term aim is to use intelligent scripting to provide cascading search facilities, in other words, to search highest-value fields first (titles and subject terms), then other metadata fields (if no matches are found), then full-text searching or cross-searching.

Learning materials

In the absence of time or funding to spend on authoring learning materials, the GDL approach has been to semi-automate the creation of educational resources. This was possible to an extent by drawing on the values of controlled metadata fields for people, organisations and dates to automatically generate illustrated indexes linking related items, drawing out themes, timelines and inter-relationships between objects. Better results could be obtained by additional research and hand-crafting of materials, but this simply was not possible. The automated process was feasible, and the added value created was judged to be worth the effort involved. It is also satisfying to see metadata being used to worthwhile effect. All the library contents can still be accessed as independent digital objects and assembled in different ways for different purposes.

Copyright

Copyright restrictions caused inconvenience for the GDL rather than major problems, as much material is historical and out of copyright. In other cases the standard requirement was followed by requesting permission from copyright holders before digitising any copyright material. The main implementation decision was to proceed anyway in those few cases where the copyright holder could not be traced.

---

[12] The ease of importing Access databases into SQL Server made this the simplest solution to implement, with ASP or Cold Fusion scripts controlling the interface and search requests.

Preservation

A complementary principle to 'think globally, act locally' is 'think long-term, act short-term'. The GDL aims to create, describe and manage content with an indefinite life-span, including historical material that may still be of interest in hundreds of years time. There are three main categories of concern: physical storage media (disks, CDs, tapes etc.), content format (relational databases, Word documents, web pages, image files etc) and information structures (MARC, DC, LCSH etc.). For content and metadata, the solutions are in structures and standards. Textual content held in a consistent manner in a structured database can always be exported to another format. Storage media are more of a problem, as there is no knowing what technical developments will take place in future, so the policy is to keep master copies of data in two formats (CD and disk) while being prepared to migrate in future.

Conclusions

Digital library developers can only do what is possible with the resources available. The solutions adopted will vary from case to case, but a clear understanding of the issues involved and techniques available can help maximise value obtained from limited resources. Few of the solutions adopted for the GDL to date have been technologically innovative, but they were achievable, they suited its purpose and philosophy, and they sustained its potential for long-term scalability and interoperability with other digital libraries.

References

Andrews, J & Law, D 2003, *Digital libraries: Policy, planning and practice*. Ashgate, Aldershot, Hamps.

World Wide Web Consortium 2003, *Web content accessibility guidelines*. <http://www.w3.org/TR/WAI-WEBCONTENT/>.

APPENDIX 2
Glossary

ABN Australian Bibliographic Network (*see* Kinetica).

Aggregator A service that sells publications from a variety of publishers as a single package, typically by licensing customers such as libraries to access its database.

Algorithm Set of step-by-step rules, used to solve problems.

ALU Arithmetic and Logic Unit: the part of a CPU that performs arithmetic and Boolean operations.

Analogue Form of data transmission in which signals are sent as continuous waves. Contrast with digital.

AND A logical operation in which the output is true only if all inputs are true; otherwise it is false. Contrast with OR and NOT.

ANSI American National Standards Institute.

Applications software Software designed to perform specific functions, such as text retrieval or circulations control. Applications software acts as an interface between user and system software.

Artificial intelligence The use of human-like methods of reasoning by computers, e.g., expert systems.

ASCII American Standard Code for Information Interchange: a binary code used to represent characters. ASCII was specifically developed for data communications.

Assembly language A second-generation programming language, which consists of mnemonic alphabetical abbreviations. Assembler is a language translator that translates the step-by-step instructions of an assembly language program into machine code, on a one-to-one basis.

Asynchronous Refers to a form of serial data transmission in which each transmitted byte is preceded and/or succeeded with special start and stop bits. These start and stop bits are used to control the flow of data for the receiving device. Contrast with synchronous.

Authority file In general terms, a file that contains the preferred form of terms (words or phrases) used to access a main file, e.g., authors' names, titles and subjects. In the context of library management systems, an authority file is a file that is separate from the main bibliographic file and stores terms in their preferred forms. Compare with thesaurus.

Automation platform Used to refer to the operating system and hardware on which library management software runs.

Back-up Copy of a program or file that is made in case the original should be lost. Magnetic tapes and diskettes are typical back-up media.

Bandwidth The capacity, measured in bits per second (bps), of a communications channel.

Barcode A set of parallel lines (bars) which represent data using factors such as the width of the lines and the distance between them. A barcode label is affixed to items, which can uniquely identify the item. A barcode scanner is used to read barcodes to assist in fast accurate data entry.

Batch processing Type of data processing in which data accumulated over a period (e.g., a day's circulations transactions in a mobile library) are processed as a single job. Contrast with real-time processing.

Baud rate The rate at which a communications medium (e.g., a telephone line) changes state (not necessarily the same as bits per second).

Bibliographic database Database made up of surrogate records that identify and describe bibliographic items. Bibliographic file refers to a single file containing surrogate records. Contrast with full-text database.

Binary A numbering system using only the digits zero and one. Data in binary form are also said to be in digital form.

Bit A Binary digIT: either a zero or a one: the smallest unit a computer can recognise.

Bit-mapped An image that is stored and displayed by a computer as a matrix of tiny spots or pixels (picture elements). Each pixel is represented by a bit.

Bits per second *See* bps.

Boolean operator A mathematical means of representing logical functions with operators such as AND, OR and NOT. *See also* AND, OR and NOT.

Bookmark Means of recording links to sites, such as websites, to which users may wish to return.

Bps Bits per second: a measure of data transmission speed.

Browser In the context of the Web, a piece of client software used to access the Web; also used in the context of hypertext to refer to a mapping device used to represent graphically where a hypertext node is in relation to associated nodes.

Buffer A type of computer memory used for temporary storage of data sent from one device to another, e.g., from a CPU to a slower device such as a printer. Buffers allow the CPU to perform other functions without having to wait for a device to finish.

Bug Program error.

Bus The channel along which data travel within a computer system. The number of bits a bus can transmit simultaneously is called the word length. Also refers to a local area network topology in which each device on the network is connected to a backbone cable. Contrast with ring and star.

Byte A group of eight bits that is used to represent a single character.

Cache A type of computer memory which is extremely fast and is used to store frequently accessed software or data.

CAI Computer-Assisted Instruction: a software package that provides users with educational or instructional material.

Cathode-ray tube A tube in which electrons strike a phosphorus-coated screen to form an image. Used in televisions and as a form of computer screen (hence CRT terminal).

CCITT Comité Consultatif International Télégraphique et Téléphonique, one of the sources of international communications standards.

CD-R (CD-Recordable) A CD that can typically be written to once and then cannot be written over or erased – also known as WORMs (Write Once, Read Many disks). Those CDs that can be written to more than once are correctly termed **CD-RW** or Compact Disk Re<u>w</u>ritable.

CD-ROM Compact Disk Read-Only Memory: a type of optical medium.

Central Processing Unit *See* CPU.

Check sum A method of detecting transmission errors by which each transmitted byte is treated as a binary number and added to the following byte. The final sum is called the check sum and is transmitted to the receiving device for validation.

Chip *See* Microchip.

Circuit switching A method of data transmission which involves sending a message once there is an uninterrupted link between sending and receiving devices.

Client/server model The model underlying much communication on the Internet, it involves the linking of a client (the user's local system) with a server, a 'remote' system that handles data and files and deals with requests via clients for access to data and files. The model requires special client software and server software in order to function.

Clock A small IC (integrated circuit) within a computer system that oscillates at regular time intervals measured in MHz. It is used to coordinate activities within a computer system.

Coaxial cable (coax) Cable used in data communications, consisting of a single insulated wire, surrounded by a conductive sheath and further wrapped in an outer insulated jacket.

COM Computer output on microform. A COM recorder is a device that outputs data stored in a computer system in microform format, e.g., reproduces bibliographic data in the form of a microfiche catalogue.

Command An instruction from a user, generally via a terminal, telling a computer to perform a particular function or execute a particular program. A command-driven interface is one which requires the operator to enter commands that are not displayed as options on the screen. Contrast with menu-driven interface and GUI.

Common command language (CCL) Standard command language used for communication across different networks (e.g., ANSI standard Z39.58).

Communication The act of one computer system transferring data to another computer system.

Compact disk *See* CD-ROM

Compiler A language translator that translates the whole of a computer program into machine code before execution. Contrast with interpreter.

Compression Use of an algorithm to reduce the size of a file: another algorithm is used to decompress a file when it is required. Applications include the storage of bit-mapped images and data communications.

Computer Output Microform *See* COM.

Computer system A system that comprises computer hardware, computer software and data.

Consortium A group of organisations (such as libraries) that combine to cooperate on a specific project or a number of projects, e.g., on an automation project.

Control field In MARC, a field that contains information about a record that is not necessarily contained in data fields.

Control unit The part of the CPU that coordinates the activities within the CPU and computer system.

Conversion on the fly The creation of brief bibliographic records at the point of issue.

Copy cataloguing Copying existing catalogue records, e.g., by downloading them from a bibliographic network. Contrast with original cataloguing.

CPU Central Processing Unit: the part of a computer system that performs all processing and control functions. It consists of the ALU, the Control Unit, and main memory.

Crosswalk In the area of metadata standards, a crosswalk is a means of mapping the elements in one standard (such as Dublin Core) to those in another.

CRC Cyclic Redundancy Check: a method of detecting transmission errors by which the transmitted data are treated as one long binary number. This number is then divided by an agreed on constant. The remainder after division is transmitted to the receiving device for validation.

CRT Cathode-ray tube; hence a CRT terminal is a terminal that contains a cathode-ray tube.

CSMA/CA Carrier Sense Multiple Access/Collision Avoidance: a technology used in Ethernet networks in which each device monitors network traffic and follows transmission rules on the network in such a way that data collisions with other devices are avoided.

CSMA/CD Carrier Sense Multiple Access/Collision Detection: a technology used in Ethernet networks in which each device monitors network traffic and can transmit data on the network. If two devices transmit simultaneously, a collision is detected and the two devices wait a random time interval before re-transmitting the data.

CTS Clear To Send: the signal sent by the receiving device to the sending device in hardware flow control, indicating that the receiving device is ready to receive more data. Contrast with RTS.

Cursor A special character on a computer screen that users can move in order to point to options displayed on the screen, e.g., an arrow that can be moved over an icon in order to select the object represented by the icon.

Cyclic Redundancy Check *See* CRC.

Data The raw, unprocessed facts input into a computer system. Contrast with information.

Data communications The transmission of data from one computer-related device to another.

Data dictionary Part of a database management system that contains information such as what files are in the database and descriptions of the data contained in the files.

Data processing system An information system in which well defined data (e.g., loans data) are transformed according to well defined rules to some normal form (e.g., a completed loans transaction). The DP system generates information, such as operational information (e.g., lists of overdue items).

Data redundancy Storing the same data more than once in a computer system.

Database A collection of related computer files stored in a computer system.

Database management system (DBMS) A type of computer software that manages a collection of computer files (database). It consists of the database, applications software to handle enquiries from users, systems software to manage the computer hardware and a data dictionary.

Decision support system (DSS) A kind of information system used by a manager to work through management problems based on a formal model of the organisation, e.g., the use of a spreadsheet program to predict the results of a 'what-if' scenario.

Dedicated line A line that can be rented from the supplier of a telephone network and used permanently to connect two devices (also called a leased line).

Default Value that is automatically entered by an applications program unless the user specifies an alternative value.

Delimiter A symbol indicating the end of a set of data, such as a record, field or subfield.

Diagnostics The running of software designed to identify and correct errors.

Digital The term refers to the binary format in which computers store, manipulate and transfer data. In data communication it describes the form of data transmission in which signals are sent as discrete, on/off signals. Contrast with analogue.

Digital service A data communications service that supports the transmission of data using digital signals, e.g., ISDN (Integrated Services Digital Network).

Digitisation The process of converting a document or other information resource into digital format.

Discussion list A form of electronic mail, in which messages from members of a discussion list are forwarded via a server to all members on the list. Also known as mailing list or listserv.

Diskette A magnetic storage medium consisting of a thin flexible plastic disk inside a harder plastic jacket. A secondary storage device (also known as a floppy disk).

DOS Disk operating system: an operating system that uses disk drives to store and make available data files and programs.

Down-time Time when a computer-based system is not operating.

Downloading The process of copying data (e.g., bibliographic records), for instance from a server to a client or from a CD-ROM workstation to a diskette. Contrast with uploading.

Drive Input/output device used to read/write data on a secondary storage medium, such as magnetic diskette, magnetic tape or CD-ROM.

DTD (Document Type Definition) A set of rules that define the elements that make up a specific type of document (for example, journal article) and encode them in such a way that text within the document can be retrieved, displayed and exchanged across different platforms. HTML, for instance, was developed as a DTD of SGML.

Dumb terminal   Terminal that can send digital signals to a computer and display the signals that are sent to it, but has no data processing facilities of its own.

DVD-ROM   Digital Versatile Disk - Read-Only Memory: a type of optical medium. Data are stored on both sides of the disk and on two layers on each side using MPEG-2 technology. Similar to a CD-ROM.

EBCDIC   Extended Binary Coded Decimal Interchange Code: a binary code used to represent characters, developed by IBM.

EDI   Electronic Data Interchange: the electronic transmission of trading documents, such as purchase orders and invoices.

EEPROM   Electronically Erasable Programmable Read-Only Memory.

Electronic mail   A means of transmitting electronic messages, between computers or between a computer and another device, such as a fax machine.

Electronic publishing   Form of publishing in which resources are disseminated by electronic means, e.g., as HTML documents on the Web. Not to be confused with desktop publishing, which uses electronic means to produce print-based products.

Embedded pointer   A data element that is part of each record segment in a hierarchical or a network database management system, linking each record segment to related segments.

EPROM   Erasable Programmable Read-Only Memory: a form of ROM that can be erased and re-written to.

Ergonomics   The design of technological systems using studies of human physique and behaviour.

Ethernet   A physical layer protocol, developed by Xerox Corporation for LANs, that utilises either CSMA/CD or CSMA/CA technology.

Expert system   A type of computer software that can act like a human expert in a narrowly defined area of knowledge, e.g., online intermediary.

Export   Transferring or copying data or files from one application into another application (e.g., from a library management system to a spreadsheet package) or from one system to another system.

Extension   The three-letter code that appears at the end of a computer file name, enabling the computer to recognise the file type.

Fax   Facsimile transmission: the transmission of images (text and graphics) over a telecommunications link.

Fibre optic   *See* Optical fibre.

Field   An element of data, often described as the smallest element of data to make sense to a user (e.g., author or title). Fields are sometimes also referred to as data elements or attributes.

File management system   A system which is used to process only one file (also file manager).

File-save   The process of creating a back-up file.

File server   A computer that is used for the storage and distribution of files, e.g., in a local area network. *See also* client/server model.

File Transfer Protocol   *See* FTP.

Firewall Special security software, typically run on a proxy server, that helps to protect an intranet from external threat by examining the content and source of every message passing through the server.

Fixed length field Field that has its length determined in advance: typical of fields in database management systems. Contrast with variable length field.

Flash memory A special kind of EEPROM that can be updated, giving hardware added functionality without having to purchase new hardware.

Floppy disk A magnetic storage medium consisting of a thin flexible plastic disk inside a harder plastic jacket. A secondary storage device (also known as a diskette).

Flow control The method by which two devices communicate when transferring data asynchronously. Flow control can be either software or hardware.

Form filling Type of data entry in which the system displays what looks like a blank form, with labelled spaces for data entry.

Format Used in relation to diskettes and disks to refer to the number of tracks and the position of sectors.

Fourth-generation language (4GL) A near-English language that can be used to develop some software applications.

Free text search A search for a term across a computer file or database, not limited to a particular field.

Freeware Computer software that is quite often written by an enthusiastic individual and is offered to others for no charge. Similar to shareware.

Front-end software A type of computer software that acts as a user-friendly interface between a client and a server.

FTP File Transfer Protocol: a TCP/IP protocol used to download or upload files between a client and a host on the Internet.

Full duplex A method of communication where data can travel between two devices, simultaneously. Contrast with half-duplex.

Full-text database A database that contains information resources in electronic format and not merely surrogate records. Contrast with bibliographic database.

Function keys A set of numbered keys at the top of some keyboards, to each of which is assigned a particular function (e.g., the help function).

Gateway A device consisting of software and hardware, allowing two different networks to be connected and hence share resources.

Gb Gigabyte: 1,024 Mb.

GIF (Graphics Interchange Format) An image file format commonly used for Web delivery, principally for greyscales.

Gopher A piece of communications software that accesses remote servers for a user, finding its way through various communications protocols with the user's requests and allowing the user to navigate gopher sites by selecting options from a hierarchical set of menus. Largely supplanted by the World Wide Web.

GUI Graphical user interface: a user interface which allows users to select actions, commands or options that are displayed on the screen as graphical representations called icons. A GUI is sometimes referred to as a WIMP environment.

Half-duplex A method of communication by which data can travel between two devices, but only in one direction at a time. Contrast with full duplex.

Hard copy A printed form of computer output, e.g., on paper or microfiche, as distinct from the temporary display of data on a computer screen (soft copy).

Hard disk A magnetic storage medium consisting of a hard disk inside a protected, air tight container. A secondary storage device.

Hardware The physical, 'touchable' parts of a computer system. Contrast with software.

Heuristics A rule of thumb type of reasoning, used in expert systems. It may involve forward chaining (working forward from information in a knowledge base), backward chaining (starting with possible solutions and searching a knowledge base for relevant facts) and a mixture of both techniques. Contrast with algorithm.

Holdings file A file used in some library management systems to hold item-specific data required for the circulation of library material. Fields include record identifiers, item identifiers, item statuses (e.g., 'missing') and item descriptions.

HTML (HyperText Markup Language) International standard code that is used to determine the format of Web pages and to embed links to other pages/publications in specified text, thus enabling clients to identify the various parts of a web document and present them to the user correctly. A development of SGML (Standard Generalised Markup Language).

HTTP (HyperText Transfer Protocol) Protocol used to move copies of hypertext files between HTTP servers and HTTP clients.

Hub A hardware device for connecting sections of a LAN.

Hybrid library Term used to refer to the typical library that provides users with access to a range of electronic, audiovisual and print information resources.

Hypermedia The same as hypertext (see below), except that what is linked is not just text but also other media, e.g., graphics, audio and animation.

Hypertext Type of software used to create a textual database, in which text is stored as 'nodes' of text, links are created between nodes and users can follow associative links between nodes, generally using a GUI (graphical user interface).

IC Integrated Circuit: a complete semiconductor circuit printed on a single piece of silicon. Also known as a microchip or a chip.

Icon A graphical representation of a particular option on a computer screen.

Identifier In general terms, a field (data element) that uniquely identifies a record, e.g., an ISBN. In relational database management systems, an identifier forms a link between two relations. Also referred to as a key.

IEEE Institute of Electrical and Electronic Engineers.

ILANET An electronic mail network used primarily for transmission of inter-library loans requests and run by the State Library of New South Wales.

Image retrieval system A text retrieval system that stores images of documents or pictures in electronic form and links these to index files containing access points such as title and subject descriptor.

Image scanning The scanning of a document, such as a page of text or a graphic, and the conversion of each page or picture into a digitised or bit-mapped image (also referred to as imaging).

Impact printer Printer that produces characters by striking a ribbon against paper (e.g., using hammers).

Import The process of bringing data or files that have been exported from an application or system into another application or system (e.g., bringing records from a bibliographic network into a local system).

Index file In information retrieval, a file of terms that have been automatically extracted from a main file, with a view to speeding up the retrieval process, e.g., an inverted file index.

Inference engine The part of an expert system that applies the rules held in the system's knowledge base to the information provided by the user to produce conclusions.

Information Processed data output from a computer system. Contrast with data.

Information system System that represents objects in a physical system, e.g., books in a library. A computerised information system comprises computer software, computer hardware, representations of objects (e.g., book orders) and people.

Infra-red Light waves of greater frequency than red and hence invisible. Infra-red signals are used to transmit data between devices located within about ten metres of each other.

Input The process of entering data into a computer system in machine-readable form.

Input/output device A device that allows human operators to communicate with a computer system, entering data and retrieving data or information; e.g., a terminal.

Integrated circuit *See* IC.

Integrated system Software package in which different applications can share the same data, e.g., bibliographic data.

Interface board A piece of circuitry which can plug into a computer for purposes of data communication (also referred to as an interface card).

Internet A large international network of interconnected networks.

Internet Relay Chat (IRC) A form of interactive conferencing using the Internet.

Interpreter A language translator that translates a computer program into machine code and executes it, one line at a time. Contrast with compiler.

Intranet A network internal to an organisation that employs web standards and technologies, such as HTML, HTTP and the use of a web browser client.

Inverted file An index file, used, for example, in text retrieval systems to list indexed terms from a main file along with references to their occurrences in the main file.

Invisible web Those parts of the Web that are not indexed by any search engines such as those which have been 'blocked' by their web masters.

IP (Internet Protocol) number A number that uniquely identifies host computers on the Internet.

ISBN International Standard Book Number, unique to each edition of a book.

ISDN Integrated Services Digital Network: a digital network supplied by telecommunications organisations enabling the transmission of digital data.

ISO International Standards Organisation: an international body responsible for the development of data communications standards.

JPEG An image file format developed by the Joint Photographic Experts Group.

Kb Kilobyte: 1,024 bytes.

Kernel The core component of an operating system which coordinates the activities of software and the CPU.

Key A field (data element) that uniquely identifies a record, e.g., an ISBN. In relational database management systems, key also refers to the identifying field that links two relations. Also known as an identifier.

Keyboard A hardware device used to input data into a computer system. It consists of numerous alphabetic keys, numeric keys and other special keys.

Kilobyte *See* Kb.

Kinetica System used to support Australia's national bibliographic network.

Knowledge base Part of an expert system that contains facts and rules about solving problems within a defined knowledge domain. Expert systems are sometimes referred to as knowledge-based systems.

LAN Local area network: a network of computing devices usually confined to a single office or building. Contrast with WAN.

Land The area between the pits on an optical disk, such as CD-ROM.

Language translator A program that translates from one computer language to another, e.g., assemblers, compilers and interpreters.

Laptop computer Portable computer, generally small enough to fit inside a briefcase.

Layered protocol A protocol is a set of rules or conventions that governs the use of communications channels. A layered protocol is a suite of rules and conventions in which each layer addresses specific aspects of control (such as physical connection).

Leased line A line that can be rented from the supplier of a telephone network and used permanently to connect two devices (also called a dedicated line).

Library management system A computerised system used to perform everyday library functions such as cataloguing, circulations and acquisitions and to generate management information.

Light-pen A light-sensitive device (also referred to as a wand) that is passed across a barcode label to read the data encoded in the barcode. The signal generated is passed to a barcode reader, which transmits the data to a CPU. In some computer systems, the term 'light-pen' also refers to a kind of pointing device, used to select options on a computer screen.

Line protocol A set of rules or conventions that governs the use of communications channels.

LISTSERV A common piece of electronic mail server software that supports discussion lists (or mailing lists), in which messages from members of a list are forwarded via a server to all members on the list. Sometimes listserv is used synonymously with discussion list.

Local area network *See* LAN.

Logging on Process of gaining access to a software application, file or account, typically by identifying the application, etc., and entering either a password or a user name and password. Logging off or logging out is a common procedure for ending a session.

Logic gate An electronic switch which behaves in special ways. *See* AND, OR and NOT.

Machine code A hardware specific programming language, which is written in binary code and describes each step that the hardware must take. Also known as machine language.

Macro A facility in some applications software packages that allows a detailed set of instructions to be recorded and then to be executed (when required) by use of a single keystroke.

Mailer Software package used to handle electronic mail. Sometimes also referred to as an emailer.

Mailing list *See* Discussion list.

Main memory The area of the CPU where data and programs can be stored during execution. Also referred to as primary storage.

Mainframe computer A large computer with greater processing capabilities and memory than a minicomputer or a microcomputer. Typically used in large organisations such as local councils and universities.

Management information system (MIS) A system that provides regular, predefined information, which helps a manager to measure organisational performance.

MARC Machine-readable code or machine-readable cataloguing: a standard specifically designed for the exchange of bibliographic data using magnetic tape (based on an international standard, ISO 2709).

Mb Megabyte: 1,024 Kb.

Megahertz *See* MHz.

Menu-driven interface An interface in which the user is offered a choice of options (e.g., programs or commands) from which to select.

Meta search engine Search engine that will send users' search terms to a group of different search engines and then display the search results from each.

Metadata Structured data about data, often used to refer to the descriptive elements required to describe Internet resources and so make these resources easier to access (e.g., the Dublin Core Metadata Element Set).

MHz Megahertz: millions of Hertz. A measure of frequency.

Microchip An integrated circuit, i.e., a complete semiconductor circuit printed on a single piece of silicon. Also known as a chip.

Microcomputer Small computer which has less processing capabilities and memory than a minicomputer and can cope with fewer peripherals than it can. Sometimes referred to as a personal computer.

Microfiche Sheets of transparent film containing small images which can be enlarged and displayed using a microfiche reader. Also referred to as fiche.

Microform Generic name for film containing small images which can be enlarged and displayed using an appropriate reader, e.g., microfilm and microfiche.

Microprocessor A microchip that combines all three components of a CPU, or at least the Arithmetic and Logic Unit and the Control Unit.

Microwave A transmitted high frequency radio signal used in data communications. Special microwave dishes are used to receive and transmit microwave signals.

MIME Multipurpose Internet Mail Extension, a standard that enables people to send non-textual documents by electronic mail.

Minicomputer A smaller computer than a mainframe, with less processing capabilities and memory than a mainframe but more powerful than a microcomputer.

MIPS Millions of Instructions Per Second: a measure of the speed of a computer system.

Modem MOdulator DEModulator: a hardware device used to convert the digital signals from a computer (modulate) to the analogue signals used in telephone wires and to convert the analogue signal received from the telephone wires into the digital signal used by computers (demodulate).

Module A subsystem that can perform as part of a larger system (e.g., a circulations module within a library management system).

Monitor An output device which presents a temporary display of data and information to the user on a screen. Also known as a Visual Display Unit (VDU).

MOO Stands for MUD (Multi-User Dungeon) Object-Oriented and is effectively a form of Internet conferencing that appears to be based loosely on the role-playing model of MUDs.

Mouse A pointing device that can be rolled around on a desktop causing a pointing symbol to move around a computer monitor. A mouse has one or more buttons that can be used to select commands or options on a screen.

MS-DOS Microsoft – Disk Operating System: operating system software developed for IBM compatible computer systems.

Network An arrangement of computers, computer peripherals, communications media and a control mechanism, designed to share data, information or components of a computer system.

Newsgroup A special form of electronic mail in which messages from members of a newsgroup are sent to a server and stored there for other members of the group to read.

Nibble Half a byte, i.e., 4 bits.

NISO National Information Standards Organization: an American standards organization.

Node In hypertext applications, a card or page or chunk of text, typically representing a single concept, such as an encyclopedic entry. In general usage it can mean an intersection and so in data communications it can also refer to a workstation or other device in a computer network.

Noise Distortion in transmitted data signals caused by electromagnetic interference, resulting in data corruption.

Normalisation In data management, the process of organising small data structures (relations) in a relational database management system. The main purpose of normalisation is to reduce data redundancy.

NOT A logical operation in which the output is true only if the input is false, otherwise it is false. Contrast with AND and OR.

OCLC Online Computer Library Center: US-based bibliographic network.

OCR Optical character recognition: software designed to convert scanned/digitised text into characters.

Offline Condition in which there is no communications link between a device and a computer, e.g., the offline preparation of a search strategy on a local microcomputer before establishing a communications link with a remote host computer.

Online Condition in which there is a communications link between a device and a computer, e.g., a circulations terminal and a circulations control system. Data processing conducted online is said to be real-time processing.

Online catalogue Catalogue in electronic format that can be accessed via a terminal or a client acting as a terminal. Also known as OPAC (Online Public-Access Catalogue) or PAC.

Open Systems Interconnection *See* OSI.

Operating system Software designed to manage the hardware resources of a computer system and provide an interface for application software to the hardware.

Optical character recognition *See* OCR.

Optical disk A computer storage medium, the production and reading of which typically exploits laser technology, e.g., CDs and videodisks.

Optical fibre A communications medium in which pulses of light are sent along thin glass tubes.

OR A logical operation in which the output is true if any of the inputs are true, otherwise it is false. Contrast with AND and NOT.

Original cataloguing Creation of cataloguing records by examining the information resources to be catalogued and providing bibliographic descriptions that are consistent with an established set of cataloguing standards. Contrast with copy cataloguing.

OSI Open Systems Interconnection: a data communications system designed by the ISO.

Output device A computer device that displays information to humans.

Packet switching service A data transmission service that splits messages into standard-sized packets, sends them along the most convenient circuits and reassembles them at the other end.

Parallel A form of data transmission that involves sending eight bits simultaneously. Contrast with serial.

Parameter A variable value that can be established by the owner of a computer system, e.g., loan periods in a library management system.

Parity bit The extra bit used in data communications to check for transmission errors. If for example both sender and receiver are using even parity, the parity bit is added to ensure that each transmitted byte contains an even number of ones.

PC-DOS The (pre-Windows) disk operating system used to run IBM microcomputers. Similar to MS-DOS.

PDF (Portable Document Format) A proprietorial format (developed by Adobe) that has become a *de facto* standard for the distribution of electronic documents.

Peripheral Any hardware device that is attached to, but separate from, the main computer unit.

Personal computer (PC) A microcomputer generally for personal use: typically refers only to IBM microcomputers or compatible machines.

PICK An operating system tailored for database applications and which, like UNIX, has become an industry standard.

Pixel Picture element: the smallest graphical element on a computer screen that can be manipulated.

Platform Used to refer to the operating system and hardware on which application software runs.

Point of issue Time and place at which a library item is issued.

Pointer *See* Embedded pointer.

Pointing device An input device that allows a user to move the cursor on a computer screen and thus indicate an option that is to be selected.

Portal A resource that acts as a gateway on to the Internet, offering its users a range of resources and services such as free email and information services.

Postings file In information retrieval, a file used to link an index file and a main file and to alert users to the number of matches a particular search term has achieved.

Primary storage The area of the CPU where data and programs can be stored during execution. Also referred to as main memory.

Printer A peripheral device used to produce text and graphics on paper.

Program Set of instructions that direct the operations of a computer. Programming refers to the writing of a program, i.e., translating a set of specifications into an appropriate computer language.

Prompt A question or statement from a computer system that requires a response from the computer operator.

Protocol The set of rules and conventions governing the transmission of data.

Proximity operator Search operator, used to specify how close search terms must be (e.g., whether they are to be in the same field).

Proxy server The hardware device through which communications between an organisation's internal network and the outside world typically must pass – uses special software.

Pull down menu A menu that is normally hidden from view until selected by a pointing device such as a mouse. When selected, numerous other menu options are revealed to select from.

Query language A very high level computer language used to access, manipulate and retrieve data from a database, e.g., SQL (which is an industry standard).

RAID Redundant Array of Independent Disks: combinations of two or more hard drives combined in such a way as to increase the performance and fault tolerance of the hard drive.

RAM Random Access Memory: the part of main memory to which data and applications are temporarily copied, prior to being used. The contents of RAM are lost when the computer is switched off. Contrast with ROM.

Reading The process of transferring data from a secondary storage device (e.g., a CD-ROM drive) or from an input device (e.g., a light-pen and barcode reader) to a CPU. Read-only memory (ROM) is memory into which data and/or programs are entered at the production stage and which cannot subsequently be altered or added to.

Real-time processing Data processing which provides immediate updating of files. Contrast with batch processing.

Record A set of fields (data elements) treated as a unit within a computer file, e.g., bibliographic and subject description of a work.

Register A part of the CPU used to hold one datum or one instruction during the execution of a program.

Relational database management system (RDBMS) Database management system in which data are organised in small data structures called relations or tables. Relations are linked through the data themselves.

Relevance ranking Ranking of search results by relevance, based, for example, on the frequency with which search terms appear in a document.

Repeater A network device used to regenerate an analogue or digital signal before re-transmitting to the next device on the network, thus minimising data corruption.

Report generator Software that allows the extraction of ad hoc reports from a database and the definition of regular statistical and exception reports that are to be generated.

Resolution The amount of detail that can be displayed on a computer screen: the greater the number of pixels (picture elements), the greater the resolution.

Retrospective conversion The process of converting existing records (e.g., catalogue cards) into electronic format.

RF (radio frequency) technologies Technologies that support wireless communication, in which data are transferred over the air, with little need for direct connection.

RFI Request for information: a request to system vendors/developers, giving a brief overview of system requirements and asking vendors if they could supply appropriate systems.

RFP Request for proposals: a formal document requesting system vendors/ developers to submit proposals for system development and giving each vendor/developer sufficient information on which to base its proposal, such as functional and technical specifications.

Ring A LAN topology in which each device on the network is connected to form the shape of a closed loop. Contrast with bus and star.

ROM Read Only Memory: computer memory from which data can be read from but not written to. The contents of ROM are etched into the ROM chip during production and cannot be changed. Consequently, the contents of ROM are not lost when the computer is switched off. Contrast with RAM.

Router A networking hardware device used to re-direct transmitted messages towards other networked devices.

RS232 An international standard for the configuration of serial ports.

RTS Request To Send: the signal sent by the sending device to the receiving device in hardware flow control, asking whether the receiving device is ready to receive more data. Contrast with CTS.

Satellite An object which orbits the earth and is used to bounce microwave signals from in order to overcome transmission distance problems due to the curvature of the earth.

Scanner A hardware device used to scan text, graphics and barcodes and convert them into digital images.

SCIS Schools Catalogue Information Service, a service for Australian and New Zealand schools, run by Curriculum Corporation.

SDI Selective dissemination of information: service that supplies individuals and organisations with information on requested topics at regular intervals. Typically based on a set of user-profiles.

Search engine A searchable index by means of which people can locate Web resources. It automatically indexes a Web resource and then follows hypertext links across the Internet adding to the index and following still further links.

Secondary or auxiliary storage Computer memory external to a CPU and used to supplement main memory. Generally used to store data and programs not currently being used.

Security Protection of data from unauthorised use (e.g., by use of passwords).

Selective dissemination of information *See* SDI.

Semiconductor A device which can act as both a conductor and insulator. Semiconductor circuits are made by printing transistors on to silicon wafers.

Sequential searching Accessing items in the order in which they are stored on a secondary storage medium.

Serial A form of data transmission that involves sending data one bit at a time. Compare with parallel.

Server The term refers to both a host computer that stores data and files and makes them available to clients (*see* Client/server model) and to the special software required to handle data and files and provide access to them.

SGML (Standard Generalized Markup Language) A widely adopted non-proprietary mark-up language that specifies characteristics of electronic text for publication. It is the basis for a series of other electronic publishing standards, including HTML.

Shareware Like freeware, shareware is computer software that is typically written by an enthusiastic individual and is offered to others for no charge, but, unlike freeware, is generally accompanied by a request for payment, in return for which the purchaser may receive extra functionality or documentation.

Shell That part of operating system software that enables communication between the user and the rest of the computer system.

Simplex A method of communication in which data travel from one device to another in one direction only.

Smart barcode A barcode that has an encoded number which already corresponds to an identifier in a computer's files. In cataloguing, a smart barcode would be generated when a bibliographic record is created.

SNA Systems Network Architecture, IBM's layered protocol.

Software The set of instructions that tell the computer what to do. Contrast with hardware.

Spooling The process of storing data on a secondary storage medium, until a device (such as a printer) is ready to use the data. Some printers have an area of memory for such purposes, called a spooler. *See also* Buffer.

Spreadsheet An applications program that allows a user to process, manipulate and display large amounts of mainly numerical data.

SQL Structured Query Language.

Stack In hypertext, a matrix of nodes, through which a user can follow links.

Star A LAN topology in which each networked device is connected to a central hub. Contrast with bus and ring.

Stemming In information retrieval, the shortening of search terms in order to broaden a search to include all occurrences of text that share a common stem; achieved by leaving characters off the end of the term, e.g., 'librar?' (a form of truncation).

Stop word A word that is not to be used for retrieval, e.g., a preposition or an article.

Streaming tape Magnetic tape (generally in a cartridge or cassette) that is used for back-up.

Structured database Databases, such as bibliographic databases, in which data are organised into fields.

Structured Query Language (SQL) A database query language used to manipulate and retrieve data in a relational database management system. Developed by IBM, it is now an industry standard.

Subfield A data element that is smaller than a field and which is the smallest data element to make sense to a user.

Subject directory A web resource that consists of hierarchically-organised lists of websites that have been compiled by human developers, as distinct from search engines which are indexes compiled by robots or 'spiders'.

Surrogate record A record in a computer file that represents something in the physical world (e.g., a book order or the book itself).

Switched line The type of line available on the normal telephone exchange system.

Synchronous Serial transmission in which each bit is sent one after the other until all data have been transmitted. Serial transmission relies heavily on the sender and receiver having synchronised system clocks. Contrast with asynchronous.

System Something formed of parts, each of which interacts with other parts to achieve a common purpose.

System analysis First stage in a structured process of system development. It includes an analysis of the functional requirements of the proposed system.

System design Second stage in a structured process of system development, in which the logical model derived from the analysis stage is transformed into a detailed set of physical requirements.

System development life cycle A structured process of system development.

System software A set of programs that directs computer hardware to perform the instructions encoded in applications software, e.g., operating systems, language translators and utility programs.

Tag A three-digit number that precedes and identifies each field in a MARC record. Each field is referred to as a tagged field.

Tape drive Input/output device used to read/write data on a magnetic tape.

Tb Terabyte: 1,024 Gb.

TCP/IP Transmission Control Protocol/Internet Protocol: a suite of protocols used by the Internet and a standard in academic and government environments.

Telecommunications The process of using communication facilities, e.g., the telephone system or television, to send data, information, sound and images over a long distance.

Telnet A TCP/IP protocol used to login to a remote host and execute instructions as if they were being typed into the host machine itself.

Terabyte *See* Tb.

Terminal An input/output device, combining a keyboard and a monitor or visual display unit, that allows a user to communicate with a computer system.

Text retrieval system A system designed to facilitate the location of text in a textual file or database.

Thesaurus A product (printed, online or ondisk) that allows users to explore a controlled vocabulary (e.g., a list of subject terms). Compare with authority file.

Thread In newsgroups, a thread is a means by which postings (messages) that relate to previous postings are linked to it, making it easier for members of the group to follow specific discussions.

TIFF (Tagged Image File Format) An image file format that offers high quality images.

Toggle A device (e.g., a key on a computer keyboard) that generates one of two options.

Token ring A physical layer protocol designed by IBM for ring topologies. A token (a pattern of bits) is sent around the ring and is used to control the flow of data and prevent data collisions.

Topology The method by which a LAN exchanges data. Also referred to as the LAN's architecture.

Touch screen Type of computer screen that allows a user to make selections from the screen by physically pointing to the displayed option.

Trap A procedure in a circulations control system which interrupts certain transactions, e.g., blocking loans of certain material or categories of material, or alerting staff to problems, such as borrowers exceeding their loan entitlements.

Truncation Shortening search terms in order to include all occurrences of text that share common characters, e.g., 'lab?or' might locate labor' and 'labour'. *See also* Stemming.

Turnkey system A library management system in which hardware and prewritten software are supplied by the one vendor.

Twisted pair A cable media used in data transmission, mainly in LANs. It consists of two insulated copper wires twisted around each other.

Unicode A 16-bit code for data representation that provides sufficient combinations of code for complex languages such as Chinese and Japanese – now a standard for the leading computer manufacturers.

UNIX A multi-user, multi-tasking, multi-processor operating system, developed by Bell laboratories that can be used on a wide range of computer systems.

Uploading Transferring a copy of data or files (e.g., a bibliographic record) to a computer, e.g., from computer tape to a local system or from a local system to a remote server.

URL (Uniform Resource Locator) A unique address for Internet resources, made up of the retrieval method (typically, HTTP), the host server and domain name, and the directory-type address of the resource on the host server.

URN (Uniform Resource Name) An attempt to find a unique naming convention for web resources, intended to provide a more permanent form of identification than the URL and so solve the problem of broken links.

User friendly A term used to describe how easy a software package is to learn and use. The more user friendly a software package is, the easier it is to learn and use.

User interface The software and hardware that allow the user to maintain a dialogue with the computer system; the medium through which humans communicate with computers.

Utility program A type of system software that can be purchased as a small discrete program. Utility programs perform specific tasks, such as performing diagnostic and debugging procedures. Sometimes regarded as part of an operating system.

Variable length field Field that does not have its length fixed in advance and is therefore only as long as it needs to be: typical of text retrieval systems. Contrast with fixed length field.

VDU *See* Monitor.

Videodisk An optical disk, larger than a CD-ROM, and designed to include video (moving images) and audio, as well as text and graphics.

Virtual memory The extra memory provided by secondary storage devices when they are used to extend main memory through the process of swapping programs and data between main memory and secondary storage. Also called virtual storage.

Virus A program that is designed to destroy other programs or data.

Volatile A description of computer memory from which data and programs are lost when the power is switched off, e.g., used to describe RAM.

WAN Wide Area Network: a network of computing devices dispersed among cities or countries.

Web (World Wide Web or WWW) In general terms, used to refer to the Internet resources that can be accessed using Telnet, FTP, Gopher, WAIS and HTTP, but a more precise definition might be that it comprises the large number of Internet servers that use hypertext to store and link files.

Web browser A piece of client software used to access the Web; also used in the context of hypertext to refer to a mapping device used to represent graphically where a hypertext node is in relation to associated nodes.

Web server The computer device and the software required to run it which together store website files and respond to messages that have been submitted using HTTP (or an associated protocol).

Webcasting A one to many form of communication (like broadcasting) that allows users to 'publish' multimedia presentations (including video, audio and powerpoint) via the Internet.

Wide Area Network *See* WAN.

WIMP Window, Icon, Mouse, Pull down menus: the four major components of GUIs.

Window A discrete area of a screen used to display a document or an application, different from those displayed in other windows.

Windows 95 A multi-tasking operating system developed by Microsoft for small office and home use.

Windows NT A multi-tasking, multi-processor, multi-user operating system developed by Microsoft for corporate use.

Word The bus width of a computer system. This may vary from computer to computer.

Word processing The use of a computer and word processing software to produce textual material, such as staff manuals or correspondence.

Workstation A configuration of hardware and software components required to perform a specific function, e.g., searching an online or ondisk database, or performing cataloguing functions.

World Wide Web *See* Web.

WORM *see* CD-R.

Writing The process of transferring data from main memory to a secondary storage medium, such as magnetic tape or an erasable optical disk.

XML (Extensible Markup Language) A subset of SGML, designed as the universal format for the exchange of structured documents and data on the Web.

Z39.50 An applications layer protocol, standardised in 1988 by NISO, that provides a uniform method for users to access information resources such as online library catalogues.

Zip drive A special input/output device used to read/write data on a high-capacity magnetic 'zip disk', typically external to the main computer hardware component.

APPENDIX 3
Answers to review questions

Chapter 1

1. A listserv is a common piece of mail server software and the term is often used to denote a discussion list or mailing list.

2. A thread is a useful device for following discussions that have taken place in a newsgroup. In a thread, responses to a posting are displayed under the original posting with a common subject header.

3. The client/server model is the one used for networking and internetworking and involves using local, client computer systems to access data, software etc. stored on remote servers or hosts (which are generally more powerful computers).

4. To telnet is to open a link between a client and a server.

5. A protocol is a set of rules or conventions that governs the use of communication channels. Examples discussed in this chapter are telnet, FTP (File Transfer Protocol), HTTP (HyperText Transfer Protocol) and Z39.50.

6. The search operators that narrow a search (at least in this chapter) are the boolean operators 'AND' and 'NOT' and the three proximity operators mentioned (those specifying terms that are near each other, together in the same element or adjacent).

7. HTML (HyperText Markup Language) is a means of formatting web pages, so that documents can be presented properly on clients, and of embedding hypertext links in web documents (i.e., links with other parts of a resource or with other resources altogether).

8. A URL (Uniform Resource Locator) is a means of addressing web resources and consists of the retrieval method (typically HTTP), the host and domain name and the pathway on the host server.

9. A web browser is a piece of client software that allows users to access the Web, e.g., by using retrieval methods such as HTTP, and presents web resources to them.

10.   The parts of a web page that are indexed by the common search engines vary, for example, WebCrawler and Lycos will index the contents of web pages but some others will index only certain elements, such as title and URL.

Chapter 2

1.   A field is defined as an attribute or the smallest data element that makes sense to a user.

2.   The main components of an online information retrieval system are a database, retrieval software, a microcomputer or terminal, a communications link and communication software.

3.   The most common indexing parameters applied to text retrieval systems are words that are not to be indexed (stopwords), fields in which words are to be indexed and fields in which phrases are to be indexed.

4.   The main techniques for narrowing a database search are field specification, use of field delimiters, use of boolean operators AND and NOT, and use of proximity operators.

5.   Three kinds of help facility available include help documentation, access to indexes and access to thesauri.

6.   The two solutions to the limitations of boolean searching discussed are term weighting and relevance ranking.

7.   The main elements that make up a user profile in SDI are topics of interest, associated keywords and sample citations considered useful by the user.

8.   The difference between the index file and the subject index or descriptor field is that the index consists of a list of terms used in the main file that is automatically generated, whereas the subject index consists of terms assigned to an information resource (generally by a human indexer) to describe what it is about.

9.   The decisions to be made in the development of an inhouse database include the type of system considered appropriate, what information to include, whether the database should be structured into fields, length of fields (if appropriate), what to do about repeating elements in fields, which fields should be used for retrieval and whether to have a thesaurus.

10.   The main technologies that contribute to the development of document delivery services were said to be networks, electronic mail, CD-ROMs and delivery technologies, such as fax or image scanning (combined with email).

Chapter 3

1.   Three files that you might immediately associate with online catalogues are bibliographic files, holdings files and authority files. From your reading of last chapter, you might have added index files.

2.   The term 'OPAC' might refer in general terms to the bibliographic database and the means of accessing the database (terminal, retrieval software etc.), but it is sometimes used to refer to the actual terminal.

3.   The main disadvantages of CD-ROM catalogues are that they are not as up to date as online catalogues, production is relatively expensive and they cannot tell users the status of an item (e.g., on loan).

4.   MARC refers to a variety of formats used to identify bibliographic records and their data elements for purposes of exchange.

5.   MARC data fields correspond to bibliographic elements such as title and statement of responsibility area, whereas control fields contain additional information about records, e.g., the language of the publication.

6.   National libraries are sources of copy cataloguing (new titles and older ones for retrospective cataloguing), cataloguing standards, such as subject headings (in the case of Library of Congress) and authority lists.

7.   A common method for recompensing libraries is to work out the value of their input and recompense them in uncharged copy cataloguing.

8.   Libraries in a bibliographic network share bibliographic standards, authority control, database development and maintenance, hardware and software costs, information resources, and technical support and advice.

9.   Technologies used to copy catalogue records from a bibliographic network to a local system include 'downline loading' using communications links, ordering records on magnetic media such as diskettes (floppy disks) or tape, or downloading from a CD-ROM.

10.   The main costs of shared cataloguing are financial support for network administration and maintenance of a central bibliographic database, extra equipment (e.g., communications hardware) and telecommunications costs.

Chapter 4

1. Parameters are values that need to be determined by librarians before library management systems can become operational. The point is that they allow librarians to customise systems so that they operate in accordance with the library's policies and procedures.

2. The main features of a cataloguing subsystem are original cataloguing, importation of records from external sources (copy cataloguing), catalogue enquiry, editing of catalogue records, deletion of catalogue records, authority control, and output of stationery.

3. Examples of parameterisation available in cataloguing subsystems include (a) fields to be presented for data input and (b) level of cataloguing.

4. Authority files are lists of authoritative terms, such as personal names, but in the context of LMS they also refer to computer files in which particular authoritative terms, such as personal names, are stored only once and are linked to the bibliographic records in which they occur.

5. The main features of an acquisitions subsystem include bibliographic checking, creation and despatch of orders, receipt of orders, fund accounting, claiming for outstanding orders and cancellation of outstanding orders.

6. A default in data entry is a value that can be assumed and which is automatically input by the system itself unless another value is input by the operator. An example in acquisitions is financial currency, for which the default is normally the currency of the country in which the order is made.

7. The data files that need to be set up before a basic library management system becomes operational include fund, supplier, bibliographic, holdings and borrower files.

8. The parameters that need to be established for a circulation control subsystem include loan periods, loan quotas, calendars, renewal restrictions and fines schedules.

9. The provisions that can be made for down-time in a circulations department include (a) transaction sheets on which to manually record loans and returns and (b) portable data-capture units that can record and store transaction data in electronic form.

10. Transaction information is used in the everyday running of a library (e.g., data processing systems alert library staff to overdue items) whereas management information is used to help evaluate library performance and is regarded as a component in management's control function.

Chapter 5

1. The point of an index file is that it speeds up retrieval by storing terms that are required for retrieval in a separate file from the larger main file in which the records are held, where they can be manipulated for faster retrieval (e.g., by alphabetical sorting).

2. One alernative to a sequential computer search through an index file is a binary search, which involves splitting the alphabetically sorted file into two parts and progressively dividing in two that part of the file which contains the search term.

3. A relation in database management is a small data structure, such the set of data elements used to describe holdings information, and resembles a small file in non-relational systems.

4. Two relations are linked in a relational database management system by data that is common to both relations, e.g., a system-generated bibliographic record number might link a bibliographic relation to a holdings relation, or a bibliographic relation to an order relation.

5. The difference between a query language and a fourth-generation language is that a query language is used to access, manipulate and retrieve data from a database, whereas a fourth-generation language is a tool used to develop new applications.

6. Text retrieval software offers fast retrieval speeds, compared to DBMS, and good search facilities, whereas database management systems offer fast updating speeds, a minimum of data redundancy and good data manipulation.

7. The three main retrieval techniques in a hypertext package are selection of associative links between nodes, performance of keyword searches across stacks and use of graphical browsers.

8. The main components in expert systems software are a knowledge base, an inference engine and a user interface.

9. The main features of personal bibliographic software are relative ease of use, pre-defined data structures, pre-defined output formats, generation of a bibliography from a manuscript, boolean searching, batch importation of records, flexible sorting of selected records, output to a printer or to a disk file, duplicate detection, search and replace and global addition of text, merging of databases, production of structured bibliographies and access to index files.

10. The main features of spreadsheet software are creation of spreadsheets, provision of built-in functions, editing, changing formatting of cells, macro programming, graphical presentation, print output, and saving and filing of spreadsheets.

Chapter 6

1.   The four main categories of hardware are input, processing and control, storage and output.

2.   The control unit's tasks are to coordinate the flow of data through the computer system and to tell the other parts of the computer system what to do and when to do it.

3.   The two types of storage are primary and secondary. RAM, the first of two types of primary storage, is where data and programs are transferred to, from secondary storage, when the CPU requires them. The contents of RAM are temporary and only exist while the computer is on. ROM, the second type of primary storage is permanent, and is used to store data and instructions that never change. Secondary storage, on the other hand, is used to store data and programs for later retrieval and adopts either magnetic or optical storage technologies. Unlike RAM, secondary storage is not lost when the computer is turned off.

4.   Each character is represented using an eight bit binary code. These eight bit codes are defined in either the ASCII (American Standard Code for Information Interchange) or the EBCDIC (Extended Binary Coded Decimal Interchange Code) table. Every computer system uses one of these tables, with the ASCII table being the most common among personal computers and EBCDIC popular with IBM mainframe computer systems.

5.   The three types of software are operating system software, utility software and application software. Operating system software enables the user and the other types of software to access the various resources of a computer system. Utility software is designed to maintain and diagnose a computer system only and is not necessary for the computer system to function. Application software is used to enable users to perform various functions such as word processing, database management, games and many more.

6.   Bit stands for Binary digIT and is used to represent a single binary digit such as zero (0) or one (1). A byte is a grouping of 8 bits and a Megabyte is 1,024 kilobytes, where a kilobyte is 1,024 bytes.

7.   The three building blocks for all functions within a computer system are the three logic gates of AND, OR and NOT. The AND gate can have numerous binary inputs but only one output. The output is 1 (on), only if all inputs are 1 (on), otherwise it is 0 (off). The OR gate again can have numerous binary inputs but only one output. The output is 1 (on) if any of the inputs is 1 (on) and 0 (off) if all inputs are 0 (off). The NOT gate on the other hand has only 1 input and 1 output. If the input is 1 the output is 0 and vice-versa. From these three logic gates, circuits can be constructed to perform addition, subtraction, multiplication, division, comparisons as well as storage. In fact all computing operations can be built from these three basic logic gates.

8. A GUI is a Graphical User Interface. It represents one of three interfaces that exist between humans and computers. It is designed to present users with all possible choices instead of forcing a user to remember all possible commands that can be given to a computer (as is the case with a command-line user interface). GUIs make extensive use of Windows, Icons, Mice and Pull-down menus and hence are sometimes referred to as WIMP environments.

9. When data are stored digitally they can be stored, manipulated, and duplicated within a computer system. They can be used as input into other computer systems and shared among many people. Data stored on paper, on the other hand, are less permanent and can be viewed by one person only. Paper eventually deteriorates unlike some forms of digital storage and cannot be manipulated or used as input into other computer systems.

10. User-friendly is a term used to describe how easy a software package is to learn and use. Since humans and computers 'speak' different languages, the user-interface between humans and computers is crucial. A user interface that is user-friendly provides a more efficient means of utilising computer system resources. A computer without a user-interface is like a car without a dashboard.

Chapter 7

1. By networking, computer systems resources can be shared among many computers and users, for instance, a single printer can be shared among many users, saving costs on maintenance as well as multiple purchases. Hard drives can be shared, enabling many users to save and share files amongst themselves. Networking also enables users to share data and information and thus collaborate on ideas and projects.

2. The difference between a LAN and a WAN is purely geographical. Local Area Networks, as the name suggests, are limited to a local area. Usually LANs are found within or between neighboring buildings. Wide Area Networks, on the other hand, are for networking between cities or counties. The grey area that exists between LANs and WANs is sometimes referred to as Metropolitan Area Networks (MANs).

3. Common communications media include:

    Twisted pair – two insulated copper wires twisted around each other. It is used in most of the world's telephone systems. The wires are twisted around each other to help cancel out line noise.

    Coaxial cable – an insulated copper wire surrounded by a grounded shield of braided wire and plastic. The shield helps reduce line noise while the centre wire is used to carry signals. Although coaxial cable is more expensive than twisted pair, it can carry more signals and is less susceptible to interference.

Optical fibre – glass like tubes, thinner than a human hair, that are used to carry signals in the form of pulses of light. Although dramatically smaller in size than coaxial cable and twisted pair, and less expensive, fibre optic cable can carry up to 26,000 more signals than twisted pair and at very high speed. It has better security than coaxial cable and twisted pair since optical fibre cannot be tapped.

Infrared – used in wireless communications where the sender and receiver are within about 10 metres of each other. Infrared has a wavelength greater than that of red light and hence is just out of the visible spectrum for humans.

Microwave – high frequency radio signals used to transmit data between transmitter and receiver. It relies on line-of-sight and hence transceivers are placed on hilltops to maximise the distance between towers. Data can be transmitted at very high speeds and hence it is a good solution for linking buildings or academic campuses together instead of expensive cabling.

Satellite – works similarly to microwave in that it relies on line-of-sight between transceivers. The difference is that a communications satellite is used between transceivers to achieve transmission distance that normally wouldn't be possible due to the curvature of the earth.

4. In serial transmission, data are transmitted one bit at a time while in parallel transmission, data are sent eight bits at a time. In synchronous communications, data are transmitted serially and both the sender and the receiver have synchronised system clocks to ensure that each device knows exactly when each bit is to be transmitted and received. With asynchronous communication, data are sent serially in blocks (usually one byte at a time). The sender and receiver keep each other informed by special signals so that each device knows when the other is ready to transmit or receive data. Data sent asynchronously usually have start and stop bits to indicate to the receiver the start and end of each block of transmitted data.

5. Three common error detection and corrrection methods are:

Parity checking – an eighth bit is added to ASCII characters such that the total number of one's is even (for even parity) or odd (for odd parity). If the receiving device calculates either an odd number of ones (if using even parity) or an even number of ones (if using odd parity) then an error is detected and the data are re-transmitted.

Check sum – each byte sent is treated as a binary number and the numbers added together. At the end of transmission, the sum of all the bytes is transmitted and then compared against the sum that was calculated by the receiving device. If they differ, an error is detected and the data are re-transmitted.

CRC – or cyclic redundancy check: the transmitted data are treated as one huge binary number. This number is divided by a constant, agreed upon between sender and receiver. At the end of transmission, the remainder after division is transmitted and compared against the remainder that was calculated by the receiving device. If they differ, an error is detected and the data are re-transmitted.

6.   Protocol means the set of rules and conventions governing the transfer of data between computer systems. They are essential to establish successful communications between computer systems, since without them, each device would not know the answers to questions such as:

- When are the data going to arrive?
- Which format are the data going to arrive in?
- Are the data compressed?
- Are the data being sent serially or in parallel?
- Are the data being sent asynchronously or synchronously?
- What error detection method is going to be used?
- How does the sender know that the receiver is ready?
- And many more...

7.   The Open Systems Interconnection (OSI) Reference Model was created by the International Standards Organisation (ISO) to assist in the transfer of data between devices. It consists of seven layers for defining the various aspects of transmission control. The seven layers, starting from the physical link are: physical, data link, network, transport, session, presentation and application. This OSI Reference Model has been well accepted by organisations. The ISO have also developed protocols for each of these seven OSI layers, however, these have not been accepted very well due to a number of popular protocol suites already being in widespread use.

8.   TCP/IP stands for Transmission Control Protocol/Internet Protocol, two protocols spanning the Transport and Network layers respectively. By itself, IP is a connectionless protocol concerned with the delivery of data to a destination only. When combined with TCP, it provides a connection between the sender and receiver and ensures that data are delivered successfully and that the packets of data arriving at the destination are ordered (since packets may arrive out of order). TCP/IP is the protocol used on the Internet.

9.   A gateway is a combination of software and hardware used to connect networks of differing protocols. Generally gateways are used to connect WANs together or LANs to WANs. A bridge on the other hand is used to connect two LANs together, irrespective of the protocols used on each. Bridges simply forward packets of data without performing any processing on them (unlike gateways).

10. Modems are required to convert the digital signals from a computer system to the analogue signals used by the telephone system (MOdulate), and vice versa (DEModulate). Modems are serial devices that attach to the RS-232 serial port on the back of the computer. Modems won't be with us forever since most of the world's telephone infrastructure is being replaced with digital fibre optic cabling. This means that no conversion process is required between computers and telephone systems since both operate in digital.

Chapter 8

1. The main options for systems development in libraries are development of an inhouse system, purchase of a turnkey system, purchase of library-specific software, purchase and development of generic software, contract with a bibliographic network, formation of a consortium or use of the facilities of a parent organisation.

2. The advantages of using general purpose software are that it is well tested, well documented and relatively inexpensive. Libraries may also have access to such software already, e.g., through parent organisations.

3. Benefits associated with membership of a bibliographic network include sharing of data, sharing the costs of hardware and software development and sharing systems administration.

4. The disadvantages associated with 'traditional' structured systems analysis and design are time taken to develop and test software, errors, dependence on skilled staff or consultants and escalation of costs.

5. The main costs associated with systems development are hardware/software costs, purchase of manuals, training, file conversion, site preparation, consumables, maintenance costs or contract, software enhancements and extra staff salaries.

6. The first step to make in the selection of one system from a shortlist is the elimination of those systems that do not meet mandatory requirements.

7. Five main steps in the process of implementation are site preparation, installation of software and hardware, staff training and preparation of documentation, creation or conversion of databases and running the system.

8. Ergonomics refers to design of technological systems that takes into account studies of human physique and behaviour.

9. Smart barcodes have encoded numbers that are already linked to a specific bibliographic record, with the result that barcode labels must be attached to a specific work, whereas dumb barcodes can be attached to any item because it is not until then that a link between that particular barcode number and a bibliographic record is created.

10. Strategies for converting from an old to a new system are direct conversion, phased (stage-by-stage) conversion, parallel conversion (both systems run for some time) and pilot conversion (i.e., use of test sites).

INDEX